From Boas to Black Power

D1571195

From Boas to Black Power

Racism, Liberalism, and American Anthropology

Mark Anderson

Stanford University Press
Stanford, California

Stanford University Press
Stanford, California

©2019 by the Board of Trustees of the Leland Stanford Junior University.
All rights reserved.

No part of this book may be reproduced or transmitted in any form or by any means, electronic or mechanical, including photocopying and recording, or in any information storage or retrieval system without the prior written permission of Stanford University Press.

Printed in the United States of America on acid-free, archival-quality paper

Library of Congress Cataloging-in-Publication Data

Names: Anderson, Mark, 1969- author.
Title: From Boas to Black power : racism, liberalism, and American anthropology /
   Mark Anderson.
Description: Stanford, California : Stanford University Press, 2019. |
   Includes bibliographical references and index.
Identifiers: LCCN 2018031407 (print) | LCCN 2018035364 (ebook) | ISBN 9781503607880 |
   ISBN 9781503607286 (cloth : alk. paper) | ISBN 9781503607873 (pbk.)
Subjects: LCSH: Ethnology—United States—History—20th century. | Anti-racism—
   United States—History—20th century. | Liberalism—United States—History—
   20th century. | Race—Study and teaching—United States—History—20th century. |
   Racism in anthropology—United States—History—20th century. | United States—
   Race relations—History—20th century.
Classification: LCC GN308.3.U6 (ebook) | LCC GN308.3.U6 A49 2019 (print) |
   DDC 305.800973/0904—dc23
LC record available at https://lccn.loc.gov/2018031407

Typeset by Newgen in 10/14 Minion

Cover design by Kevin Barrett Kane

Contents

Acknowledgments

THIS BOOK HAS BEEN AWHILE in the making and I have accrued numerous debts along the way. The idea for the project was first sparked by an undergraduate course I have taught several times over the past dozen years at the University of California, Santa Cruz, called "Race and Anthropology." The many students who have taken that course helped me identify the core thematics of this work and convinced me of their enduring relevance. Wherever you may now be, thank you!

Fantastic editor Michelle Lipinski and the staff at Stanford University Press have made the publication of this book as smooth as I can imagine. Michelle enthusiastically embraced the project and expertly guided it through completion, allowing me the freedom to keep it my own. I also appreciate her selection of excellent anonymous reviewers, who helped me identify errors and omissions and clarify key arguments. The remaining flaws are on me.

I would also like to thank the staff of various institutions housing manuscript collections I consulted for this work. These include the Archives and Special Collections Library at Vassar College, the American Philosophical Society, the Northwestern University Archives, the National Anthropology Archives at the Smithsonian Institution and the Schomburg Center for Research in Black Culture.

Versions of parts of this book have been presented at the American Anthropological Association annual meetings, the UCSC Center for Cultural Studies, and the Ethnographic Engagements workshop in the anthropology department at UCSC. Chapter 3 is derived, in part, from the article "Ruth Benedict, Boasian Anthropology, and the Problem of the Colour Line," published in *History and Anthropology* Volume 25, Number 3, 2014, 395–414 and available online at: https://doi.org/10.1080/02757206.2013.830214. The cartoon illustrations from the pamphlet *Races of Mankind* in Chapter 3 have the following credit line: "Illustrations" from *Race: Science and Politics* by Ruth Benedict, copyright © 1940, 1943, 1945 by Ruth Benedict; copyright renewed © 1968, 1971, 1973 by Robert G. Freeman. Used by permission of Viking Books, an imprint of Penguin Publishing Group, a division of Penguin Random House LLC. All rights reserved. Any third party use of this material, outside of this publication, is prohibited. Interested parties must directly apply to Penguin Random House LLC for permission.

I am blessed to have an intellectual community at UC Santa Cruz full of incredibly smart and generous people willing to engage my work. Faculty of the anthropology department provided unflagging support and never questioned my turn from ethnography to disciplinary history. At a time when faculty are increasingly valued by grant getting and publication quantity, having the institutional space to do what you want is a precious thing. I don't take it for granted. The graduate students have also been a constant source of inspiration; special thanks here to Patricia Alvarez, Kim Cameron Domínguez, Roosbelinda Cardenas, Brent Crosson, and Bill Girard.

I am particularly grateful to friends, students, and colleagues who read and commented on portions of the manuscript at various times: Noriko Aso, Jim Clifford, Kim Cameron Domínguez, Mayanthi Fernando, Susan Harding, Kate Jones, Dan Linger, Marc Matera, Dean Mathiowetz, Triloki Pandey, Carolyn Martin Shaw, Vanita Seth, and Megan Thomas. They helped me refine and clarify the arguments, led me to new sources and lines of inquiry, and pushed me to make this story not just about U.S. anthropology but about American liberalism. A totally unexpected benefit of the project is that it has drawn me closer to Jim and Susan, who may have rearranged their schedules in retirement but remain as intellectually engaged (and brilliant) as ever. Somehow they never pull rank even when I prattle on about an era they lived through and that I only know through text and image. Marc and Mayanthi read large chunks of the draft manuscript. Marc and I, bonding over a shared love of records and basketball, had innumerable conversations on Black intellectual history that deeply informed the project. Mayanthi pushed me the hardest, her critical acumen exceeded only by, and reflective of, her fierce commitment to friendship. Vanita and Kate have been constant sources of intellectual engagement, emotional rescue, and fabulous dinners. Other friends may not have read the manuscript but provided various kinds of advice and companionship; thank you, Jennifer Goett, Kate Gordy, Kate Knight, Casey Coneway, and all those who come to the parties. RIP Cafe Pergolesi.

My greatest debt is to Megan Thomas, my companion of fifteen years. Megan shared and suffered every excitement and frustration of the project, helped me develop arguments, edited several chapters, assuaged my anxieties, and otherwise made this work possible. She is a brilliant scholar whose devotion to students and dogged determination to fight for the university continually inspires. I will refrain here from embarrassing her further by relating what she means to me.

Finally, I would also like to thank my father, brother, and their/our families, who allowed me to become the academic I am and continue to provide love and support. I dedicated my first book to my deceased mother, Dorothy Anderson. This one I dedicate to the students, past, present, and future.

Prologue

The Custom of the Country

ON AUGUST 26 AND 27, 1970, Margaret Mead and James Baldwin held a recorded conversation of seven and a half hours, which was transcribed into the book *A Rap on Race* (Mead and Baldwin 1971). They discussed race and society against the backdrop of the Black Power movement, the Vietnam War and the Atomic Age.

Mead, 71 at the time, was the most famous anthropologist in the United States. Her highly public career devoted to making Americans "culture-conscious"[1] spanned nearly half a century. From her early ethnographic projects on gender and sexuality in "primitive" societies of Samoa and New Guinea to her work in intercultural education to her "culture and personality" studies of "modern" nations, she urged Americans to tolerate cultural differences and to permit the expansion of individual freedoms across racial and gender distinctions. Her discipline, a science of race and culture, had played an important role in constructing and disseminating a liberal anti-racist discourse. Although the influence of Mead's theoretical models in anthropology had waned by the 1960s, she remained its most prominent public figure, serving as a kind of matriarch of liberal consciousness. She was also an optimistic white voice for the progressive possibilities of America.

Baldwin, 46, was one of the most acclaimed American writers of his time, the author of several important novels, plays, and essay collections that probed the destructive dynamics of racial, sexual, and class distinctions in Europe and the U.S. He also played a prominent public role as a spokesperson for the civil rights movement, though his rejection of heterosexual normativity made him suspect within and beyond the movement. Baldwin voiced a humanist Black perspective that expressed deep ambivalence about his country and its role in the world. He managed to combine the passionate protest against white American racism expressed in the Black Power movement with a critical distance from Black nationalism that appealed to a white liberal audience.

The conversation between Mead and Baldwin was staged as a largely unstructured "rap" between racial progressives, not as a debate. But as their encounter progressed, disagreements emerged and intensified. The issues at stake reflect some of the paradoxes of U.S. liberal thought on race and racism that, this book argues, cultural anthropologists helped construct.

Early in the conversation, Mead and Baldwin agreed that the Black Power movement that emerged from civil rights struggles had called attention to the inherent problems of racial integration premised on normalized whiteness. Mead offered some critical self-reflections on the strategies she used to combat prejudice in the 1940s. In that era she had participated in efforts to develop forms of intercultural education to alleviate prejudice, promoting forms of cultural exchange between ethnic groups (Burkholder 2011).

> Mead: I was speaking in those days about three things we had to do. Appreciate cultural differences, respect political and religious differences and ignore race. Absolutely ignore race.
> Baldwin: Ignore race. That certainly seemed perfectly sound and true.
> Mead: Yes, but it isn't anymore. You see it really isn't true. This was wrong, because—
> Baldwin: Because race cannot be ignored. (Mead and Baldwin 1971, 8)

Baldwin elaborated on the generational shift associated with the Black Power movement, which brought to the fore the issue of white power as a characteristic feature of the republic.

> Baldwin: What they are doing is repudiating the entire theology, as I call it, which has affected and destroyed—really, literally destroyed—black people in this country for so long. And what this generation is relating to, what it is saying, is they realize that you, the white people, white Americans, have always attempted to murder them. Not merely by burying them or castrating them or hanging them from trees, but by murdering them in the mind, in the heart.
>
> By teaching a black child that he is worthless, that he can never contribute anything to civilization, you're teaching him how to hate his mother, his father, and his brothers. Everyone in my generation has seen the wreckage that this

has caused. And what black kids are doing now, no matter how excessively, is right. They are refusing this entire frame of reference and they are saying to the Republic: This is your bill, this is your bloody bill written in my *blood*, and you are going to have to pay it.

Mead: But don't you think, also, that it is not only the disillusionment of this younger generation, which I understand perfectly, but also it's a sensible position that you've got? That the integration position was a one-sided one?

Baldwin: Yes, it was.

Mead: And, of course, it was one that was shared in by both black and white. It was what, in a sense, many black people thought they wanted as individuals. They thought they wanted it, and then they had to learn it was one-sided.

Baldwin: Yes.

Mead: That's what Fanon said when he wrote *Black Skin, White Masks*. But his point, that what the black man is offered as civilization is *white* civilization, deals more with French civilization that it does with American.

Baldwin: It's clearer.

Mead: It's much clearer. But, nevertheless, the offer—which is substantially the way I would phrase it—the offer that well-intentioned white people made is: "If you will be like us—

Baldwin: "You could join our clubs and come to our houses—

Mead: "And we'll pretend that you're just like us."

Baldwin: Yeah.

Mead: Which means of course that we'll deny you.

Baldwin: Exactly. (11–12)

Mead repudiated the color-blind position of ignoring race she once promoted and came to understand integration as maintaining the refusal of recognition to Blacks, as Blacks. She was aware of the limitations of integration into an American society and culture coded as white. Yet she also defended her attachment to the nation and the hope "America" could offer the world. In one exchange Mead identified the origins of the nation in people who came "for political and religious reasons"—for freedom—and solicited Baldwin's identification with that American ideal.

Mead: So this part of our image of what is American, yours and mine, because our ancestors came here together. We share a notion of a kind of people that formed the ideals of this country and the ideals against which we have always

been measuring the country and finding it faulty. But the ideals were here. I
mean, Jefferson did postulate ideas of democracy that one could follow.
Baldwin: Yes, but he also owned slaves.
Mead: Sure he did. But he set down the statements on the basis of which one
could fight for the vote for everybody in this country. The fact that he owned
slaves is one thing. The principles he laid down are something else. (151)

Throughout the conversation Mead articulated a vision of "America" as an exceptional country based on ideals of freedom and democracy. If in practice
these ideals were violated—by slavery, genocide, and racism—they retained
redemptive value for the republic. Baldwin, in contrast, refused to accept the
distinction, highlighting not simply the failure of the country to live up to its
ideals but the violent racial exclusions inherent in becoming and being American. In an exchange that began as a disagreement on Israel and Baldwin's comparison of himself, as a Black American, to "the Arab at the hands of the Jews"
(210), Mead accused Baldwin of racism. Baldwin emphasized that he was not
engaging in anti-Semitism. Mead responded skeptically, waiting for his "but,"
and Baldwin replied:

Well then, the "but" is that the Jewish American, the Italian American, the Greek
American—anyway, all white Americans—all came to America probably to become Americans, and the price for becoming an American, the badge, is very
much like being Indian and having a white man's scalp. In this case, it is my
scalp. And it is not the color of the skin that matters, it is the custom of the
country. (213)

Baldwin not only drew a distinction across the color line between those that
can become white American and those, like himself, forever denied that possibility. He held that the price of being/becoming American was participation
in racism, specifically anti-Black racism. He thus highlighted the deep association between whiteness, violence, and "America," albeit via the overburdened
image of the scalp-taking Indian. For Baldwin, endemic racism and the violent
exclusions of the color line were "the custom of the country," as much a part of
American culture as the compromised ideals of freedom and democracy they
exposed. He could not share Mead's identification with America in the terms
she posited them.

The irreconcilable differences between Mead's and Baldwin's relationships
to America were reflected in their understanding of their own subject posi-

tions. Baldwin self-consciously spoke from the standpoint of a Black American, "the despised bastard of the Western house" (93), abjected by his white countrymen as the price of their belonging. Although living in exile, he insisted on his responsibility for the crimes and pathologies of his country that existed in "terror of the world" (84). Mead spoke as a white American free from racial prejudice and as a cosmopolitan anthropologist familiar with world cultures. She positioned herself as a universal subject. She also chided Baldwin for his particularistic standpoint, accusing him of reducing American problems to race and painting a one-sided, negative portrait of America and its Western Christian foundations. In the end, Mead offered some telling reflections on the difficulties they had in having a conversation.

Baldwin, she contended, could have had a more productive exchange with a white person with a personal history of racial prejudice, a "scarred oppressor" prepared for reconciliation. A white American who had "converted" from a position of white supremacy would be better suited to dialogue with Baldwin. Mead was not that person, she asserted, because she had been raised in a family entirely free of racial prejudice. "I have never been in the position of believing that I had any right because I was white . . . I never felt one moment of white supremacy in New Guinea, and I simply do not have the feeling which is one component in this country" (235–236). She, unlike Baldwin and the white oppressor, had not suffered because she did not bear the scars of participation in white supremacy. Here, Mead figured white supremacy as a matter of individual attitude and feeling. Her stance reflects what Jane Hill refers to as a core element of white American "folk ideology" that racism is a matter of individual belief and attitude (2008, 6). Growing up without racist sentiments—"lifted out of the situation that grips this country and is destroying it" (Mead and Baldwin 1971, 236)—she allowed herself to claim, "I have neither been scarred nor specially benefited by being white" (237).

Baldwin did not challenge her directly on this assertion but, searching for a point of identification, suggested that they shared a common condition as exiles "from the mainstream of life in this country" based on their knowledge of it. Mead refused the identification: "I am not an exile. I am absolutely not an exile. I live here and I live in Samoa and I live in New Guinea. I live everywhere on the planet that I have ever been, and I am no exile" (237). Nicholas De Genova comments on this exchange: "Mead is remarkably adamant about her own anthropological (white and imperial) cosmopolitanism. In the guise of a universal humanism, she may go abroad 'as an American' and avowedly feel secure that her identification with the human condition ensures that she will be 'at home' everywhere on the planet" (2007, 256). She thereby rejected the invitation to reject a political identification with America, to "disavow her own effective identification with the racial and imperial order that has materially and practically constituted her social privilege and anthropological conceit" (256). This position was enabled by Mead's faith in her own liberal subjecthood. Her avowed ability to see past race allowed her to personally disavow the scars and privileges of white supremacy as an American. But what if, as Baldwin insisted, white supremacy was a "custom of the country," deeply woven into the patterns of American culture and social structure?

A Rap on Race puts in unusually bold relief quintessential paradoxes of U.S. anti-racist liberalism as represented by the most publicly influential anthropologist in the U.S. Mead held deep attachments to liberal principles as equated with American nationalism in ways that attenuated her recognition of the structural power of whiteness in the republic. She was particularly adamant in her disavowals, but her positions reflected broader trajectories of thought characteristic of U.S. anthropology in the twentieth century. Mead was, after all, the foremost living representative of Boasian anthropology, an eclectic collection of intellectuals composed of the "father" of U.S. anthropology, Franz Boas, and his students at Columbia University, who helped refashion U.S. intellectual discourses on race, critiquing scientific racism and biological determinism while promoting culture consciousness in projects of liberal reform. Boasians such as Mead and Ruth Benedict were important figures in a politics of what Gary Gerstle calls "civic nationalism"—a view of the U.S. nation as tied together by values of freedom, democracy, and equal opportunities regardless of race and religion. From the 1940s to the mid-1960s, "the movement for racial equality was civic nationalist to the core, identifying itself with the pilgrims, Founding Fathers and the American Dream." However, by the end of that period, the failure of civil rights victories to advance racial equality led to the emergence of Black Power, "an ideology that rejected America as hopelessly compromised by racism" (Gerstle 2001, 9–10). The frustrated dialogue between Mead and Baldwin reflected these disparate views.

At the time of their conversation, a critical perspective on anthropology had emerged in response to decolonization, revolutionary movements, feminism, and mobilization of people of color, including the Black Power movement. Anthropology was under fire as a discipline complicit with colonialism and imperialism, its image of progressivism in question. A battle over the history and politics of anthropology ensued that continues today. In the early 1970s, African American anthropologist William Willis—who entered the Columbia University anthropology graduate program in the 1940s because of its anti-racist legacy—published one of the most scathing indictments of the discipline ever written. He defined anthropology as, essentially, the study of people of color by white people for the benefit of white societies and as a liberal practice that perpetuated white supremacy (1972). Compare that perspective to the comment by George Stocking the foremost historian of anthropology, that

> In the long run, it was Boasian anthropology—rather than the racialist writers associated with the eugenics movement—which was able to speak to Americans as the voice of science on all matters of race, culture, and evolution—a fact whose significance for the recent history of the United States doubtless merits further exploration. (1968, 307)

Whereas Stocking upheld the progressive legacy of anthropology and its contribution to civil rights and racial integration against scientific racism, Willis cast anthropology as a science complicit in white domination of the "colored world" (1972, 123). This book explores the question: What if they were both, in the essentials, correct?

Introduction

THIS IS A BOOK ABOUT HOW U.S. cultural anthropologists wrote about race, racism, and America between the 1920s and early 1970s as a window into U.S. anti-racist liberalism. Over these fifty-odd years anthropology, initially under the leadership of Franz Boas, was consolidated as the academic discipline we know today. It expanded dramatically after World War II only to confront a sense of crisis generated by the political upheavals initiated in the 1960s. Culture became anthropology's paradigmatic concept but race would remain its shadow.

Many U.S. anthropologists have, for quite some time, taken pride and comfort in the anti-racist legacy bequeathed by Franz Boas and his students. A story we often tell goes something like this: In the nineteenth century anthropology was, alas, a racist discipline. Anthropologists measured skulls to scientifically prove the innate superiority of whites and ranked the world's peoples on a scale of civilizational achievement with "modern" Europeans at the top and "primitives" at the bottom. But then along came Boas, a Jewish German immigrant to the U.S. who refashioned the discipline and its discourses on race and culture. Boas refuted biological racism, asserting that the most important differences between groups of people derived from cultural (learned) rather than biological (innate) inheritance. He simultaneously argued against the ethnocentric ranking of cultures in evolutionary hierarchies. Boas thus established anthropology as an anti-racist science. This story is often told with greater nuance than this abbreviated version, but its moral, I believe, is a common component of the anthropological legacy.[1] The lesson: anthropology is a racially progressive discipline that has repudiated its racist past and has played a key role in creating a racially progressive future. The story resonates with a common narrative of racial progress in the U.S., which is no mere coincidence because anthropology has contributed to that narrative.

Close examination of anthropological discourses on race and racism from the time of Boas forward complicates any simple story of the discipline's racial progressivism. On the one hand, scholars have recognized the powerful role the Boasian intervention played in combating racism not only in the scientific community but in the wider public sphere. On the other hand, many of the same scholars have identified tensions and contradictions within the Boasian paradigm. George Stocking (1968)—whose nuanced appreciation of Boas informs all subsequent assessments—was careful to note that Boas never fully escaped the nineteenth-century evolutionism he challenged. Vernon Williams (1996; 2006) has elaborated on what he calls the Boasian paradox: the contradiction between Boas' liberal egalitarian politics and his retention of inegalitarian tenets of physical anthropology. Race itself remained a valid biological category of human difference, even as Boasians sought to minimize its importance. "In retrospect, the Boasians could not perceive that race was a culturally constructed way of looking at and interpreting human variation" (Smedley 1993, 280).

Other scholars expand further on the paradoxical legacies of the Boasian intervention. Kamala Visweswaran (1998) provides one of the more pointed critiques. She argues that by defining culture against biology and relegating race to biology, Boasians left the study of race to the biological sciences and thereby ironically fueled "the machine of scientific racism" (1998, 70). She also contends that "after World War II, race dropped off the agenda of the cultural anthropologist in part due to the very success of the Boasian maneuver that argued that culture, not race, was a more meaningful explanation of significant differences among groups of people" (75). Michel-Rolph Trouillot (2003) similarly argues that a reified race-culture distinction ultimately left culture as a fetish for anthropological objectification, disconnected from the structural dynamics of power. These assessments suggest that the very touchstone of Boasian thought—the distinction between race and culture—produced a legacy in which cultural anthropologists came to avoid racism, particularly as a structural feature of contemporary society. Faye Harrison (2008a) puts the point succinctly: "Many sociocultural anthropologists assumed that race was not useful for understanding social distinctions. This led to a silence concerning structural racism." According to Lee Baker, it also contributed to liberal and conservative color-blind discourses in the U.S. that minimize racism as a social reality (1998, 210; 2010, 219).

These arguments represent a profound challenge to any straightforward narrative of anthropology's progressive history on race and racism.[2] They inform my own analysis of the Boasians in the first half of the book, though I will have occasion to modify, complicate, and challenge various aspects of them. I depart from these critical perspectives—in the dual sense of starting from and differing from—in three general ways.

First, whereas most engagements with Boasians focus on their conceptions of race as a physical/biological phenomenon, I am interested in their explicit and implicit engagements with what I call the social life of race. If, to be sure, the main import of the Boasian intervention was to undermine biological determinism, Boas and his students also provided accounts of racial consciousness, prejudice, discrimination and conflict as social phenomena. Boasians did not simply assume that the public dissemination of scientific knowledge or proper thinking about the race concept would resolve race "problems." They were not so naïve as to believe that the debunking of scientific racism alone could fundamentally transform race relations. Ruth Benedict was quite explicit on this point, noting that the anthropologist "has no illusions that proofs of what race is or is not will change racial attitudes" (1941, 74). She viewed racial "conflict" and prejudice as social facts amenable to cultural investigation.

> The sociologist and the cultural anthropologist must begin their study where the physical anthropologist, the psychological student of race, the geneticist and the physiologist conclude theirs. If racial conflict is not written in biological laws, it is nevertheless before us in America as a social fact which we cannot blink. It is no less real for being man-made. (1941, 74)

This was a clear statement that racial conflict and prejudice (though not race itself) were realities produced by social and cultural dynamics. As we will see, Benedict's historical explanation of racism ultimately minimized the need to investigate it (Visweswaran 1998), but her thought cannot be reduced to a reflex of the race-culture distinction. Boas himself explored the social dimensions of race, identifying the cultural variability in the significance of race in defining social groups across world regions. For him, the race problem in the U.S. was particularly intractable because there social group distinctions were defined by race. Indeed, for quite some time Boas contended that the *"Black*

problem" in the U.S. could only be resolved by the lightening of the Black popu-
lation via miscegenation between Black women and white men. Understanding
why he took this remarkable and troubling position—a subject neglected in the
literature—requires an examination of how Boas understood the relationship
between race, social categories, national identity, and white subjectivity in the
U.S. More generally, examining how anthropologists theorized the social life of
race and imagined a progressive racial future provides insights into anthropological anti-racism and its paradoxes.

Second, I approach the Boasians as key thinkers within the broader intellectual tradition of American liberal anti-racism who, when interpreted
critically, help illuminate paradoxes of that tradition. Understanding race in
anthropological thought requires an inquiry into the political ideals, motivations, and worldviews informing anthropological understandings of race and
racism. It also requires reading anthropological anti-racism through the lens
of anthropologists' engagements with "America" and liberalism. I refer to the
"Americanism" of U.S. anthropologists to call attention to the various ways U.S.
anthropology was a project in which an imagined America—as nation, people, society, and/or culture—figured prominently. Boasian anthropology was
a political project with powerful associations with liberalism and with deep
commitments to America. U.S. society, culture, and peoplehood were an object
of sustained concern, whether or not anthropologists understood themselves
as directly studying the U.S. (Gilkeson 2010). Dorothy Ross has observed that
the disciplines of economics, political science, and sociology in the U.S. were
distinctively American precisely in the influence that ideologies of American
exceptionalism—"the idea that America occupies an exceptional place in history based on her republican government and economic opportunity"—had
upon them (1991, xiv). As I will show, this was no less true of U.S. anthropology
even as anthropologists promoted liberal reform in U.S. society. In referring
to the "Americanism" of U.S. anthropology, I am concerned with how anthropologists imagined and constructed America, with how perceived American
(liberal) ideals informed their thought, and with how their relationships and
commitments to America affected their figurations of race and racism. This
approach, in turn, allows for a reconsideration of their public impact in U.S.
intellectual life.

Finally, my inquiry departs from previous accounts in examining how U.S.
cultural anthropologists engaged the social life of race in the period after World
War II. As I will show in more detail later, cultural anthropologists did not

abandon the study of the social life of race, and the Boasian separation of race and culture did not logically inhibit such inquiries. The issue then is not why did cultural anthropologists relinquish race but what happened to the study of race by cultural anthropologists in the wake of the Boasian intervention. I focus here on two moments. On the one hand, in the 1950s and 1960s there were efforts to extend and move beyond the Boasians in the historical, ethnographic, and comparative study of the social life of race, represented most prominently by two of their successors at Columbia, Charles Wagley and Marvin Harris. On the other hand, by the late 1960s a critical perspective on the racial politics of the discipline emerged as a crucial but today neglected part of the wider effort to decolonize the discipline. Voiced primarily by anthropologists of color and influenced by a Black Studies perspective that identified white racism as a constitutive feature of the nation and its institutions, this critique called into question the image of anthropology as a racially progressive discipline, echoing the doubts that had arisen concerning the realities of American liberal democracy.

The Arguments

The book is organized into two halves, chronologically divided by World War II. The first part treats Boasian anthropology, with primary chapters focusing on Franz Boas (Chapter 2) and Ruth Benedict (Chapter 3). Chapter 1 provides an overview of the Boasian intervention on race in the wider social and political context of the U.S. in the 1920s and 1930s. The second part analyzes significant trajectories of post-Boasian cultural anthropological engagements with race and racism. Here, another overview chapter (Chapter 4) provides an account of transformations in anthropology in the post-war era. Primary chapters focus on the work of Marvin Harris and Charles Wagley (Chapter 5) and the reconceptualization of race and anthropology at a moment of disciplinary crisis, as represented in the writings of William Willis, Diane Lewis, and Charles Valentine (Chapter 6).

The central argument of the first half is that cultural anthropology in the Boasian tradition was an Americanist liberal project that contributed to key paradoxes of liberal discourses on race and racism in the United States. I use the term liberal here in the most general sense of an ethical and political stance promoting the freedom of humans to realize their potential as individuals. Generally recognized as rooted in Enlightenment thought and enshrined in political documents such as the U.S. Constitution and Declaration of Independence, American liberalism from the start rested on constitutive contradictions

(Wilder 2005) between the notion of equal endowment across humanity ("all men are created equal") and the delimitation of full political rights to a "community of the free" restricted to propertied white men. Whiteness itself became a form of property integral to a U.S. body politic characterized by racialized exclusions and hierarchies (Harris 1993; Hartman 1997). "The principle of racial equality became a constitutive element in liberal identity only from the mid-twentieth century onwards" (Losurdo 2011, 322). Boasians helped forge that identity, seeking to expand liberal principles across the color line and instructing Americans—particularly white Americans—on how to reconcile liberal principles with racial differences. Yet the deep relationships between racism and liberalism integral to the U.S. body politic proved exceptionally difficult to dissolve and were reproduced in the anthropological imagination. Anthropology, in turn, helped produce a liberal imagination of American race and culture that reinscribed in new terms the equation between whiteness and America.

I focus on two sets of conundrums in Boasian anti-racist thought. If the Boasians' view of racism as a cultural phenomenon made its elimination imaginable, their theorization of the tenacity of tradition and the power of culture to shape individual consciousness provided a formidable obstacle to liberal reform. The implicit question emerged: How could U.S. whites—socialized into racist attitudes toward non-whites—become liberal subjects who treated individuals as individuals? Education, especially socialization into liberal principles from an early age, was the most ready solution, but Boasians also doubted its efficacy. Most striking, Boas himself was pessimistic that white Americans could be educated into becoming liberal subjects who could ignore race in the evaluation and treatment of Black individuals. However, rather than confront this social-political problem as a reflection of deep associations between whiteness, liberalism, and American national identity formation, he deferred it by proposing a biological solution—the lightening of the Black population through miscegenation. Benedict pursued a different tack, attempting to reconcile the coexistence of white racism and liberal democracy in the U.S. by representing liberal democratic principles as core values in American culture. Overall, Boasians ultimately deferred a confrontation with racism, the color line, and the power of whiteness as constitutive features of the U.S. social order.

Moreover, Boasian thought reflected and perpetuated a typically tacit, sometimes explicit, equation between whiteness and American even as it contested dogmas of white supremacy. Boasians argued that culture rather than race provided the best scientific explanation for group differences, but they did not deconstruct the race concept (Teslow 2014). Rather, they reconstructed race to signify a global division of humanity into three primary classifications: Caucasoid, Negroid, and Mongoloid. This had the effect of sharpening a distinction between whites and non-whites—the color line in its most basic sense—under the authority of science (Jacobson 1998). Race continued to matter in Boasians' thought as a category of biological difference and social belonging in the U.S., as evidenced in the care they took to insist that European immigrants were racially white rather than members of distinct races or sub-races. Although Boasians recognized racism as a problem created by white Americans and acknowledged the social importance of the color line, they nonetheless modeled the overcoming of racism facing non-whites on the assimilation of European immigrants. These immigrant analogies contributed to the effacement of the power of racial distinction and whiteness in structuring U.S. society while reproducing an equation between whiteness and America.

In sum, Boasian thought was an important part of a larger stream of twentieth-century liberal anti-racist Americanist discourse that simultaneously contested, instantiated, and denied white domination. Seeds for alternative approaches, however, were apparent from within Boasian thought itself as well as in subsequent cultural anthropological engagements with racism discussed in the second half of the book.

In the post-war era, the Boasian critique of biological determinism was deployed in advancing a civil rights agenda within the U.S. and a human rights agenda within the international sphere (Baker 1998). As in the previous era, many anthropologists would support scientific anti-racism without devoting their work to the study of the social life of race and racism. There were exceptions. Most prominently, Marvin Harris and his mentor Charles Wagley produced a substantial body of comparative work on race, racial classification, and discrimination in Latin America and the U.S. in the 1950s and 1960s. This work was initiated by a study of race relations in Brazil sponsored by the United Nations Educational, Scientific and Cultural Organization (UNESCO) with the goal of determining conditions of "racial harmony." Wagley and Harris departed from the Boasian tradition in devoting sustained ethnographic attention to the social dynamics of race and racism and, in the case of Harris, developing a materialist perspective to explain social variance in forms of racial classification and discrimination. Their comparative analysis had the potential to generate a structural account of racism and white domination across the Americas.

That potential was unrealized as they minimized race as a factor in social domination in Brazil despite early ethnographic insights from Harris that racial ascription was a key factor in social stratification and class formation. Wagley and (ultimately) Harris projected an image of race in Brazil as a society free of systemic racial discrimination, relying on an interpretation of Brazilian society as a kind of inverted projection of the rigid "caste-like" race relations of the U.S. I argue that this account better reflected their liberal desires for the possibility of a post-colonial, post-slavery society free of racism than their ethnographic data. Their theoretical frames minimized racism in Latin America and circumvented the nascent possibility of a project of a comparative and hemispheric study of whiteness as a form of social power. Moreover, Wagley and Harris deployed modernization discourses and immigrant analogies that perpetuated problematic comparisons between whites and non-whites in both the U.S. and Brazil that contributed to the normalization of whiteness. Like the Boasians they succeeded, Wagley and Harris contributed to liberal anti-racist discourses that tacitly confirmed the cultural power of whiteness.

The entanglements between U.S. anthropology, racism, and liberalism came under self-conscious anthropology scrutiny in the late 1960s as a crucial but neglected component of a critical turn in the discipline in which the traditional subjects of anthropologists, as well as anthropologists themselves, began to question the ethics, politics, and relevance of the discipline. The critical turn was itself related to a crisis in American liberal nationalism generated by ethnoracial movements at home, decolonization abroad, the Vietnam War, the rise of the counterculture, and domestic repression. Emergent accusations that anthropology was a form of knowledge production beholden to colonialism and imperialism clearly implicated racism, but the best-known voices involved in the critical turn devoted little attention to a revitalized anthropological approach to race and racism. However, a set of anthropologists—most of them anthropologists of color—articulated a critical race agenda for the discipline and offered a profound challenge to anthropological self-satisfaction as a progressive, anti-racist discipline.

Chapter 6 traces these developments through a focus on the critical diagnosis of anthropology by William Willis, Diane Lewis, and Charles Valentine. Influenced by the Black Studies movement, these scholars developed approaches for analyzing the color line and white supremacy as structural features of America and global imperialism while casting into radical doubt the progressive legacy of the discipline. They developed early critiques of anthropological culture as a concept that, like biological racism, could justify racial and ethnic hierarchies. They advocated structural approaches to race/racism that refused to reduce racial and ethnic dynamics to class and capitalism, and they called for a "native" or "insider" anthropology. They exposed the normalization of whiteness in American social institutions, including the university and anthropology, which they identified as a predominately white liberal practice. The reinvention of anthropology, they suggested, would have to go beyond the critique of biological determinism and scientific racism to confront the racial contradictions of American liberalism reflected in the discipline itself. The Conclusion reflects on the legacies of these interventions.

The Caveats

This is a partial history of U.S. anthropological thought on race and racism—and of the paradoxes of liberal anti-racisms—not a comprehensive one. My focus is on cultural anthropology rather than biological anthropology, even though some anthropologists worked across the two fields. Until Chapter 6, I concentrate primarily on anthropologists affiliated with Columbia University as either faculty or graduate students (or both). This was not my intention when I conceived the project, but it turned out that even in the post-war era many cultural anthropologists addressing the social life of race were associated with Columbia (see Chapter 4). Even within this frame, I had to be highly selective in the figures I chose to examine. Several volumes could be written on the Boasian intervention alone if we were to consider in depth figures such as Alexander Goldenweiser, Paul Radin, Melville Herskovits, Margaret Mead, Zora Neale Hurston, Gilberto Freyre, Otto Klineberg, Ashley Montagu, and other lesser-known intellectuals. Many of these will make appearances in the text, but I have chosen to focus on Boas and Benedict both because of their prominence and because, in my estimation, they provided some of the most compelling (if also paradoxical) reflections on the social life of race and racism.

Columbia University was one major site for the production of anti-racist anthropology in the period under consideration. The other was the University of Chicago, where Lloyd Warner directed several projects in the social anthropology of race relations in the U.S. Warner was a key figure in what is sometimes called the caste school of race relations, and he developed an analytical frame focusing on the relationship between class stratification and the racial divisions perpetuated by harsh strictures against exogamy (McKee 1993, 145–180). His students included African Americans Allison Davis, who conducted studies of race relations and their effect on African American psychology in the rural South (Davis and Dollard 1940; Davis, Gardner, and Gardner 1941), and St. Clair Drake, who co-authored a now classic study of the African American community in Chicago (Drake and Cayton 1962). I do not focus on the social anthropologists (but see Chapter 1) because their work was marginalized within mainstream anthropological currents, was associated more with sociology than anthropology, and because full treatment of it would expand this project beyond the bounds of a single book. Drake, however, does make several appearances in my account. In the mid-1970s he provided important reflections on African Americans in anthropology, which I use to contextualize the racial politics internal to the discipline. Throughout his career he emphasized the central role of struggles of the racially oppressed in transforming structures of power, a perspective the Boasians studiously avoided. His attention to Black subjectivity and self-professed ambivalence toward white liberalism in some ways anticipated the critiques of anthropology I discuss in Chapter 6. I have not, however, produced an account with the central goal of recuperating marginalized figures for the discipline.[3] With the exception of the lesser-known scholars discussed in Chapter 6, my focus is on scholars who had a prominent status within the discipline during their lifetime.

I write this work for two audiences: anthropologists curious about the history of the discipline, particularly with regards to race and racism; and non-anthropologists interested in the history of U.S. liberal thought on race and racism. The goals overlap. I hope that anthropologists come to recognize the liberal Americanism at the heart of twentieth-century anthropology and that non-anthropologists see the discipline as having played an important role in U.S. liberalism. The agenda driving this work is to identify and interrogate the paradoxes of Americanist liberal anti-racism in association with U.S. nationalism. Along the way, I hope to convince the reader that anthropological thought on race and racism has been more extensive, nuanced, and troubled than previously imagined. The point is not to condemn or "trash" anthropology or anthropologists. I consider all of the authors I discuss to be sophisticated thinkers with sincere anti-racist commitments. That is why they are worth engaging critically.

Critical responses to critiques of earlier anthropologists typically insist on locating those anthropologists within their particular social, political, and intellectual contexts. I agree, but discerning such contexts is no simple affair once we take into account not only the orthodox intellectual and political currents of a particular era but the variable heterodox currents also available at a particular moment. For example, our interpretations of the Boasians look different if we locate their thought in relation to the pervasive biological racism of eugenicists and segregationists or in relation to the contemporaneous anti-racist thought of Marxists or radical Black intellectuals.[4] In my analysis of anthropologists I juxtapose their work with those of other intellectuals engaging similar themes in order to discern the particular trajectory anthropology took in relation to other available options. I am particularly concerned with African American engagements with anthropological thought, a subject that merits far more extensive treatment than I can provide here. I nonetheless hope that this book, especially Chapter 6, can contribute to a dialogue between anthropology and Black Studies.

Approaching Race and Racism

Since this book concerns how intellectuals wrote about and theorized race and racism, I should say a few words about the theoretical approach to race and racism that informs my analysis. To be clear, my intent is not to articulate a developed theory of race and racism and use it to measure the virtues and defects of previous scholarship. My goal is to develop a robust narrative of a complex anthropological tradition on race and racism, a narrative that both is sensitive to the historical context of the scholars I discuss and provides critical analysis that illuminates that tradition and its legacies. However, it would be foolish to claim that my own ways of thinking about race and racism—influenced by scholarship produced after the period in question—did not inform my reading of earlier anthropology. How could they not?

Race is both a highly charged topic and a slippery concept to pin down, having a "chameleonic" character (Goldberg 1993) and operating as a "floating signifier" (Jhally and Hall 2002) with variant referents and meanings across time, space, and context. The *Oxford English Dictionary* offers a definition of race as "each of the major divisions of humankind, having distinct characteristics." Those characteristics are, in common usage, typically understood as physical, biological, and/or genetic. Viewed in this way, races, as divisions of humanity, appear to be based on an extra-discursive referent identifiable in human bodies and ancestry. For many contemporary social scientists, myself included, race should be understood, alternatively, in terms of a discourse invented by (some) humans to differentiate humanity (and sub-humanity). "Race is the framework of ranked categories segmenting the human populations that was developed by western Europeans following their global expansion beginning in the 1400s" (Sanjek 1994, 1).[5] Viewed in this way, race is a social construct and, many of us are quick to add, a social reality.

The OED definition is useful, however, in the sense that it minimally points to a version of the race concept with long-standing endurance, applicable to, say, the taxonomy of race posited by Linnaeus in the eighteenth century, as well as to the Boasian embrace of Mongoloid, Caucasoid, and Negroid as "major divisions" of humanity in the first half of the twentieth century. Scientific discourse on race transformed dramatically between these periods, but a "conceptual kernel" (Trouillot 2003)—that humanity could be described in terms of "major divisions"—unites Boas and Linnaeus. In contrast, the constructivist view I hold locates the origins of those differences—indeed, the effort to locate difference—not in the characteristics of those divided but in the social apparatus of division. This apparatus includes, but is not limited to, the sciences and their modes of classification. In other words, race is best seen as a discursive and social mechanism of differentiating humanity rather than as a means of describing human difference. It is thus intimately imbricated with power relations, providing a modality for their articulation, development, and naturalization.

This constructivist approach to race differs from that of the Boasians, but it does not provide me with a set of master keys for deconstructing Boasian thought. To be sure, I will emphasize that the Boasian embrace of the tripartite division of humanity into Mongoloid, Caucasoid, and Negroid had important implications. It did not, however, prevent Boasians and subsequent anthropologists from grappling with the social life of race, with how racial distinctions and the meanings associated with them informed social relationships. It did not, for example, prevent them from examining how classification in the name of race proceeded in socially variable ways, exploring how "race consciousness" varied in intensity across different social formations, identifying racial prejudice and discrimination as imminently social phenomena, or positing the idea of "social race." It is precisely these aspects of anthropological thought, its struggles to comprehend the social significance of race and the production and reproduction of racial hierarchies (racism), that have been neglected in the historical scholarship.

Here, some reflections on the term racism, and how its meaning has expanded over time, are in order. The word racism, dating to the early twentieth century, was not commonly used by scholars until Ruth Benedict helped popularize it in *Race: Science and Politics*. In her usage, racism referred to an ideological phenomenon, a belief and "dogma" concerning the innate superiority and inferiority of races as characterized by immutable biological differences.

> Racism is the dogma that one ethnic group is condemned by nature to congenital inferiority and another group is destined to congenital superiority. It is the dogma that the hope of civilization depends upon eliminating some races and keeping others pure. It is the dogma that one race has carried progress with it throughout human history and alone can ensure future progress. It is a dogma rampant in the world today and which a few years ago was made into a principal basis of the German polity. (Benedict 1940, 153)

If the term racism only entered into common usage with the condemnation of Nazism, Boasian anthropologists had, for years, attacked lay and scientific dogmas of racial inferiority and superiority in the U.S., insisting that the primary determinants of human difference were cultural rather than biological. They were also aware of the social inequities and oppression perpetrated by dominant whites, referring to racial prejudice, antipathy, persecution, conflict, and discrimination. Although Boasians did not use the *term* racism until Benedict's work in the 1940s, they were concerned with the ideologies, mental-affective states (e.g., racial prejudice), and practices (e.g., racial discrimination) referenced by the *concept* of racism as the term is often used today.

From the standpoint of the present, then, Benedict's use of "racism" appears limited, particularly for those who think of racism in structural terms. Indeed, even in the 1940s Oliver Cox, a Black Marxist sociologist, argued that those who—like Benedict—used the term "conceive of it as an ideology or philosophy of racial superiority" and "usually make the assumption that racism is the substance of modern race antagonism." In the process, they focused on the study of an idea rather than the study of "social facts and situations" (Cox 1948, 482), mistaking cause for effect and ignoring how "modern race relations developed out of the imperialistic practices of capitalism." (483). For Cox, terms like "race relations" and "race antagonism" were more inclusive in addressing the "social facts and situations" than the term racism. Ironically, the term racism itself became, for many scholars, a term with broad meaning, referring not only to ideologies but also to practices and, eventually, structures and/or systems. For example, in his widely read *Racism Without Racists*, Eduardo Bonilla Silva identifies "racism as a structure, that is, as a network of social relations at social, political, economic and ideological levels that shapes the life chances of various races" (2014, 26).

My own thinking embraces a structural approach to racism, and I use the term to denote the imbrication of race and power through systems of domination, oppression, inequality, and exclusion. I also use the term to refer to a subject of attention and concern of the anthropologists at the heart of this work, even though, as noted above, they may not have used the term racism in this way or used the term at all. I do so because they were concerned with understanding and combating the production and reproduction of racial inequalities, oppression, segregation, and so on. The question of how they theorized these phenomena cannot be reduced to their use of a word; it requires an extended exegesis of how they conceptualized the differentiation of humanity within relationships of power.

Developing this account by no means precludes a critical perspective. My approach here is to identify and explicate tensions and paradoxes internal to anthropological thought (a key focus of Chapters 2, 3, and 5), developed out of close readings of texts, particularly as they relate to Americanist liberalism. Doing so does not negate the importance of the Boasian intervention and its legacies. Its insistence on a distinction between race and culture, however problematic, helped lay the intellectual grounds for analysis of race as a social phenomena and a social construct. It challenged discourses of biological determinism and cultural hierarchy in ways that students still find illuminating. Avowed white supremacists vilify Boas and his successors for a reason (Baker 2010, 156–219). Their project *was* anti-racist. It also deferred a full confrontation with white supremacy and the color line, disavowed the possibility that racism was a constitutive feature of the U.S. social order, and reproduced a foundational presupposition of the republic that equated "America" with whiteness. Those legacies too must be confronted.

A Personal Orientation

In the chapters that follow I provide background information on the major authors under consideration, with the conviction that their personal histories, politics, and subject positions informed their work. It seems appropriate then to provide the reader with a sense of who I am and the personal and intellectual trajectory that led me to write this book. If this becomes tedious, dear reader, move on.

I am a white, middle-ageing, heterosexual man from a family with a Protestant background. I was born in Louisville, Kentucky, in 1969—in the midst of the creative and tumultuous period that marks the end of my inquiry—and raised in the early years of the post–civil rights era. My parents were the first in their families to go to college, beneficiaries of a post-war expansion in university education. My father went on to law school, worked under Attorney General Robert Kennedy, and returned to Louisville to work for a corporate law firm. My mother worked as a middle school teacher to support my father in law school and then became a homemaker.

I grew up in a suburban enclave, the product of a wealthy childhood we called "upper middle class." Of the hundred or so households in our neighborhood, almost all were white, mostly Protestants like us, though there were a handful of Catholic and Jewish families and others from a few foreign countries: Yugoslavia, Iran, and India come to mind. No African Americans lived in our neighborhood. This was not to say that my childhood was entirely segregated, at least in the public schools I attended. In 1975, when I was five years old, the Louisville school district was forced by court mandate to begin a busing program to integrate city schools segregated by entrenched racial geographies and white flight. Black kids were sent to suburban schools and white kids to inner-city schools. Some eight to ten thousand whites came out to protest busing, and their clashes with the police were only put down when the governor called in the Kentucky National Guard. I, of course, only learned about busing and the white riots later. In the early 1980s my older brother spent his last two years of high school in an inner-city school and reported that his experiences of school integration were largely limited to gym, given that his placement in the "advanced program" meant he spent most of his class time with fellow white deportees. By the time my high school years arrived, busing was replaced by a magnet system.

My parents were probably more liberal than those of most of my friends and by and large retained the political values of their parents, New Deal Democrats. They believed in the welfare state and were chagrined by the history of white racism. They did not send their kids to private schools to avoid busing. My mother, the daughter of a carpenter, made sure we understood the good fortune of our class position and, I think now, never appeared comfortable in a class scene that looked down on the world she came from. At the same time, she worked hard to ensure her children had the cultural capital that counted.

She corrected me if I talked too Southern or too Black. She fought like hell with school principals to get me in the advanced program, knowing full well that was the track to a good university. Although I did not have the terms, I had a sense of what class and white privilege meant.

The great divides that defined the world I grew up in, besides gender and sexuality, were the class distinctions between whites and the racial-class division between white and Black. The distinctions between Protestants, Catholics, and Jews also mattered but made relatively little impression upon me. Since my family did not go to church, religion did not mean much aside from the pervasive fear that if God existed I was in trouble. Catholic mostly signified you might go to a Catholic school. As with Catholics, I had Jewish friends I knew from school or tennis, went to their birthday parties and Bar Mitzvahs, stayed over at their houses. Early on, the only thing I noticed about the Jewish kids was they got to skip school for their different holidays. Later I realized they had their own country club and to a certain extent their own suburban neighborhoods. Some of the other white kids occasionally derided them behind their backs. In high school my friend Mike—more outspoken in his Jewish identity than most—was teased for wearing a *kippah* (yarmulke), but he gave as good as he got. In Spanish class the teacher told us we could chose our own names and he picked Jesús. They battled the entire year, Mike always insisting she call him by his chosen name. Overall the Jewish kids I knew were upper-middle-class whites like me; they of course might have seen things differently.

The Black-white distinction was of a different order. We lived worlds apart even when we shared the same space. I do not recall much overt hostility or direct racist comments on the part of whites, certainly not in my own family. I identified such racism—and that is probably what racism meant to me— mostly with the whites we were socialized not to be: rednecks and white trash (local parlance my parents never used). Yet there was always a divide no one, speaking for the whites at least, cared to breach. Neither my friends nor I had Black friends. If dating between Blacks and whites occurred, I do not remember it. I do remember two occasions the subject came up in conversation. The mother of a friend told us cardinals and blue jays don't mix, so why should white and Black? Another friend said he did not see anything wrong with it, but think of the rough time children would have. Such were some of the ways the color line was preemptively protected in 1980s Louisville. Race was a morally charged space many whites avoided discussing, even with each other. But my childhood heroes were the Black basketball players of the University of Louisville. My brother and I were proud that our team had been integrated by our parents' alma mater before our archrival, the University of Kentucky. When I fantasized about the awesome basketball team I was the star of, my teammates were two of my (white) best friends and two Black schoolmates I hardly knew. Perhaps that was the only safe space for a white masculinist liberal desire for social integration.

I give this account of my childhood sensibilities of whiteness and the color line—revolving around a Black-white binary—because they inform my subjective experience of race in this country and surely shape my ways of thinking about it in ways I do not fully perceive. A recent body of scholarship has analyzed the complex history of the racialization of Jews and other European populations (e.g., Italians, Irish, Slavs) in the United States.[6] The Boasian reinvention of race was, in part, a confrontation with the use of the race concept to define meaningful biological distinctions between these populations and "Old Americans" (deemed Anglo-Saxons and Nordics), identifying them all as falling within the category Caucasian. By the time I grew up, that understanding of race had achieved the status of common sense. It is thus, I admit, more difficult for me to grasp the racialization of European immigrants in the nineteenth and early twentieth century than to recognize racialization across the color line, particularly the Black-white divide. Having said that, I am ready to defend the argument that efforts to analogize the situation of European immigrants and peoples of color is a well-established habit in the U.S. social sciences—and public discourse—that has contributed to a misapprehension of racial dynamics in ways that reinforce racial hegemony.

My particular concern with the Black-white divide in this book is also a product of an intellectual trajectory that has focused on the African Diaspora in the Americas. When I entered graduate school in anthropology at the University of Texas, I did not intend to become a scholar of race. I had been an undergraduate philosophy major at the University of North Carolina at Chapel Hill, which allowed me plenty of space in my schedule to tour the liberal arts. I pursued anthropology because it allowed me to combine a burgeoning interest in Central America with my attraction to critical theories of modernity. My assigned advisor at Texas was Edmund (Ted) Gordon, an African American who spent nearly a decade in Nicaragua working in the middle of a tense relationship between Afro-Nicaraguan Creoles and the Sandinista revolutionary government (Gordon 1998). Through my courses with him, I developed an interest in the politics of race and ethnicity in Central America, eventually deciding to do research on an Afro-indigenous people known as Garifuna in Honduras. My work was informed by an emerging focus on transnationalism and diaspora that called attention to the production of social identities and political affiliations across the borders of nation-states (e.g., Gordon and Anderson 1999; Anderson 2009).

It is thus notable that my inquiry into the twentieth-century history of race and anthropology has led me back to the nation-state and a determined focus on white U.S. anthropologists as "Americans." The literature informed by transnationalism and diaspora, as well as colonialism and empire, has convincingly argued against the constraints of the nation-state as an analytical frame in imagining phenomena ranging from social movements to knowledge production.[7] The anthropology of the African Diaspora has itself long been informed by intellectual exchange across the borders of colonies and nation-states (Yelvington 2006; 2011). Moreover, transnational analytical frameworks have allowed us to apprehend how comparisons of racial dynamics across nation-states have helped produce discourses of race and racism within them (Seigel 2009). As we will see, anthropological accounts of racial classification and discrimination (or purported lack of discrimination) in Latin America have long informed academic figurations of race and racism in the U.S. These comparisons not only tended to minimize racism in Latin America; as I argue in Chapter 5, they attenuated recognition of the scope and nature of white domination in the U.S.

My own examination of anthropological discourse on race has led me back to the nation-state because of the importance of "America" and Americanist commitments to the thought of prominent U.S. anthropologists. The critical sensibility toward the nation-state generated in the aforementioned literature facilitates a critical apprehension of the power of nationalist discourse in a discipline often imagined as historically disinterested in the U.S. So too a burgeoning literature within critical race studies and whiteness studies has called attention to the conflation between whiteness and America in constructs of race and nation.[8]

Here, I also owe a debt to Brackette Williams' now classic critique of anthropological literature on "ethnicity" (1989), a topic of considerable interest to the discipline in the 1970s and 1980s. Her key move was to view terms such as "ethnic" and "minority" not as neutral descriptors for particular kinds of groups but as meta-labels that do ideological work in the world. Most pointedly, Williams identified how those terms often operate in relationship to an unmarked, racialized dominant category. Ethnicity, she insisted, had to be understood in relation to the broader field of categorical distinctions, including racial distinctions, operative in a society and nation-state that privileged some kinds of bodies and heritage over others: "To do otherwise is to make the mistake many of our informants make—to believe, for example, that a nonwhite can 'whiten' into invisibility" (428). Those categorized as "ethnic," particularly those rendered as racially distinct from the "majority"—think of the "ethnic" aisle in the supermarket—occupy a troubled position within the nation. "Groups labeled 'ethnic,' minority, 'subnational,' or 'subcultural' pit themselves against the state-backed race/class conflation that becomes the ideologically defined 'real producers' of the nation's patrimony" (434). In the United States, white "middle-class" identity and culture have long been tacitly conflated with "America." Williams notes of anthropologists: "Taking ethnic groups and the race/class/nation conflation as givens in the world to be analyzed, all too often they have paid insufficient attention to the conceptual contradictions" inherent to the categorical distinctions of discriminatory national identity formation (434–435).

I would go further to assert that anthropologists, like other social scientists, are themselves producers of categorical distinctions, forever debating categories and meta-categories of difference and their proper labels. They have contributed in key ways to discourses of race, culture, and ethnicity in the U.S. Williams' critique of the failure of anthropologists to fully comprehend the conceptual conflations between race, nation, and culture can be extended back to the Boasians and the work of Wagley and Harris. Margaret Mead's *And Keep Your Powder Dry* (1942)—a wartime examination of U.S. culture that self-consciously represented America as a nation of white immigrants in a plea for national solidarity—is an egregious example (Hazard 2014). But I do not focus on Mead as a primary subject of this work. I am more interested in exploring the nuances of anthropological positions—for example, tacit writing practices that conflate America with white, reconstructions of racial classification systems, immigrant analogies between whites and non-whites—to critically reflect on the contradictions of influential currents of anthropological anti-racism. Rather than simply highlight the inadequate treatment of race and racism by anthropologists, I explore the ways they participated in, contributed to (and challenged) the conflation between America and whiteness in their struggles to reconcile American liberalism and racism.

In the body of this work, I avoid—as best I can—extemporizing on the contemporary politics of race in the U.S. with the hope that readers will make their own evaluation of the relevance of my analysis for thinking about our troubled times. Nonetheless, in the Conclusion I grapple with a set of questions this history poses for the present. In the age of Trump, what should those of us invested in racial justice make of Americanist liberal anti-racism and critiques of it? In the face of direct assaults on that tradition by resurgent white supremacist nationalism—resonant with the early twentieth-century nativism the Boasians confronted—is the moral and political imperative to defend the Americanist liberal tradition? Do struggles to defend anti-racist liberalism perpetuate the continued misrecognition of white power throughout American society? Does the liberal shock at the election of Trump betray a continued inability of the social sciences to grasp the realities of the social life of race and racism in this country? What did anthropology do with the critiques of liberal anti-racism voiced in the early 1970s? Where does the discipline now stand in relation to its liberal anti-racist legacy and the project, announced fifty years ago, to decolonize it?

1 The Anti-Racist Liberal Americanism of Boasian Anthropology

IN 1924, THE UNITED STATES CONGRESS passed the Johnson-Reed Act, an immigration law designed to dramatically reduce the number of immigrants and populate the country with a particular type of white person. The law excluded from entry any person ineligible for citizenship on the basis of race or nationality. The 1790 Naturalization Act, still in force, reserved for free whites naturalization as a path to citizenship. This act had been modified to allow for the naturalization of "aliens of African nativity and to persons of African descent" in the Reconstruction era. The Johnson-Reed Act thus prohibited all Asian immigration. For Europe, the law devised a quota system figured at 2 percent of each country's U.S. immigrant population as recorded in the 1890 census. The year was not arbitrary. From the 1890s forward, the European immigrant population entering the United States had shifted from northwestern Europe (e.g., Germany and the United Kingdom) to southern and eastern Europe (e.g., Italy and Russia). The Johnson-Reed act tried to ensure that the right kind of whites—those understood to be racially Nordic—would arrive in greater proportion than undesirable Europeans (Ngai 2004, 21–55). Moreover, enforcement of the law nearly completely halted the arrival of European colonial subjects, most notably Black West Indians who had been arriving in significant numbers in the post-war era (Putnam 2011). In sum, the law encoded a dual logic of white exclusivity and differentiated whiteness in a racialized vision of the American people—past, present, and future.

The Johnson-Reed Act represented a political victory for a prominent set of East Coast eugenicists. Among them were H. H. Laughlin, Madison Grant, Henry Fairfield Osborn, Theodore Lothrop Stoddard, and Charles Davenport.

Through organizations such as the Immigration Restriction League, the American Genetic Association, and the Eugenics Records Office, they campaigned against immigrants from eastern and southern Europe as biologically unfit for American citizenship and civilization. The eugenicists, invoking the authority of biological science, physical anthropology, and racial psychology, played a key role in structuring immigration policy. Laughlin, for example, was the leading expert on genetics for the House Committee on Education while Grant served as the chair of the Eugenics Committee of the United States Committee on Selective Immigration. Grant's *The Passing of the Great Race* (1916) was a highly influential work in the 1920s and has been described as "the Ur-text of modern American nativism" (Guterl 2001, 8). He divided humanity into a tripartite scheme of Caucasians, Mongols, and Negroes, sub-dividing Caucasians into Nordics, Alpines, and Mediterraneans, echoing an influential taxonomy established by economist William Ripley. Grant's book focused on the protection of Nordic racial purity from Alpines and Mediterraneans, but there was little doubt that Negroes and Mongols were, for him and other eugenicists, members of "primary" races occupying the lowest positions on the global racial hierarchy. Grant also helped manufacture Virginia's Racial Integrity Act (Guterl 2001, 47; Spiro 2009, 252–258), which prohibited sexual relations between "white" and "colored" and defined as white any person "who has no trace whatsoever of any blood other than Caucasian" (Wolfe 2015). In this instance, the overarching distinction that mattered was white/non-white. This law was also passed in 1924, a year Spiro calls "the high point of scientific racism in the United States" (2009, 328).

Racial science was not, however, simply the handmaiden of Nordic racism but a contested field in which a cadre of anthropologists, led by Franz Boas, attempted to reorient understandings of racial difference in their political and intellectual struggles against eugenicists (Spiro 2009, 297–327). In the early months of 1925, the magazine *The Nation* published a series of articles critical of "the Nordic Myth." Boas and three former students—Alexander Goldenweiser, Melville Herskovits, and Edward Sapir—wrote four of the articles. As Handler notes, these short pieces collectively embodied the main tenets of Boasian thought on race:

> that race "antagonism" is not instinctive; that American racial categories could not be correlated with fixed biological facts; that "civilization" included "contributions" from all peoples (not just the "Nordics"); that there was no

relationship between a people's cultural achievements and the biology of the group; and that such sciences as eugenics were little more than rationalizations of commonsense prejudices. (2014, iv)

Boas (1925) argued that mental differences between groups should be traced not to racial affiliation but to family ancestry and social environment. Herskovits (1925) criticized the conflation between race and nationality underlying immigration policy and identified flaws in intelligence testing purporting to show innate racial hierarchies in mental ability. Goldenweiser catalogued civilizational achievements of Mongols, Arabs, (East) Indians, and Negroes, urging whites to accept these peoples as comrades on the "chariot of history" rather than "persist in forcing them to do the pulling while we wield the whip of race pride and domination" (1925, 462). Finally, Sapir lampooned the mania for racial classification and abuse of inadequate knowledge of heredity, suggesting that the "reasonable man" forgo thinking in racial terms (1925, 213). If the 1924 laws enshrined a vision of white/Nordic supremacy, *The Nation's* issue on the Nordic Myth reflected the rise of university-based Boasian anti-racism as a liberal public intellectual project that would gain increased traction over the next two decades.

This chapter provides an overview of the Boasian intervention on race in the 1920s (and beyond) in the broad contexts of race making and imperial power, contests over the meaning of race and America, and the consolidation of anthropology as a university-based discipline in the United States. First, I discuss the professionalization of anthropology in the early twentieth century in relation to ongoing patterns of racial domination and exclusion inherited from the nineteenth century: settler colonialism; anti-Black terrorism; and racialized anti-immigrant agitation. I highlight how American national belonging was built on the foundation of an original racial distinction between whites, Indians, and Blacks, a foundation that Boasian anti-racism never fully interrogated or subverted. The second part of the chapter treats Boasian anthropology as a university-based field of knowledge production and a multivalent public political project concerned with the reformation of modern U.S. society based on liberal principles. I provide an account of the main tenets of the Boasian critique of scientific and popular racisms, with a critical eye toward the different implications it held for those it considered white and non-white. The final section extends this discussion with a comparison of Boasians with Black intellectuals associated with the Harlem Renaissance and the social anthropology of the University of Chicago to begin to lay bare some of the paradoxes and limitations of Boasian anti-racism.

Foundational Distinctions of the Republic

The post–World War I racisms of American nativism were the products of the recent past and long-term dynamics of racialized exclusion and domination characterized by white supremacy. Saidiya Hartman succinctly captures how, in the history of U.S. racial formation,

> liberty, property, and whiteness were inextricably enmeshed. Racism was central to the expansion of capitalist relations of production, the organization, division, and management of the laboring classes, and the regulation of the population through licensed forms of sexual associations and conjugal unions and through the creation of an internal danger to the purity of the body public. Whiteness was a valuable and exclusive property essential to the citizen-subject and the exemplary self-possession of the liberal individual. (1997, 119)

In the U.S., whiteness was a key marker of "fitness for self-government" reflecting the colonial opposition between white settlers, indigenous peoples, and African slaves. Black enslavement and Indian displacement were constitutive conditions for the realization of American independence and remained central to the development of the republic. In its early years, "what a citizen really was, at bottom, was someone who could help put down a slave rebellion or participate in Indian wars" (Jacobson 1998, 25). Native American peoples were forced west of the Mississippi and rendered "domestic dependent nations" (28) denied citizenship. Indian displacement was facilitated by treaty, federally sponsored war, legalized dispossession, and vigilante terror. The 1887 Dawes Severalty Act furthered the process of expropriation, reducing by half the lands controlled by Indians (Painter 2010, 234). By the 1890s, the census bureau declared the frontier of continental expansion closed, though armed Indian resistance—sometimes referred to as the Indian Wars—continued intermittently until 1924. The institution of Black slavery in the South and some of the western territories persisted long after American independence, abolition coming only as a result of the Civil War. African American advances toward enfranchisement during Reconstruction in the South were short-lived, whites reconstituting power through law and terror and creating a system of segregation upheld by the Supreme Court in 1896. Although Black subjugation was particularly intense in the South, structural discrimination afflicted Blacks throughout the country.

Black soldiers who fought in World War I returned only to be confronted with race riots in over twenty U.S. cities and a resurgent Ku Klux Klan with a mass presence within and beyond the South (Schneider 2002).

The foundational tripartite division between white, Indian, and Black provided the scaffolding for other racial distinctions and discriminations. For example, it informed the treatment of Mexicans occupying the vast territory acquired by the United States in the Mexican-American War (1846–1848). Although the treaty ending the war stipulated that Mexicans who remained could choose to become U.S. citizens, the federal government considered Indian communities as a distinct legal category (and "problem")[1] and devolved the right to determine individuals' citizenship status to the governments of the new territories and states. Those governments all limited full political rights to persons deemed white, though they used different criteria of blood quantum in determining who was white, Indian, or Black and implemented varying strictures on those deemed non-white (Menchaca 2001, 215). The racial status of Mexicans crossing the border in the early twentieth century remained structured by racial distinctions. The *Dictionary of Races and Peoples*, written under the auspices of the Bureau of Immigration, noted that individuals counted as Mexican were considered white while Mexicans deemed Black or Indian were counted under those categories (United States Immigration Commission 1911, 96). The 1924 immigration law did not create a country quota for Mexico—in deference to the need for agricultural labor in the Southwest and California—but did establish the Border Patrol, which operated to regulate border crossings and effectively established the category of illegal immigrant (De Genova 2005, 213–249; Ngai 2004, 56–90).

In the second half of the nineteenth century, Asians became considered a problem on the West Coast. Labor and white supremacist organizations agitated against the Chinese. In 1882, the federal government passed the bluntly named Chinese Exclusion Act. In 1908, President Theodore Roosevelt established the Gentlemen's Agreement with the Japanese government to severely limit Japanese immigration. Five years later, California passed the Alien Land Law—forbidding agricultural land ownership by persons ineligible for citizenship—that targeted Japanese. In 1917, the federal government expanded immigration restrictions to a "barred Asiatic Zone" extending from Afghanistan to the Pacific (Ngai 2004, 18). The 1924 immigration law, combined with contemporary Supreme Court decisions, definitively established that persons from throughout Asia and the Pacific were not white, even if racial science suggested that some of these persons (e.g., "Hindus") were "Caucasian." For the purposes of U.S. law, being white became equated with European ancestry, a notion that may not have had entirely clear boundaries but nonetheless divided Europe from non-Europe in reckoning American belonging as white right and privilege (Jacobson 1998, 223–245; Ngai 2004, 37–50).

The race concept was also used to differentiate populations within Europe. The meaning and boundaries of whiteness, beyond its distinction from blackness and indianness, were not subjects of major concern until the mid-nineteenth century and the mass immigration of Germans and Irish. Beginning in the 1840s, Germans and especially Irish became subjects of nativist anxiety and were cast as Teutonic and Celtic races in the racial science of the era. By the end of the century, such anxieties were increasingly directed to southern and eastern European immigrants. By the 1924 law, Irish and German ancestry had largely become folded into an Americanist Nordicism purportedly requiring protection from mongrelization by the problematic stocks of southern and eastern Europe. Although racialized understandings of non-Nordic immigrant inferiority, incapacity for self-government, and dubious capacity for assimilation were fiercely contested, particularly by the immigrants themselves, they were pervasive within U.S. media culture, racial science, and political institutions (Jacobson 1998, 39–90).

From this all too brief overview we can highlight the co-existence of two modalities of racial differentiation in the United States in the late nineteenth and early twentieth century. The first, still with us today, revolved around the social construction of white/non-white distinctions built on the foundational opposition between whites, Blacks, and Indians in which whiteness became a form of property (Harris 1993). Indian and Black blood—the enduring heritage of the conquered aborigine and the enslaved African—were the elemental differences that made the white nation, and made the nation white. The "Mongolian" or "Asiatic" races were also located beyond the bounds of whiteness. The meanings and boundaries of whiteness were never entirely fixed or clear, but the white/non-white distinction—the color line—was a pervasive feature of the sociopolitical order and national belonging since the founding of the republic. The second modality of racial differentiation revolved around distinctions within whiteness. Here, hegemonic American whiteness, equated with terms such as Anglo-Saxon, Teutonic, and/or Nordic, was opposed to the denigrated others of European provenance, peoples racially classified and sub-classified as Alpine and Mediterranean or Semitic, Celtic, Slavonic, and so on.

The classification system found in the *Dictionary of Races or Peoples*, a report of the United States Immigration Commission (1911) authored by anthropologist Daniel Folkmar, represents one prominent effort to develop a schema to classify the racial relationships among various immigrant groups, focusing especially on distinctions within the category Caucasian.[2] Reading from left to right in Figure 1, the schema begins with Johan Blumenbach's eighteenth-century classification of "races" as Caucasian, Mongolian, Malay, Ethiopian, and American (Indian). It then adapts the work of U.S. anthropologist Daniel Brinton to subdivide Caucasians at the levels of "stocks," "groups" and finally "peoples," themselves also figured as "races" (thus the *Dictionary of Races or Peoples*, not "Races *and* Peoples"). The final column presents an alternative scheme for sorting Caucasian peoples under the subdivisions Teutonic, Alpine, and Mediterranean developed by William Ripley in 1890. All of the significant European immigrant populations fell under the category Caucasian, although the classification of Hebrews (Jews) as "Semitic" placed them in an ambiguous position. This taxonomy represented racial difference as a series of nested categories with the implication that the taxonomical distance among the various Caucasian peoples/races was far less than that between Caucasians and the other principal races, especially "Ethiopians" ("Negroes") and American Indians. The dictionary was not overly concerned with differences within the latter categories. For example, it noted that while scientists disagreed on whether the "Hottentots" and "Bushmen" of South Africa, the "Negritos" of Malaysia, and the Papua New Guineans were "Negroes," for the purposes of immigration they could all be classified as such: "They are alike in inhabiting hot countries and in belonging to the lowest division of mankind from an evolutionary standpoint" (100).

Being Caucasian was, in social life as in scientific discourse, by no means a monolithic affair. English, Russian, Italian, and Jew were peoples/races deemed more or less fit for inclusion in the American republic. Jews were a particular source of anxiety, blurring the boundaries of whiteness. Goldstein argues that in the late nineteenth and early twentieth century, Jews—cast as clannish, ambitious, and successful—represented a "mirror of American modernity" reflecting ambivalence about modernity itself (2006, 36). Anti-Semitism became particularly prominent in the inter-war era, as Jews became associated with communism and universities imposed quotas on Jewish enrollment. Throughout the 1920s and 1930s, "few Americans could part with their belief that Jewish racial characteristics presented a significant obstacle to the stability of white

Based on Brinton (cf. Keane).			People.	Ripley's races, with other corresponding terms.
Race.	Stock.	Group.		
Caucasian..	Aryan.....	Teutonic	Scandinavian: Danish...... Norwegian........ Swedish......... German (N. part)..... Dutch...... English (part)......... Flemish...........	I. TEUTONIC. H. Europæus (Lapouge). Nordic (Deniker). Dolicho-leptorhine (Kohlmann). Germanic (English writers). Reihengräber (German writers). Kymric (French writers).
		Lettic........	Lithuanian.........	
		Celtic.......	Scotch (part)........ Irish (part).......... Welsh...............	Part Alpine.
		Slavonic.....	Russian............. Polish.... Czech: Bohemian........ Moravian........ Servian............. Croatian............ Montenegrin......... Slovak.... Slovenian........... Ruthenian........... Dalmatian........... Herzegovinian....... Bosnian.............	II. ALPINE (OR CELTIC). H. Alpinus (Lapouge). Occidental (Deniker). Disentis (German writers). Celto-Slavic (French writers). Lappanoid (Pruner-Bey). Sarmatian (von Hölder). Arvernian (Beddoe).
		Illyric.......	Albanian............	
		Armenic.....	Armenian...........	
		Italic.......	French.............. Italian (part)......... Roumanian..........	Part Alpine. Part Mediterranean.
			Spanish............. Spanish-American.... Mexican, etc......... Portuguese..........	III. MEDITERRANEAN. H. Meridionalis (Lapouge). Atlanto-Mediterranean and Ibero-Insular (Deniker). Iberian (English writers). Ligurian (Italian writers).
		Hellenic.....	Greek...............	
		Iranic.......	Hindu.............. Gypsy...............	Part Mediterranean. Part Teutonic.
	Semitic...	Arabic......	Arabian.............	
		Chaldaic....	Hebrew............. Syrian..............	Part Mediterranean.
	Caucasic ..	....	Caucasus peoples.....	Doubtful.
	Euskaric..	....	Basque..............	
	Sibiric....	Finnic......	Finnish........... Lappish............ Magyar............. Bulgarian (part)......	
		Tataric......	Turkish, Cossack, etc .	
		Japanese....	Japanese, Korean	
		Mongolic....	Kalmuk.............	
Mongolian .	Sinitic....	Chinese.....	Chinese............ East Indian (part, i. e., Indo-Chinese).	
Malay......	....	....	Pacific Islander (part).	
Ethiopian..	....	....	East Indian (part).... Negro...............	
American (Indian).	....	....	American Indian......	

Figure 1 Classification of "immigrant races or peoples" in the *Dictionary of Races or Peoples.*

Source: United States Immigration Commission (1911, 5)

America" (136). This anxiety reflected ambiguities in the perceived whiteness of Jews, but it did not negate their whiteness.

Historians of whiteness have struggled to come up with a term to describe the populations located in between Nordic and/or Anglo-Saxon whiteness and categorical non-whiteness. Contenders include, among others, "conditionally white," "not quite white," "situationally white," "off white," "semiracialized," "white on arrival," and "inbetween peoples" (Roediger 2005, 12–13). The racialized distinctions between groups understood as Caucasians and between those divided by the color line differed in important ways. As Roediger notes, it is important to keep in mind that the "new" European immigrants of the late nineteenth and early twentieth century experienced forms of racialization and discrimination that cannot be equated to the "hard, exclusionary and often color-based racism of Jim Crow segregation, Asian exclusion, and Indian removal" (12). However ambivalently they were located within discourses of hegemonic whiteness, the former were able to naturalize as "whites" and could make claims to whiteness via European provenance. Recognizing that the race concept worked both to differentiate types of whites and delineate a color line between white and non-white is crucial for understanding not only the history of U.S. racisms but the liberal anti-racism of Boasians.

The Professionalization of Anthropology

The Boasian intervention on race was, in no small measure, a reactive product of a racist social order supported by science, including anthropology. Most notoriously, what Europeans dubbed the "American school" of anthropology—a group of scholars who posited the multiple origins of human races—provided scientific support for the defense of slavery in the mid-nineteenth century. Their polygenic theory fell out of favor with the ascendance of the Darwinian evolutionary paradigm, but their techniques of measuring skulls to rank the intelligence of races, undergirded by presumptions of innate white superiority, persisted in physical anthropology (Baker 1998, 11–53; Smedley 1993, 231–254; Stocking 1968, 42–68). Although the ethnologists who studied the customs and languages of living humans might express sympathy and admiration for American Indians, they too largely began and ended with assumptions of racial hierarchy. Daniel Brinton, the first anthropology professor in a U.S. university, was typical in contending that visible physical differences among races reflected mental differences such that global races could be organized in hierarchical terms, with whites at the top and Blacks at the bottom (Baker 2000, 405).

Anthropology did not begin to develop into the university-based professional academic discipline we know today until the late nineteenth and early twentieth century. Throughout most of the nineteenth century, anthropology was largely practiced by gentleman scholars affiliated with localized scientific societies (Darnell 1998, 12). According to Darnell, anthropology began to be professionalized under the Bureau of Ethnology (later the Bureau of American Ethnology [BAE]), a government agency created in 1879. The first head of the bureau was John Wesley Powell, whose studies of American Indians were an outgrowth of his geographic work in western territories undergoing white settlement. He justified the establishment of the bureau on the grounds that detailed knowledge of Indian languages and customs would prove useful in addressing the "Indian Problem" and document primitive cultures before they disappeared (Baker 2010, 70–73; Darnell 1998, 37). The first effort to institutionalize anthropology by creating a corps of paid professionals was thus intimately bound up with settler colonialism. The BAE remained important to anthropology into the twentieth century, funding some of the work of Boas and his graduate students. Museums would also play a key role in the development of the discipline, combining the collection of artifacts for public display with sponsorship of ethnological research. Ultimately, it was the university that became the primary institutional locus for anthropological knowledge production; Franz Boas would play a key role in the process.

Boas (1858–1942) was, it is commonly recognized, the most influential figure in the formation of twentieth-century U.S. anthropology. He was born in Minden, Germany, in a secularized Jewish family devoted to political liberalism. He received a PhD in physics from the University of Kiel (1881), where he also studied geography. His move to anthropology developed out of an interest in the relationship between the human mind and the natural environment and his encounters with Inuit people. Boas immigrated to the United States in 1887, inspired, he later said, by the republican and individualist ideals associated with American democracy and the relative freedom of scientific inquiry possible in a young country. The suppression of liberalism and resurgence of anti-Semitism in Bismarck's Germany also likely played a role (Cole 1999, 84). Naturalizing as a citizen in 1889, he worked in a variety of positions in his early years in the U.S. and conducted research on indigenous peoples on the Northwest Coast.

He was hired at Clark University in 1889, resigning in 1892. He then worked as the chief anthropology assistant for the World's Columbian Exposition in Chicago. In 1896 he was appointed assistant curator at the American Natural History Museum and lecturer at Columbia University, where he was appointed professor in 1899. Cole asserts that by the early twentieth century Boas "commanded the field of American anthropology . . . becoming the leading ethnologist, American linguist, folklorist, and physical anthropologist" (285). After resigning from the museum in 1905, his primary base was Columbia, where he trained several generations of leading U.S. anthropologists.

In the late nineteenth century, United States universities began to imitate the research and graduate training model developed in Germany. Johns Hopkins University (1870), Clark University (1887), and the University of Chicago (1892) were founded on the research model while prominent institutions such as Harvard, Columbia, and the University of Pennsylvania established graduate programs. The first anthropology PhD was awarded at Clark University under Boas in 1892, and by 1901 there were seven graduate programs in anthropology: at the University of Chicago, the University of Pennsylvania, Clark, Harvard, Columbia, Yale, and the University of California, Berkeley. In the period from 1892 to 1930, Harvard and Columbia produced two-thirds of the anthropology PhDs in the U.S.[3] The influence of Boas and the Columbia program was even greater than these figures indicate when we consider that most of the academic programs in anthropology "were directed by students of Boas or men influenced strongly by him" (Darnell 1998, 175).[4] This was especially the case for cultural anthropology. The Harvard students were primarily oriented toward physical anthropology and archaeology while the majority of Columbia students concentrated on linguistic and cultural anthropology.

During the early twentieth century, anthropologists across the subfields focused heavily on Native Americans of the U.S. and Canada, with archaeologists also working on ancient societies of Latin America. Before 1920 only a handful of anthropologists focused on areas outside of the Americas, primarily on indigenous peoples in territories under U.S. control: the Philippines and Hawaii. In the 1920s the geographical range of anthropology PhD students began to expand. For example, Margaret Mead conducted her dissertation research in Samoa (under U.S. rule) while her fellow Columbia student Melville Herskovits did a library-based dissertation on the cattle complex in East Africa. Overall, however, anthropologists remained oriented foremost to the study of

North American Indians, followed by Latin American Indians, a pattern that remained largely intact until World War II (Wolf 1974, 7).

The Americanist Political Project of Boasian Anthropology

The anthropologists who studied under Boas did not study indigenous, so-called primitive societies simply for the sake of scientific knowledge. They also promoted political, social, and cultural transformations in the U.S. Boas' students came from atypical backgrounds in an era in which U.S.-born white Protestant men dominated the professoriate. Like Boas, many were from Jewish families (e.g., Robert Lowie, Edward Sapir, Paul Radin, Alexander Goldenweiser, Melville Herskovits, Ruth Bunzel, Otto Klineberg, Gene Weltfish), typically with recent roots in the United States. Moreover, many were women (e.g., Bunzel, Weltfish, Ruth Benedict, and Margaret Mead). On the whole, Boasians were an "unusually secular lot" (Gilkeson 2010, 6). They were especially attracted to liberalism as a political and moral philosophy. Some, including Boas, had socialist affinities at one time or another.

Boasian anthropologists were part of a larger network of intellectuals concerned with American nationality and the transformations associated with modernity. Susan Hegeman situates the reimagination of the culture concept associated with Boas' students such as Sapir, Benedict, and Mead in relation to modernism, a "nexus of historical, intellectual, technological and aesthetic developments" associated with the trauma of World War I, the rise of the U.S. as a global power, social revolution, new technologies, and consumer culture (1999, 19). A sense of self-conscious estrangement pervaded a New York–centered array of artists and writers, many of whom engaged in a critical evaluation of American cultural life, including its sexual and racial mores. Boasians were active participants in this movement, publishing in political and literary journals such as *The Nation, New Republic, Masses, American Mercury,* and *Dial.*

If the ethnographic object of most anthropological research was "primitive society," "modern America" was also a subject of considerable attention. Anthropology as taught by Boas provided a space to challenge the diverse forms of convention and prejudice impinging on modern lives. Benedict said of Boas: "The study of the mental life of man in other cultures was to his mind one of the best pedagogical means of making men 'free'" (quoted in Caffrey 1989, 118). Boasians addressed a range of problems in U.S. society, such as the alienation of modern existence (Sapir 1924), the psychological turmoil associated with adolescence (Mead 1928), the social production of "abnormality" (Benedict 1934), racial prejudice (Boas 1928), and "the existence and value of an American national culture" (Handler 2005, 75). A signature move of anthropologists was to use the study of "primitive" cultures to invite their American readers to reflect on the specificities—and thus potential deficiencies—of their ("our") "modern" mode of existence. As Hegeman puts it, Boasians "became experts in the manipulation of cultural estrangement for the purposes of social critique. Indeed, it is a distinctive feature of Boasian anthropology that it turned a great deal of critical attention on contemporary American life" (1999, 46). Mead and Benedict were particularly adept in popularizing the anthropological approach to culture for a general audience. It is no accident that two of the best-selling anthropological texts of the twentieth century, *Coming of Age in Samoa: A Psychological Study of Primitive Youth for Western Civilization* (Mead 1928) and *Patterns of Culture* (Benedict 1934) explicitly sought to impart lessons from the study of "primitives" for the modern U.S. Mead contrasted the anxiety-free and sexually libertine adolescence of Samoa with the psychological turmoil of becoming a woman in the U.S., advocating reforms in U.S. sexual mores and child-rearing practices. Benedict sought to make her readers aware of the cultural variance in understandings of abnormality, ending with a plea for a more tolerant attitude toward forms of behavior deemed aberrant, including homosexuality, in U.S. society (1934, 251–278). Benedict and Mead would both spend a good deal of their careers leveraging anthropological insight to publicly promote the liberalization of U.S. society.

Anthropologists today often lament the loss of the public voice the Boasians once had (Handler 2005, 5). As I discuss further in Chapter 3, that public prominence derived in part from the willingness and ability of Boasians to speak to Americans as Americans (especially to white Americans as white Americans). Attention to their critiques of American culture and society should not blind us to their commitments to and identifications with America, and the forms of nationalism this entailed. Anthropologists were keen to leverage their ability to understand other cultures in support of the U.S. government in World War II. Mead's analysis of U.S. culture in her wartime book *And Keep Your Powder Dry* (1942) provided critical reflections on American culture but was also meant to rally American solidarity. In her earlier work, Samoa served not only as an antithesis of sexual repression but as an antithesis of a genuine freedom Mead portrayed as uniquely attainable in the heterogeneous modern civilization of the U.S. (1928, 247–248). To be sure, U.S. chauvinism was tempered by cultural relativism and cultural critique, but a full accounting of Boasian anthropology must reckon with its nationalist commitments and forms of American exceptionalism. This is particularly crucial when considering Boasian interventions in discourses of race.

Boasian Anti-Racism

By the early 1920s Boasians had consolidated and disseminated a series of critiques of scientific and popular abuses of the race concept based on the earlier work of Boas (e.g., 1911a; 1912). The first line of critique derived from a standpoint of scientific skepticism: all efforts to rank races in hierarchies of physical, mental, and developmental superiority-inferiority—from craniometry to intelligence testing—had failed to meet standards of scientific evidence. Boasians further argued that there were no pure races—all peoples had intermingled over time—and racialist scientists deployed a flawed understanding of racial types. These positions did not necessarily equate to a deconstruction of the race concept or an assertion of the innate equality of all races. Robert Lowie emphasized: "Personally, I take great pains to impress upon my students that the innate equality of all races is an unproved dogma, in spite of the fact that all the demonstrations of inequality hitherto attempted are scientifically worthless" (1923, 292).

In a second line of anti-racist intervention, Boasians posited a conceptual distinction between race and culture that undermined the conflation between inherited abilities and observed behavior typically found in justifications of racial hierarchies. As Lowie put it, "arguments on racial differences have almost always been advanced on the assumption that observed differences in cultural achievement must be the expression of correlated differences in inborn capacity" (1923, 295). That assumption failed to take into account the effects of the social environment on thought, action, and physical form, as Boas (1912) had elaborated in his work on immigrants. It also failed to recognize the lack of any necessary correlation between race, on the one hand, and culture and language, on the other. Sapir was particularly pointed in arguing that race "in its only intelligible, that is biological, sense, is supremely indifferent to the history of languages and cultures," which were "no more directly explainable on the score of race than on that of the laws of physics and chemistry" (1921, 222–223). The need to conceptually separate race and culture was a veritable mantra of the Boasians.

A final line of critique focused on the evaluation of civilizational achievement and cultural differences. Boas insisted that the great inventions of

humanity were not the product of one race but of many peoples, that all normal individuals could be socialized into any culture, and that all groups could
assimilate into other civilizations. He also argued that the standards for evaluating cultural achievement were themselves culturally relative, contesting evolutionary schemas that ranked Western civilization as the universal pinnacle of
progress. These arguments further undermined dogmas of white superiority by
questioning both the biological and cultural presumptions underpinning them
(Stocking 1968, 229). Among Boasians, cultural relativism—the suspension of
judgment based on standards and values external to a culture in the study of
that culture—became a key methodological premise. This did not mean that
Boas, or his students, became complete relativists. As Stocking notes, "Boas still
found in the general development of human culture at least qualified affirmation of the specific values most central to his personal worldview: reason, freedom, and human fellowship" (231). His students would study "primitive" societies, in part, to advance such liberal values in their own societies while viewing
members of primitive societies as more bound to the unconscious constraints
of custom than themselves (Willis 1972).

Racial prejudice in the U.S. represented one arena in which the seemingly
intractable constraints of custom ran against the promotion of liberal values.
Boasians tended to address the American "race problem" from a liberal orientation, emphasizing the need for (white) Americans to abandon prejudices based
on assessments of group identity in favor of assessing individuals as individuals. I discuss this perspective at length in the following chapter, so I will offer
only a few reflections here. For Boasians, racial prejudice was not a natural
instinct but a product of socialization. As Goldenweiser put it,

> prejudice, racial prejudice is a group phenomenon, a social phenomenon. It is
> based on traditional backgrounds and is inculcated unconsciously into us early
> in life, before we know what is happening. And we cannot get rid of it unless
> we become, to a great extent, individualists, independent thinkers, persons who
> can stand on their own feet intellectually and emotionally, who are detached
> and capable of viewing things "above the battle." (1924, 134)

Similarly, Sapir urged the "reasonable man" to adopt what has come to be called
a color-blind position.

> The reasonable man will feel about all the race talk that it is an exceedingly
> muddled affair. He will adopt for his practical policy the maxim, "Let race

alone." That is, he will try to act as though for cultural purposes, race did not exist. He will do his level best to act courteously to individuals of all races and he will pay them all the compliment of assuming that they are essentially similar in potentiality to himself and his like. A healthy instinct will tell him that whatever be the alleged facts about race, it is ethically debilitating to raise it as an issue, because in doing so he shifts the emphasis from the individual to collective chimeras of one kind or another. (1925, 213)

This is a concise statement of a liberal position on racial prejudice as a violation of the principle that individuals should be treated as individuals, a position Sapir associated with the Enlightenment.

However, Sapir also identified the force of collective chimeras in preventing the realization of liberal ethics. Inherited custom was difficult to overcome and "even the reasonable man is irrational enough to hang on to what stores of prejudice he possesses under cover of philosophical innocence" (1925, 213). Goldenweiser was even more pessimistic, highlighting the limitations of education and propaganda. "I do not know of any method by means of which it would be possible to make people change their attitude toward the Negro. Education is, of course, one way. But go and try to educate the American people in an attitude favorable to the Negro. Who will do the educating?" (1924, 133). Similarly, in reference to anti-Semitism, Goldenweiser despaired: "My personal view, I confess, is that nothing can be done. Once it is on the go it gets worse whether one does anything about it or not. . . . There is absolutely no writing, no propaganda, no talking of any kind that can be done that will effectively change the thing in a favorable direction, or in any direction" (136). For Goldenweiser, racial prejudice resisted appeals to reason and represented an acute conundrum for the anthropologist as a liberal theorist attuned to the power of culture in molding thought, perception, and behavior. If individuals were socialized into illiberal attitudes toward the racial other by their culture, was the elimination of racial prejudice even possible? Did the elimination of racial prejudice require the effective elimination of the distinction between other and self?

These conundrums did not prevent Boas or his students from attempting to refashion the scientific discourse of race, educate the public, and promote liberal attitudes in the 1920s and beyond. In the 1930s Boas designed a critical study of racial prejudice in textbooks, worked to reform how race was taught in schools, and struggled against the defunding of New York public schools

(Burkholder 2011). From early in his career, Boas viewed the museum as a site for mass education. He came to view "the task of weaning the people from a complacent yielding to prejudice" (1945, 2) as "a process of resocialization in which unquestioned emotional attachment to tradition is replaced during childhood by a critical weighing of cultural alternatives" (Bauman and Briggs 2003, 288). The school was the modern institution best suited to that task; students such as Mead and Benedict also worked to reform schools (Burkholder 2011). Yet, as we will see in the following chapter, Boas also expressed serious doubts as to whether socialization into liberal principles via education could counteract enculturated prejudices, particularly anti-Black prejudices imbricated with the racial-social classificatory order of U.S. society.

In the 1920s, Boasians disseminated their critical perspectives on race and prejudice not only in scholarly journals but also in a series of New York–based magazines such as *The Nation, New Republic, Opportunity, American Mercury*, and *Menorah Journal*. The rising prominence of eugenics and notions of Nordic superiority fueled efforts to refute lay and scientific "myths" of race. Boasians thus focused particular attention on the racialist attacks on southern and eastern European immigrants voiced by figures such as Madison Grant; but they also critiqued assertions of white racial superiority over non-whites. Although he never conducted ethnographic research with African Americans, Boas repeatedly argued against dominant ideas that Blacks were incapable of participation in American civilization and citizenship and that miscegenation between Blacks and whites led to "degeneration." The "Negro Problem," as a race problem, remained a topic of commentary for Boas and students such as Herskovits and Goldenweiser in the 1920s and beyond.

Native Americans were, by contrast, largely absent in Boasian anti-racist discourse. This absence is particularly conspicuous when we consider that Native Americans were the principal subjects of ethnographic attention. Boasians undermined arguments against the biological debility of African Americans but tended to discuss the "Indian problem" in terms of cultural survival and demoralization. This may have reflected a wider tendency within the U.S. to imagine and study Native Americans in terms of "customs and languages" and African Americans in terms of "brains and bodies" that dates to the early days of the republic (Baker 2010, 10). Goldenweiser's article in *The Nation* series on the Nordic Myth suggests another reason: "Who are the races whose fate it will be to share the world in the future? The North American Indian is out of the running. Fragments of the once virile and poetic stock still linger on in a state of degeneration and dejection. But their days are counted" (1925, 462). Although Goldenweiser expressed the sentiment in stark terms, a sense of the demise of Native American peoples pervaded the anthropological imagination of the early twentieth century. Whether Boasians viewed the "Indian problem" in terms of impending genocide or, as became more common, potentially reparable cultural devastation, it appears to have largely been divorced from the "race problem." Even an exception illustrates this tendency. From 1929 to 1933 Melville Herskovits (1929; 1930a; 1932; 1933) published overviews of "race relations" in the U.S. for the *American Journal of Sociology*, dividing his treatment into sections on "The Indian," "The Immigrant," and "The Negro." His discussions of Native Americans focused primarily on government administration, promoting policies of cultural preservation and revitalization, whereas his discussions of African Americans focused on racial prejudice and discrimination.

For Boasians, discrimination against southern and eastern European immigrants, including Jews, was itself a distinctive type of "race problem" because those immigrants were not, anthropologically, members of distinct races. Herskovits contended that

> Immigration, strictly speaking, is not a "race problem." Indeed, the misuse of the term "race" and the manner in which it is applied to national groups, persons coming from various geographical divisions, or linguistic stocks is notorious. . . . However, the current misuse of the term is so deeply rooted in everyday speech that a discussion of immigration must inevitably be a part of any consideration of the race problem in America. (1929, 1132–1133)

Boasians generally preferred to use the word "race" to refer to the largest global divisions of humanity—typically Mongoloid, Caucasoid, and Negroid—inherited from the racial typologies of the eighteenth century, decrying as erroneous the use of the term race to refer to nationalities and religion-based groups (Teslow 2014). In their view, all immigrants of European ancestry were, in the racial schema, Caucasians. Indeed, anthropologists played a key role in popularizing the term Caucasian as a scientific term that encompassed all those viewed as descendants of Europeans—whether Irish, Italians, Anglo-Saxons, Germans, Poles, and/or Jews (Jacobson 1998, 91–109). When it came to the racial classification schemes inherited from the nineteenth century, the Boasian intervention worked against the effort to differentiate European immigrant populations along biological lines while reproducing the distinction between whites and non-whites. This, subsequent chapters detail, had important implications for how Boas and his students imagined a future free of racism. First, however, we can expand our account of Boasian anti-racism by comparing it to contemporaneous perspectives generated in the Harlem Renaissance and in the work of Black intellectuals affiliated with the social anthropology of the University of Chicago.

Boasian Anthropology and the Harlem Renaissance

> Generally speaking, whites did not regard African American history and culture, or the relationship between whites and blacks, as central to the story of the republic. The idea of their own "race" was unexamined; to them, the white immigrant and frontier experiences were central to Americans. Really internalizing the claims of the Harlem Renaissance would have required a more profound self-revaluation than they were prepared (or forced by circumstances) to undertake. (Hutchinson 1995, 446–447)

The book exploring in full the relationship between anthropology and what was then called the "New Negro movement"—a diverse intellectual, literary, and artistic project of Black (and American) identity formation and cultural production—has yet to be written. Some of the connections between them are well known. Most famously, folklorist and novelist Zora Neale Hurston studied anthropology at Barnard, Columbia's sister institution, in the mid-1920s. She worked as a research assistant for Melville Herskovits in his physical anthropological studies of African Americans before conducting her own field research on Black folklore in the U.S. South and Caribbean, which informed her now canonized novels.[5] Another point of contact was the relationship between Herskovits and philosopher Alain Locke, who invited Herskovits to contribute to a special issue of *Survey Graphic* magazine that became the basis for the seminal collection *The New Negro* (see below). There were other connections. University of Pennsylvania anthropology graduate student Arthur Fauset, brother of novelist Jessie Fauset, studied Black folklore with the support of Boas' close ally Elsie Clews Parsons and published in the Boasian controlled *Journal of American Folklore*. The work on Black folklore published in the journal played an important role in efforts by Harlem Renaissance intellectuals such as Locke and Arthur (Arturo) Schomburg to vindicate Black culture and document the persistence of African cultures in the New World (Baker 1998, 158). Rather than attempt anything like a comprehensive account of anthropology and the Harlem Renaissance, in this section I use the work of "New Negro" scholars, particularly Locke, to further tease out features of Boasian thought on race and racism.

In some accounts of the Harlem Renaissance, the influence of Boasian anthropology looms large (Helbling 1999; Hutchinson 1995). In his extensive treatment of the Harlem Renaissance as part of an interracial matrix of American modernism and cultural nationalism, George Hutchinson highlights how Boasian critiques of biological determinism and reformulations of the culture concept became "bedrock assumptions among 'New Negro' authors" (1995, 62). Locke, for one, expressed his appreciation of the "militant but unquestionably scientific school of anthropologists captained by Professor Boas. They have dared, in season and out, to challenge false doctrine and conventional myths, and were the first to bring the citadel of Nordicism into range of scientific encirclement and bombardment" (quoted in Hutchinson 1995, 70–71). The Boasian separation of race and culture informed a shift from a biological to a culturalist view of racial group formation and identity among W. E. B. Du Bois, Locke, and other African American intellectuals. Finally, Boasian approaches to culture provided tools for the analysis and vindication of Afrodiasporic cultures.

Yet, as Hutchinson acknowledges and other scholars have elaborated, the relationship between anthropology and the Harlem Renaissance was by no means seamless. Black intellectuals did not passively absorb anthropological concepts and arguments; they critically "adapted and adopted" anthropological insights, concepts, and methods for their own purposes (Lamothe 2008, 1). U.S. anthropology was an overwhelmingly, if not exclusively, white (including Jewish) field of knowledge production which, though ostensibly an "objective" science, was in practice structured by a perspectival frame in which a white "we" studied a non-white "other" (Willis 1972). Daphne Lamothe (2008) has shown, with considerable nuance, how Black writers such as Du Bois and Hurston developed forms of native ethnography, demonstrating a self-conscious awareness of the limitations of objective knowledge production long before those issues became a prominent concern in anthropology. Lamothe, following Baker (1998), also shows how these Black writers departed from Boasians in using anthropological formulations of culture to promote forms of Black culture, identity, and solidarity. "The New Negro intellectuals' investment in a collective project of social reform, their exploration of the limits and possibilities in racial solidarity, and their celebration of 'race consciousness' are all areas where they diverge from Boas' applications of his theories of race and culture" (2008, 40).

These divergences call attention to the characteristic position among Boasian anthropologists that the amelioration of racial prejudice required the attenuation of racial consciousness and solidarity among oppressed as well as dominant peoples. Baker quotes a letter from Boas in 1933 stating he was "absolutely opposed to all kinds of attempts to foster racial solidarity" (1998, 164). It was a position Boas long held and it was embraced by Goldenweiser, who discouraged "any narrowly race-conscious propaganda" among Blacks or whites because it "stimulates antagonism, develops excessive vanity and prevents mutual sympathy and confidence from taking root" (1923, 231). For Boas and Goldenweiser, any emphasis on Black distinctiveness and collective self-interest would exacerbate the racial feeling of whites. In the next chapter, I explore in critical detail the logics underpinning this position. Here, I focus on an alternative perspective provided by Alain Locke in *The New Negro* (1968a), originally published in 1925.

Locke identified the birth of a new "race spirit" born from the movement of Blacks from the U.S. South, Africa, and the Caribbean to the industrial North. "In Harlem, Negro life is seizing its first chances for group expression and self-determination" (1968a, 7). This was a moment of increased racial consciousness among diverse people segregated by their blackness, a moment of collective identification and cultural expression. Unlike Boas, Locke saw no opposition between the desire for self-determination and self-consciousness, as Blacks, and integration within the U.S. body politic.

> The Negro mind reaches out as yet to nothing but American wants, American ideas.... The racialism of the Negro is no limitation or reservation with respect to American life; it is only a constructive effort to build the obstructions in the stream of his progress into an efficient dam of social energy and power. Democracy itself is obstructed and stagnated to the extent that any of its channels are closed.... So the choice is not between one way for the Negro and another way for the rest, but between American institutions frustrated on the one hand and American ideals progressively fulfilled and realized on the other. (11–12)

Locke refused a dichotomy between assimilative quietude and enforced segregation characteristic of much progressive thought on the "race question." Far from casting Black solidarity as a threat to integration into American institutions, Locke viewed it as necessary for American democracy.

This view was echoed by his insistence that African American culture was simultaneously American and distinctively Black. The opening line of his essay

"The Negro Spirituals" captures this stance: "The Spirituals are really the most characteristic product of race genius as yet in America. But the very elements which make them uniquely expressive of the Negro make them at the same time deeply representative of the soil that produced them. Thus, as unique spiritual products of American life, they become nationally as well as racially characteristic" (Locke 1968b, 199). Although he spoke in terms such as "race genius," Locke did not imagine culture as determined by biology or the distinctiveness of African American culture as a product simply of an African cultural heritage. Rather, he understood racial group formation as a social process. In an essay published in 1924 engaging Boasian approaches to race, Locke (1989a) used the terms "social race" and "ethnic race" to identify a complex of "culture-heredity" that included "the sense of race" or racial consciousness of a particular group. Viewed in this light, the Spirituals were emblematic products of Blacks as a "social race" formed out of adverse historical conditions, equally expressive of that group identity and "American life."[6] Locke thus departed from the Boasians in viewing racial consciousness among African Americans as a productive response to oppression and as a spur to cultural creativity. Moreover, his account of African American culture as distinctively American culture questioned the presumption that the United States was, culturally speaking, a white nation.

Locke's relationship to Melville Herskovits helps further illuminate the issues at stake. Herskovits had recently received his PhD from Columbia when he met Locke in 1924. Locke invited him to write an article on the question "has the Negro a unique social pattern?" for an issue of *Survey Graphic*. Herskovits wrote an impressionistic piece on Harlem as a "typical American community" with social institutions, sexual mores, customs, and values that differed little from predominant patterns. Whatever particularities one might detect were "merely a remnant from the peasant days in the South. Of the African culture, not a trace" (1968, 359). Herskovits concluded: "it's the same pattern, only a different shade" (360). This account echoed Boas' account of African Americans as

a people by descent largely African; in culture and language, however, essentially European. While it is true that certain survivals of African culture and language are found among our American Negroes, their culture is essentially that of the uneducated classes of the people among whom they live, and their language is on the whole identical with that of their neighbors. (1911a, 127–128)

Herskovits, like Boas and Goldenweiser, rejected the promotion of race pride and consciousness as an effective response to oppression and exclusion.

That they [Negroes] have absorbed the culture of America is too obvious, almost, to be mentioned. They have absorbed it as all great racial and social groups in this country have absorbed it. And they face much the same problems as these groups face. The social ostracism to which they are subjected is only different in extent from that which the Jew is subjected. The fierce reaction of race-pride is quite the same in both groups. But, whether in Negro or in Jew, the protest avails nothing, apparently. All racial and social elements who live here long enough become acculturated, Americanized in the truest sense of the word, eventually. They learn our culture and react according to its patterns, against which all the protestations of the possession of, or of hot desire for, a peculiar culture mean nothing. (1968, 359–360)

Walter Jackson calls this passage "a ringing affirmation of the assimilative power of American culture" (1986, 102). It also reveals certain presumptions about American culture as white. If Blacks had "absorbed" American culture, they were by that account not original producers of American culture but adapters of it. Like European immigrants, they had learned "our culture." Although that position was voiced toward the anti-racist end of demonstrating Blacks were capable of participating in American culture, it reinscribed the exclusion of that which might be distinctively Black from the idea of American culture. In other words, there was no space in Herskovits' early account for Locke's sensibility that African Americans could be, culturally speaking, distinctively American.

Famously, Herskovits would change his perspective on African American acculturation, becoming an ardent proponent of the thesis that African culture endured in the Americas, including the U.S. By the end of the decade, he had articulated an ambitious research agenda focused on African cultural survivals (Herskovits 1930b).[7] In *The Myth of the Negro Past* (1941), he drew comparisons between African cultures and "New World Negro" cultures, as well as between New World Negro cultures themselves, to argue that the trained anthropological eye could find significant African retentions in the U.S. Herskovits suggested that demonstration of the persistence of African culture among African Americans and its transmission to white Americans would not only subvert racist views of African American culture and history; it would help position African Americans like European immigrants.

Let us suppose, in short, it could be shown that the Negro is a man with a past and a reputable past; that in time the concept could be shared that the civilization of Africa, like those of Europe, have contributed to American culture as we know it today; and that this idea might eventually be taken over into the canons of general thought. Would this not, as a practical measure, tend to undermine the assumptions that bolster racial prejudice? (1941, 30)

Herskovits departed in significant ways from dominant social science paradigms that emphasized the destruction of the African cultural heritage, earlier Boasian positions on the overcoming of anti-Black racism, and his own account of Harlem. Rather than minimize Black cultural distinctiveness to emphasize that Blacks were capable of adopting U.S. civilization, he figured African Americans as participants in a pluralistic American culture, historically contributing to white American culture. For him, what made anti-Black prejudice particular was the myth that denied African Americans a worthy cultural past. Recognition of that cultural past would help position African Americans as similar to European-derived minorities in the process of being accepted as American. Herskovits thus retained and reworked the analogy between European immigrants and African Americans toward a pluralist vision of American integration.

The Myth of the Negro Past echoed key themes in the New Negro movement: the importance of a renewed and dynamic understanding of African American culture and history; the promotion of Black pride in cultural achievement; the political promise of cultural recognition in the American body politic. Locke, however, reacted ambivalently. On the one hand, he praised the work for its deconstruction of stereotypes, documentation of slave resistance, and valorization of an African cultural background (1989b, 224). He particularly appreciated that the book was "a story of reciprocal cultural interchange and influence, of Negro on white, and white on Negro" that offered a "pioneer contribution to the ground problems of acculturation" (225). On the other hand, Locke argued that Herskovits overplayed his emphasis on the "sturdy, stubborn survival" of African cultural retentions and worried that it replaced the stereotype of "the Negro as empty-headed, parasitic imitator" with that of the "incurably atavistic nativist."

> The extreme logic of such a position might, as a matter of fact, lead to the very opposite of Dr. Herskovits' liberal conclusions, and damn the Negro as more basically peculiar and unassimilable than he actually is or has proved himself to be. . . . In fact, because of his forced dispersion and his enforced miscegenation, the Negro must eventually be recognized as a cultural composite of more than ethnic complexity and cultural potentiality. (225)

Locke's critique, thought not entirely fair to the complexity of Herskovits' approach to acculturation, highlights a crucial difference in their understandings of the distinctiveness of African American culture.

Herskovits, despite his theorization of acculturation as a dynamic, two-way process of cultural contact, maintained an opposition between cultural survivals (African) and assimilative influences (Euro-American) inherited from Boas via an evolutionary framework (Yelvington 2011). His emphasis on African retentions and the tenacity of African culture located the primary source of African American distinctiveness *in African culture.* In contrast, Locke emphasized the distinctiveness of African American culture as the product primarily of the *particular conditions of Black existence in America*, including "forced dispersion" and "enforced miscegenation." For Locke, "To be 'Negro' in the cultural sense . . . is not to be radically different, but only to be distinctively composite and idiomatic, though basically American, as is to be expected, in the first instance" (1989b, 213). From *The New Negro* forward, he struggled to articulate an account of African American culture as rooted in the Americas.[8] On these grounds, he identified a paradox in Herskovits' vindicationist representation of African Americans that rendered them as, culturally speaking, more foreign to America than they actually or historically were.

Locke had another critique of *The Myth of the Negro Past.* If Herskovits overemphasized Africanisms, he also overplayed his contention that recognition of the African American cultural past would ameliorate prejudice. This stance was "scarcely realistic enough to justify the moralistic departure from scientific objectivity" (1989b, 224). E. Franklin Frazier, an intellectual opponent of Herskovits on the question of African cultural survivals, made a similar critique in more pointed fashion. "It is generally recognized by white Americans that Chinese, Hindus and Japanese have a cultural background, but this fact does not affect their status in the United States" (1942, 196). Frazier implied that recognition of the cultural past of Blacks would have little impact on ameliorating racial stratification, hierarchy, and exclusion. This critique calls attention to Herskovits' continued reliance on the analogy between African Americans and European immigrants in the imagination of the overcoming of racism. Replacing an account that emphasized the lack of cultural differences between Blacks and whites with one that emphasized the integrity of a distinct African American culture, Herskovits maintained a sense that Black integration would follow the pattern established for European immigrants. This was a key presumption of Boasian anthropology—and liberal ideologies of American democracy—that demands continual interrogation.

Boasian Anthropology and Black Social Anthropologists

Despite their view that racial consciousness, prejudice, discrimination, and conflicts were the product of particular social histories and formations, Boasians—with the partial exception of Benedict (see Chapter 3)—did not make sustained analyses of the social life of race, social relations between racially defined groups, or the structural conditions of racism. In his 1925 article for *The Nation*, Boas noted: "Whatever the outcome of scientific discussion may be, the existence of racial antagonism among ourselves cannot be denied. The inquiry should be directed toward an investigation of the conditions under which they have grown up and of the soundness of the arguments supporting racial discrimination" (1925, 89). The Boasian intervention focused far more attention on the latter than the former over the next two decades.

This reflected, in part, the consolidation of a disciplinary division of labor in the 1930s. Anthropologists played a key role in redefining the race problem in social terms, but the academic study of race as a social problem became most prominent in sociology, which developed a veritable subfield in "race relations" (McKee 1993, 103). This division was never absolute. In the 1920s, it was common for Boasians to publish in sociology journals. As noted earlier, Herskovits wrote overviews of "race relations" for the *American Journal of Sociology* in the late 1920s and early 1930s. Yet in the early 1940s, after anthropology was separated from sociology at his institution, he was drawing clear distinctions between the focus on culture in anthropology and the study of race relations (Anderson 2008). Beyond Boasian circles, however, some anthropologists did engage the field of race relations. Most notably, in the 1930s Black anthropologists Allison Davis and St. Clair Drake, trained in social anthropology at the University of Chicago, conducted ethnographic fieldwork bearing on interracial relations in the U.S. Their works *Deep South* (Davis, Gardner, and Gardner 1941) and *Black Metropolis* (Drake and Cayton 1962) became classics in sociology but were largely ignored by anthropologists until reclaimed by later generations.

A brief consideration of these two works helps further contextualize Boasian perspectives on the social life of race by pointing to alternative frameworks of inquiry and analysis available to anthropologists. Davis and Drake both worked and studied with W. Lloyd Warner, a Harvard-trained anthropologist influenced by the structural functionalism of A. R. Radcliffe-Brown. Warner joined the anthropology faculty at the University of Chicago in 1935. He is best known for the "Yankee City" studies of class, ethnicity, and the social structure of a northeastern town initiated while Warner worked at Harvard (Warner et al. 1962). As a complement to those studies, he promoted a study of class and "caste" in a region of Mississippi. The study was undertaken by a white couple (Mary Gardner and Burleigh Gardner) and a Black couple (Elizabeth Stubbs Davis and Allison Davis), as well as St. Clair Drake, a former student of Allison Davis. The Gardners focused on whites, the Davises on higher-status Blacks, and Drake on lower-class Blacks. The resulting book, according to Faye Harrison, "combined a Marxist-influenced political economy with structural functionalism to elucidate the cultural politics of terror of Jim Crow in a way that no other work published in the 1930s and early 1940s did" (2008b, 71).

Deep South developed a social structural framework integrating analysis of white domination and Black subordination (the caste system) with analysis of class status distinctions within the Black and white castes (the class system). The former provided the "fundamental division" in social organization, allocating people to membership in fixed groups classified along racial lines (Davis, Gardner, and Gardner 1941, 15). The term "color-castes" was used to highlight rigid, hierarchical distinctions between whites and Blacks as enforced endogamous groups/races and to signal the social origin of those distinctions in slavery (15–58).[9] Caste proscriptions, above all the prohibition against interracial marriage, were enforced by law and custom, terror and violence. They ensured white dominance in all spheres of social life and facilitated Black exploitation and dispossession. A series of chapters on agricultural production, land ownership, and labor control painted a dire picture of how caste power buttressed a rural economic system that left large numbers of Black tenant families in conditions of semi-starvation half of the year.

Caste power, however, did not simply imply homogeneity of class status or a static social system. The authors divided the whites into upper-, middle-, and lower-class groups (in turn divided into upper and lower) and devoted a series of chapters to analyzing family behavioral patterns in the major class divisions, social cliques, and social mobility. They also detailed a class system of status distinctions among Blacks that, owing to the caste system, placed a high premium on whiteness. Nonetheless, because caste and wealth distinctions were not absolute across the color line, economic dynamics complicated caste divisions. Some Blacks were, in income and property, wealthier than some whites, and a few Blacks were wealthier than many whites. Caste sanctions displaying white superiority and Black submission were, at times, modified according to class status or to accommodate Black consumption. Moreover, *Deep South* suggested that economic relationships were "less completely governed by caste than are intergroup relationships of any other type" (Davis, Gardner, and Gardner 1941, 454) and that the economic system, based in part on principles of private property and free competition, prevented the "full extension of caste" (478) in which all members of the lower caste (Blacks) would be in all respects below all members of the upper caste (whites). Nonetheless, overall *Deep South* painted a stark picture of how caste power—white supremacy—was foundational to the social structure. Moreover, the text documented in detail white ideologies of racial domination and revealed forms of Black critical consciousness and resistance.[10]

Black Metropolis: A Study of Negro Life in a Northern City (Chicago) provided a comparative complement to studies of Black-white relations in the South. The book, published in 1945, was the product of a massive research project at the University of Chicago in the 1930s, initially overseen by Warner and his graduate assistant Horace Cayton. Originally funded as a study of Black juvenile delinquency, the project proceeded as a study of the "entire structure of the black community" situated in the broader structure of racial and class relations in Chicago (Peretz 2004, 170). Drake joined the project after it began, researching voluntary organizations, churches, and the Black lower class. He was responsible for drafting most of *Black Metropolis* (Rosa 2012, 51).

The book begins with a history of the Black community in Chicago, proceeds to an analysis of the "color-line" and its economic, political, and social ramifications for Blacks, and then examines the institutions and class dynamics of a segregated area of Chicago known by its residents as Bronzeville (Drake and Cayton 1962). The structure of the work underscores a key premise: apprehending "Negro life in a Northern city" required a thorough understanding of the history and structure of Black-white relations defined by Black subordination along the color line. Although more flexible and contested than in the "color-castes" system of the South, the color line pervaded Black existence in Chicago. While formal legal equality allowed Blacks in Chicago access to public spaces denied Blacks in the South, whites worked to keep Blacks away from white middle-class schools and recreational areas (e.g., public swimming pools). In employment, Blacks were not allowed to compete on equal terms with whites, and restrictive covenants segregated Blacks into overcrowded, overpriced "ghettoes" (1962, 174). Segregation was most complete in spheres of social intimacy—voluntary associations, churches, friendship circles, and family; as in the South, white fears of social equality—above all interracial marriage—provided a potent bulwark against the possibility of assimilation. Correspondingly, Black struggles for equality—a key thematic of the work as a whole—focused primarily on employment and housing rather than social equality.

One reason was that although Blacks objected to the limits on free association imposed by the color line, they did not view their institutions as inferior or desire assimilation. This assessment dovetailed with the authors' account of Bronzeville as a place with "distinctive patterns of thought and behavior," undeniably similar to and shaped by larger American patterns but with its own specificity produced out of the structures of the color line and integral connections to a "larger, national Negro culture, its people being tied to thirteen million other Negroes by innumerable bonds of kinship, associational and church membership, and a common minority status" (Drake and Cayton 1962, 396). A sense of affiliation with the racially oppressed in fact extended beyond the United States, whether in struggles against "the tyrannical forces of Hitler and Hirohito, the colonial imperialism of the British Empire, or the racial imperialism of the United States" (764). In their account of Bronzeville, Drake and Cayton highlighted the diversity of its population, focusing particularly on class distinctions in perspective and behavior but also on religious affiliation and political perspective. If the chapters on lower-class life betray middle-class evaluatory precepts, the authors simultaneously exposed the class snobbery of middle- and upper-class Blacks. Accompanying this account was an attention to the complex and diverse modes of "race consciousness" (390) of Blacks, whether in forms of colorism privileging whiteness or in expressions of race pride and solidarity. Rosa notes

> *Black Metropolis* showed how a discernibly black ghetto, whatever its deficiencies, constituted a community within which a population was forced to construct a framework for an organized way of life. Moreover, at a moment when sociology seemed unaware of the potential for overt racial conflict, *Black Metropolis* anticipated the Black Power rebellions of the 1960s by acknowledging the existence of nationalistic, non-assimilative sentiment informed by race pride, on the one hand, and a long-held resentment of white oppression, on the other. (2012, 51)

The final section of the book placed in bold relief growing Black demands for equality and freedom in an American democracy "frozen and paralyzed before its Negro problem" (Drake and Cayton 1962, 765). Given the "moral flabbiness of America" and the failure of most white liberals to respond to demands for Black equality, Drake and Cayton wondered whether the "Negro question" could find an answer. They clearly doubted it would without conflict (766).

The analyses of race and class contained in *Deep South* and *Black Metropolis* were by no means flawless. Their attention to the integral relationship between the political economy of exploitation and the racial subordination of, respectively, the caste system and the color line sat uneasily with the suggestion that urbanization, industrialization, and market dynamics were making race relations more egalitarian. Moreover, their social anthropology participated in the representation of Black lower-class differences from white (and Black) middle-class norms in terms of psychological or cultural deviance commonly found in the contemporary sociology of race relations. According to some critics, the work of Davis and Drake forms part of the genealogy of post-war "poverty knowledge" pathologizing Black culture (O'Connor 2001, 74–98); Herskovits' identification of Africanisms as a key source of African American cultural distinctiveness offered a competing paradigm that attempted to relativize the evaluation of difference.

However, in other respects Davis and Drake offered modes of analysis and critique that moved beyond Boasian interventions on race and culture. Wedding structural analytics with intensive ethnography, they attended to the social life of race and racism in far more detail than those working in the Boasian tradition who, in the war era, continued to debunk scientific racism (e.g., Benedict 1940; Klineberg 1944; Montagu 1945). A focus on structure allowed for an inquiry into the relationships between racial differentiation, economic dynamics, and social class formation in systemic relations of power. The focus on conflict, struggle, and Black racial consciousness, especially evident in *Black Metropolis*, eschewed a perspective that assumed progress in race relations would be hindered by a politics of Black solidarity. Finally, a focus on the color line led Drake and Cayton to question the analogy, common to anthropology and sociology, between Blacks and European immigrants.

> As time passes individual immigrants and their ethnic groups as a whole rise in status. Many of them are "assimilated" and become socially accepted. People eventually forget the foreign antecedents of successful Americans. In the case of Negroes, however, the process stops short of complete assimilation. A Job

Ceiling limits them to unskilled and semi-skilled work and condemns them to the relief rolls during depressions. Residential segregation results in a Black Ghetto. The color-line preserves social segregation and sets the limits of advancement in politics and other non-economic hierarchies (1962, 757).

As a counterpoint, they hinted at the potentially analogous forms of structural power represented by fascism, colonialism, and U.S. racial imperialism.

Conclusion

Boasians developed and disseminated critical approaches to race that helped undermine scientific racism and the nativist defense of Nordic supremacy. Their insistence on the separation between race and culture, their rejection of biological determinism, and their promotion of culture as the key concept to understand differences among human groups had wide-ranging influence within and beyond the academy. Carl Degler contends that "By the 1930s, it was about as difficult to locate an American social scientist who *accepted* a racial explanation for human diversity as it had been easy to find one in 1900" (1989, 1), while Hegeman claims that in the same era "something like the anthropological version of 'culture' was well assimilated into the popular consciousness of many Americans" (1999, 18). In 1936, shortly before retiring, Boas appeared on the cover of *Time* magazine, feted as the most accomplished U.S. anthropologist, a champion of sensible race thinking and an ardent opponent of the Nazis. In the late 1930s and 1940s Boasians would continue to promote an anti-racist agenda, working to reform public schooling and creating popular media to educate the public on the facts of race and promote cultural tolerance (Burkholder 2011; Teslow 2014). Their arguments would ultimately contribute to Supreme Court decisions overturning segregation (Baker 1998). It is precisely because of the public influence of the Boasian intervention that its limitations and unresolved tensions require critical attention. I conclude here by highlighting some of the contradictions of the Boasian intervention and identifying domains of inquiry beyond its purview.

Boasian discourse had differential implications for European immigrants and those positioned beyond the boundaries of whiteness—Asians, Native Americans, and Blacks. For the former, it provided scientific sanction for claims to whiteness and thus Americanness. For the latter, it undermined racialist assertions of biological inferiority yet maintained a tripartite division of ancestral biological categories (Caucasoid, Mongoloid, Negroid) that continued to inform descriptions of actually existing peoples. Boasians had difficulties reconciling the implications of that difference with their vision of a more liberal, egalitarian future that relied on European assimilation into (white) America as the template for integration. They typically viewed the attenuation of difference—biological as well as cultural—as the necessary condition for dominant sectors (Nordics and non-Nordic Caucasians) to treat others (non-Nordic Caucasians and non-whites) as individuals who shared a common identity as Americans. This approach paradoxically reinscribed and elided the distinctive conditions of non-whites prevented from integration by a color line that equated America with whiteness. Even when Herskovits projected a pluralist vision of an American future that could accommodate African American cultural difference, he relied on an immigrant analogy that effaced racial distinctions.

The Boasians' blindness to the contradictions of the immigrant analogy may have stemmed, in part, from their ability to claim a white American identity. Whereas white secularized anthropologists from Protestant and Jewish backgrounds could, and often did, speak from the position of a collective we identified with a European heritage and American identity, Black intellectuals were positioned beyond the pale of unmarked whiteness. Du Bois famously articulated the conundrums and insights rising from the ambiguous position of "always looking at one's self through the eyes of others, of measuring one's soul by the tape of a world that looks on in amused contempt and pity" (1995, 45) via his notion of double-consciousness. Boasian anthropologists were less invested in discerning and analyzing the forms of ethno-racial consciousness that resulted from the dynamics and dilemmas of racialized exclusion than in promoting the diminution of racial consciousness as the necessary condition for a liberal American future. How and why this was the case is a focus of the following chapter.

Franz Boas, Miscegenation, and the White
Problem

ANTHROPOLOGIST FRANZ BOAS is known as one of the most important anti-racist intellectuals of the first half of the twentieth century. In his classic account of the history of racial thought in the U.S., Thomas Gossett asserted: "It is possible that Boas did more to combat race prejudice than any other person in history" (1963, 418). It may then come as a surprise to some that Boas ended perhaps his most extensive essay on U.S. African Americans—"The Problem of the American Negro" (1945, 70–81)—with an appeal to miscegenation—interracial sex and the production of mixed-race children—as the long-term solution to the so-called Negro problem.[1] The last sentence of this essay, published in 1921, is, to say the least, provocative:

> Thus it would seem that man being what he is, the Negro problem will not dis-appear in America until the Negro blood has been so much diluted that it will no longer be recognized just as anti-Semitism will not disappear until the last vestige of the Jew as a Jew has disappeared. (1945, 81)

Boas' assertion that miscegenation was necessary for the elimination of rac-ism has received little sustained attention in the voluminous scholarship on his work.[2] Beardsley suggests that his position involved a radical challenge to entrenched taboos against interracial marriage and beliefs in the degenerative effects of miscegenation, while noting that it "would be regarded by some today as a racist scheme, for it would solve the race issue by a gradual purge of an identifiable black race and culture" (1973, 64). Degler argues that Boas' assimi-lationist views reflected a tacit sense of cultural hierarchy where "some social groups should disappear into others," a view that implied "the disappearance of his own ethnicity" (1989, 9). Before evaluating Boas' positions, however, we need to unpack the substance of his views on interracial sexual relations and interracial marriage, and the reasoning behind his views. What we lack is a substantive discussion of his logic, the train of premises and arguments underlying his imagination of the solution to racism. How did Boas come to the conclusion that racial mixture was necessary to end racism? What was the basis of his comparison between Blacks and Jews? What broader lessons can we draw from his thought if we foreground the question of miscegenation?

Perhaps Boas' imagination that miscegenation would prove the solution to racism has received little attention because scholars tend to pay more attention to his arguments concerning the race concept, culture, and scientific racism than on his briefly elaborated speculations concerning the future possibilities for the overcoming of racism. It hardly seems fair, after all, to evaluate scholars on the basis of their predictions or their imagined solutions to social problems. We can, however, approach this issue from the perspective that intellectuals' struggles to imagine solutions to social problems provide considerable insight into their overall thought and reasoning, including their political values. This chapter provides a reading of Boas' thought on miscegenation as an important window into his thought on race and racism in relation to liberalism, nationalism, and "America." My subject, then, is not interracial sex, interracial marriage, or mixed-race identity. Rather, the chapter provides an account of how an anti-racist intellectual came to view miscegenation as necessary for the resolution of racism. Boas' writings on African Americans in the U.S. are particularly intriguing because he understood and theorized "the Negro problem" as a problem of white perception and consciousness of racial difference. He wrote: "the strong development of racial consciousness, which has been increasing during the last century and is just beginning to show the first signs of waning, is the greatest obstacle to the progress of the Negro race" (1911b, viii). The question then is how and why did Boas view racial mixture and the "dilution of Negro blood" over generations as the solution to white racism.

Tackling this puzzle requires that we understand key premises orienting Boas' politics of race and nation. His commitment to a liberal outlook promoting individual freedom from the constraints of categorical interpellation underpinned his imagination of the overcoming of racism. Boas also worked from the premise that national belonging—recognition and acceptance as co-equivalent members of a nationality—required the attenuation of publicly recognizable difference. Finally, although he critiqued ideas of innate Black racial inferiority, Boas understood Blacks and whites to be derived from "fundamentally distinct races" (1962, 89). Bringing these premises together with a sense of the deep impact of whites' enculturation into racial consciousness and prejudice in the U.S., Boas essentially derived the following position: the socially inculcated racial perceptions and feelings of whites were so ingrained that only with the lessening of physical differences between whites and Blacks would whites be able to treat Blacks as individuals rather than as members of a stereotyped group. In crucial respects, Boas' contention that African American miscegenation was the long-term solution to the "Negro problem" was driven by a deeply pessimistic assessment of the racial consciousness of U.S. whites. His promotion of miscegenation ultimately points to the difficulties he had in reconciling liberal principles with white racism and the whiteness of American nationality, a conundrum of crucial import in thinking through anthropological anti-racism.

The following pages unpack the logic of Boas' thought, with a critical eye toward its contradictions, limitations, and oversights but also an appreciative eye for its attention to whites' racial perception and consciousness and the problems that attention raises for liberal thought on racism, nationality, and "America." The chapter begins with an overview of Boas as a political theorist to provide an orientation toward his stances on liberalism and nationalism. The heart of the chapter concentrates on his writings on African Americans, focusing on his positions on miscegenation. Here, I discuss how Boas' account of white racial consciousness represented a key problem for liberal thought on racism, a problem he struggled to articulate but did not fully confront. I also call attention to a key paradox in his imagination of belonging to the American nation: American nationality was, in his view, fractured by the color line, yet Boas modeled his solution to racism on the perceived condition of European immigrants assimilating into American nationality. The penultimate section compares Boas' vision of miscegenation for the racial future of America with that of his contemporary George Schuyler, an African American intellectual familiar with the work of Boas. I use Schuyler's writings to help further tease out blind spots in the work of Boas, particularly concerning the political economy of interracial sex and the racial economy of sex and marriage. The conclusion offers some final reflections on important questions we can glean from Boas' pessimism concerning a liberal future in a thoroughly racialized American nation.

Boas' Political Principles

Boas is rarely considered to be a political theorist, but examining his political principles illuminates his thinking on prejudice and discrimination and their potential overcoming. In identifying key aspects of his political thought I draw here primarily from popular articles, public talks, and unpublished pieces drawn together by his son in *Race and Democratic Society* (Boas 1945). I focus particularly on his public pronouncements in the late 1910s as he reacted with grave concern to the super-nationalism of the war era.[3]

Boas repeatedly insisted on the importance of the principle of individual freedom, particularly freedom of thought and its expression (Lewis 2015). The actualization of freedom was difficult to achieve not only because of overt suppression of dissenting thought by state authority or public censure but, more insidiously and pervasively, because of the force of custom. In a lecture to Barnard students in 1917, Boas noted that few people understood that "true freedom means that we ourselves should be able to rise above the fetters that the past imposes on us" because they failed to realize that most of our actions were products of habit overlain with emotional value rather than products of rational discernment (1945, 179). Here was a statement of a core feature of the anthropological mission: the study of other cultures facilitated the acquisition of a critical, "non-conformist" (179) apprehension of ourselves as creatures of custom. Elsewhere, Boas noted that only a few particularly strong minds were capable of achieving true freedom of thought (157). If this sounds elitist, Boas also held that conformist thought was most characteristic of the "segregated" and "educated" classes of society because they received more training in its historical traditions than did the working populace (133–140).

Individual freedom, for Boas, did not obviate the obligations of individuals to society or the obligation of society to cultivate individuals. Boas was not the sort of liberal who imagined society as a mere collection of individuals acting out their self-interests. Humans were social beings whose formation and individuality depended on the particular society that nurtured them. Modern complex industrial societies in particular required restrictions on individuals lest their actions harm others, and the state had every right to obligate social service from individuals for the greater good, as long as it did not violate their morality. Moreover, for Boas individual freedom required equality of rights and opportunity. He did not hold that "all men were created equal" in the sense that each individual had the same identical natural endowment (165), but he did embrace the principle that "the ultimate basis of our conduct should be the preservation of the equality of rights of every new-born individual and the freedom of a social unit to develop in its own way" (183). Equal educational opportunity was foundational to democracy, but in the U.S. economic inequality, the life conditions of the poor, and inadequate school funding prevented the full realization of human potential. In a 1919 essay called "Program for Equal Educational Opportunity," Boas argued that a comprehensive program of social justice was required to remove the burden of financing child care from families to society (1945, 192–195). Such a program would require "exceedingly large expenditures" that, Boas suggested, could be funded through inheritance taxes; the lack of need for families to support children would in turn obviate one of the main rationales for property inheritance (194). If the proposal was unlikely to be realized in the capitalist U.S., it reflected a sensibility that the actualization of liberal democracy required the attenuation of economic inequality in addition to equality in civil rights. Boas was at times attracted to socialist politics, though he rejected Marxist materialism.

For Boas, the form of organization of modern societies—nation-states—represented possibilities and complications for the realization of individuals' potential. He expressed a keen ambivalence concerning nationalism, which he articulated through a distinction between devotion to national ideals and culture and imperialist, intolerant nationalism.[4] One of his more expansive reflections can be found in an article he published in *Dial* magazine in 1919 (1945, 113–124; see also 1962, 81–106). Like many early modern political theorists, Boas grounded his discussion of social solidarity and antagonism on a speculative account of their origins in primitive humanity, an account no less speculative for his familiarity with contemporary small-scale, non-Western cultures. "In early times mankind was divided into small hordes or tribes that lived in isolation and in constant fear of enemies, beast as well as man" (1945, 113). The members of these tribes had feelings of "extreme hostility" toward strangers, reserving feelings of sociability and solidarity for fellow members. Over the long course of history, the inclusiveness of those sentiments expanded with an increase in the size of social groups, but the different attitudes toward insiders and outsiders persisted, reaching a contemporary limit at the nation. A deep substratum of "instinctive social reaction" informed the strong feelings of social solidarity within nations and the equally strong disregard for the human welfare of other nations, especially under conditions of conflict (115). Likewise, race antipathy—though highly socially variable—had roots in the primitive rejection of the other.

If Boas naturalized social antipathy toward the stranger, he did not resign himself to an inevitable world of strife and war. The social solidarities of primordial group formation also produced sentiments of human fellow feeling—humanism—that could be extended beyond a social group. The formation of nation-states had extended such sentiments beyond the bonds of tribe into large social aggregates. The next stage in the attenuation of human aggression was to extend human fellow feeling across nation-states. Boas asserted as personal moral precept that when duty to humanity conflicted with duty to nation his allegiance was to humanity (178–184).[5] This did not, however, entail for him the desire to transcend the idea of the nation, or nationality, altogether. Feelings of group belonging with those in a community with shared customs were crucial to human development: "Conceived in this way nationality is one of the most fruitful sources of cultural progress. Its productiveness lies in the strength that the individual derives from being able to act in a large homogeneous social group which responds readily to his thoughts and actions because he shares with it the same cultural background" (122). His ideal then was a world of nations whose members treasured their own cultural particularity while respecting and learning from that of others. Thus, the duty to pursue individual equality and freedom was mirrored by a duty to encourage "the freedom of a social unit to develop in its own way" (183). The problem with modern nationalism was that it was not based on this sense of nationality but on the aggressive notion that the nation's ideals represented universal ideals. Modern nationalism also presumed political and economic power as the necessary condition for a strong nationality and involved the withholding of human feeling from members of other nations. Such "imperialistic nationalism" (122), cultivated by the educated classes and propagandized to the masses, was a danger to cultural progress, individual development, freedom of thought, and humanity itself.

How then did Boas, who culturally identified with Germany as well as the U.S., view the country of which he was a citizen? In a letter to the *New York Times* in the midst of World War I, he noted that when he first arrived in the U.S. he was "filled with admiration of American political ideas" and saw the U.S. as a country concerned with "perfecting its inner development" that would brook no outside interference but would not interfere with other countries and "would never become guilty of the oppression of unwilling subjects" (1945, 168). Westward expansion and the Mexican-American War appeared as mere aberrations from this idealized image of American nationality, an image exposed as an illusion with the "aggressive imperialism" of the Spanish-American War. The United States then appeared as an embodiment of expansionist nationalism with a citizenry that saw itself as "arbiter of the world" (169). One of the manifestations of that common attitude was a conviction that the U.S., and the U.S. alone, had created a model democratic government. Not only did Boas consider this a typical nationalist refusal to admit that other nations might work out equally valid institutional arrangements—a defense of Germany was never too far from his mind here (171)—he questioned whether U.S. institutions were based on American ideals. In his 1917 lecture to Barnard students, he asserted that "historically our modern democracy has very little to do with this fundamental question" (1945, 183). It was, rather, a product of individual and communal resistance to outside control that instilled deep distrust in governmental authority. Moreover, progress toward the realization of the fundamental ideals of equality in rights and independent social development was impeded by a symbolic conflation between modern democracy and the U.S. as a state. When democracy became converted into a nationalist symbol, Boas suggested, it readily became a tool of imperialist nationalism. He later reflected, "The name democracy will induce people to accept autocracy as long as the symbol is kept intact" (1928, 147). As we will see in the next chapter, Ruth Benedict, like Margaret Mead, would be more sanguine than Boas in equating "America"—and American culture—with democracy.

Boas, we might sum up, was both a complicated liberal and a complicated nationalist. He was liberal in the sense that he placed a high priority on the realization of individual human potential, especially freedom of thought, as a fundamental political and social value. Yet he insisted that the individual was always socially located and that freedom of individual development could be achieved only through social justice and equal opportunity. He was a nationalist in the sense that he embraced nationality as an incubator of intellectual-cultural development. Yet he was highly critical of existing forms of imperialist nationalism that inhibited self-realization in the nation and denied humanity to members of other nations. His doubts about the realization of liberal democracy in the U.S. were nowhere better reflected than in his assessment of the situation of African Americans.

The "Negro Problem" as a Problem of White Racial Consciousness and Miscegenation as the Solution

Although Boas concentrated his ethnographic cultural research on Native American communities and his physical anthropology focused primarily on European immigrants, he demonstrated considerable interest in African Americans. In 1906, at the request of W.E.B. Du Bois, he delivered a commencement address at Atlanta University that highlighted the civilizational achievements of African peoples to counter stereotypes of racial inferiority and inspire Black students (Boas 1974).[6] He also delivered a speech at the Second National Negro Conference, which officially established the NAACP (Boas 1910). Boas promoted the study of Black folklore through the *Journal of American Folklore* (Willis 1975) and sponsored Melville Herskovits' research on the physical characteristics and genealogy of U.S. African Americans (Herskovits 1928, 1930c). His synthetic works written for a general audience—*The Mind of Primitive Man* (1911a) and *Anthropology and Modern Life* (1928)—included discussions of the "Negro Problem" in the United States.

Boas, typically inhabiting the voice of the scientific skeptic, challenged many stock presumptions of innate Black inferiority. He criticized scientific claims to any definitive association between differences in biological type and differential intelligence or capacity for civilization; he argued against notions that races represented pure biological types and that interracial sexual relations led to deficient children and racial degeneration; he argued that the condition of African Americans in the U.S. was more a product of social conditions than of biological endowment—of displacement from Africa, enslavement, and subsequent "disorganization and severe economic struggle against heavy odds" (1911a, 272). The sum of his argument as it had developed by the time of the publication of *The Mind of Primitive Man* in 1911 was that anthropological evidence "does not permit us to countenance the belief in a racial inferiority which would unfit an individual of the negro race to take his part in modern civilization" (272). Boas did not, it must be noted, categorically pronounce that races were biologically equal (Williams 1996). Studies of brain size suggested the possibility that Blacks "would not produce quite so many men of genius as other races" (1911a, 268).[7] He also reproduced a stereotypical view of African Americans as exhibiting the undesirable qualities of "licentiousness," "shiftless laziness," and "lack of initiative," though he attributed such qualities to social conditions rather than heredity (271). On the whole, Boas emphasized that whatever racial differences might exist between Blacks and whites, there was no biological justification for denying Blacks citizenship and participation in modern society.

Crucially for my discussion, Boas did hold a view of Blacks and whites as racially distinctive, as descendant from disparate racial stocks of humanity. He developed a critical account of scientific and popular abuses and misunderstandings of the race concept but by no means abandoned it, particularly when it came to the tripartite distinction between Negro (African), Mongul (Asian), and Caucasian (European) (Teslow 2014, 32–71). In an 1899 review of William Ripley's *The Races of Europe*, he questioned the use of the term race as applied to European "types" precisely because of the contrast they collectively presented to Africans and Monguls: "I am inclined to reserve the term [race] for the largest divisions of mankind. The differences between the three European types are certainly not equal in value to the difference between Europeans, Africans and Monguls" (Boas 1966, 157; Teslow 2014, 59). Although over time he increasingly questioned the existence of substantial differences between European types, the classification schemes applied to European populations, and substantive mental differences between the larger divisions of humanity, he maintained a tripartite view of phenotypical differentiation between three global stocks of humanity. His entry "Race" in the *Encyclopedia of Social Sciences*, published in 1934, indicates this clearly:

> The special forms developed in the various races do not show that one can be considered as more advanced from the prehuman type than another. The divergences are rather in different directions. Thus the Negro is most divergent in the increased length of the legs and in strong development of lips; the Mongoloid in the loss of hairiness; the European in depigmentation, reduction in the size of the face, elevation of the nose and increased size of the brain. (1934, 32)

Boas' construction of such racial distinctions had significant consequences for his views on the "Negro problem" as a problem of white racial feeling and consciousness.

Boas addressed this problem in the speech he gave at the Second Annual Negro Conference, which Du Bois published under the title "The Real Race Problem" in the NAACP's periodical *The Crisis* (Boas 1910). He began: "The essential problem before us is founded on the presence of two entirely distinct human types in the same community." He also asserted that "the anthropologist recognizes that the Negro and the white represent the two most divergent types of mankind," that is, the most phenotypically dissimilar races (22). The first part of the essay rebuked assumptions of Black inferiority, with Boas concluding: "there is no anthropological evidence showing inferiority of the Negro race as compared with the white race, although we may assume that differences in mental characteristics of the two races exist" (23). The second part focused on the physical anthropology of race mixture, critically assessing the commonly held notion that the progeny of white and Black parentage—the mulatto—represented an inferior type in mental aptitude, vigor, and other characteristics. In the final section, Boas moved from the voice of the scientific skeptic toward a more prescriptive sociological voice.

Boas argued that the demographic facts of a large influx of Europeans and absence of new "Negro blood" from abroad combined with past and future mixture between whites and Blacks meant that the "gradual process of the elimination of the full-blooded Negro" was inevitable (25). Legislation against miscegenation might slow that process but could not halt it. Crucially, Boas attempted to allay the fears of those who saw in racial mixture the dilution of white blood by pointing toward the gendered dynamics of interracial sex and the classification of resulting children. Since the prevailing pattern of intermixture involved sexual "unions"—he did not speak of marriage here—between white men and Black women and since group membership depended upon the mother's identity, the effect of racial mixture was that the proportion of Black blood in the Black community would diminish with no effect on the white population. In other words, miscegenation led to the lightening or whitening of African Americans, but not the darkening of white Americans. The effect then was a "gradually increasing similarity of the two racial types" without a change in the white type (25).

Boas portrayed this as a positive development for the future of U.S. race relations as he reflected on the "racial feeling" of whites. He contended that the "intensity of racial feeling" in a society relied on two variables: (1) the relative proportion of the two races in contact—the greater the minority, the higher the intensity of racial feeling among the majority; (2) "the amount of difference of type"—the higher degree of physical differences between races, the greater the intensity of racial feeling. On the latter point he qualified: "This is true, at least, in all countries inhabited by north European, particularly by Teutonic, nations," suggesting a social and cultural influence on racial feeling (25). Following these premises, Boas argued that race problems would become less intense to the extent that the differences between races diminished. In other words, whites' racial feelings would diminish as Blacks became lighter over time. He indicated a social corollary to this biological process, urging Blacks to consciously minimize their differences from whites:

> From this point of view, it would seem that one aspect of the solution of the Negro problem lies entirely in the hands of the Negro himself. The less Negro society represents a party with its own aims and its own interest distinct from those of the members of the white race, the more satisfactory will be the relation between the races. (25)

Any accentuation of group feeling among African Americans, he implied, would only provoke antagonism and intensified "racial feeling" from whites. The biological diminution of physical difference was inevitable:

> it would seem that the inexorable conditions of our life will gradually make toward the disappearance of the most distinctive type of Negro, which will again tend to alleviate the acuteness of race feeling. It may seem like a look into a distant future; but an unbiased examination of conditions as they exist at the present time points to the ultimate result of a leveling of the deep distinctions between the two races and a more and more fruitful co-operation. (25)

If the "real race problem" was, Boas suggested, ultimately based on the "racial feeling" of whites, the solution required the social and biological attenuation of Black difference.

Before engaging in a critical analysis of Boas' positions, we can gain further insight into their logic and development by considering the essay "The Problem of the American Negro" (Boas 1945, 70–81), first published in 1921. The structure of this essay is similar to "The Real Race Problem." Boas first discussed the physical anthropology of race to clear away misperceptions of innate Black inferiority and miscegenation as degeneration. He then reflected on the race problem in social terms, elaborating on U.S. whites' racial perceptions and prejudices:

> Even if there is neither a biological nor a psychological justification for the popular belief in the inferiority of the Negro race, the social basis of the race prejudice in America is not difficult to understand. The prejudice is founded essentially on the tendency of the human mind to merge the individual in the class to which he belongs, and to ascribe to him all the characteristics of his class. It does not even require a marked difference in type, such as we find when

we compare Negro and white, to provoke the spirit that prevents us from recognizing individuals and compels us to see only representatives of a class endowed with imaginary qualities that we ascribe to the group as a whole. We find this spirit at work in anti-Semitism as well as in American nativism, and in the conflict between labor and capitalism. We have recently seen it at its heights in the emotions called forth by a world war. (77–78)

Racial prejudice, for Boas, appeared as one variation of a process rooted in perceptions of group differences. Prejudice was a product of a mental tendency to reduce members of a different social category to stereotyped characteristics rather than perceive them as individuals. (When Boas used the term class he referred to a social group or category rather than exclusively to a group or category based on economic status or condition.) Note that Boas represented the question of anti-Black prejudice as similar to other forms of group prejudice in which marked differences in physical type need not be present. But in the case of Blacks, phenotypical difference made a social difference: "the consciousness that the Negro belongs to a class by himself is kept alive by the contrast presented by his physical appearance with that of the whites" (78). For Boas, that visible contrast provided a crucial barrier to the attenuation and overcoming of anti-Black prejudice.

Boas portrayed the problem of racial prejudice and discrimination in liberal terms as a problem of the denial of individual recognition. Indeed, he understood the withholding of individual recognition itself as a source of suffering: "Every moment of his life, the self-respecting Negro feels the strain of his inability to overcome the prejudices that merge him in a type" rather than value him as an individual (78). He briefly hinted that a sense of group solidarity among the oppressed could serve as a foundation for self-protection—"the less feeling of unity the heterogeneous members of the group possess, the harder it is for them to bear the discrimination under which they suffer" (78)—but he elaborated no further and never suggested that group-based struggle against oppression was a viable course of action. The reason it, would appear, lay precisely in the conundrum that group classification and stereotyping posed for individual recognition.

As a devoted liberal, Boas held that only when people treat people as individuals—and not as members of a social category—could equality of condition and opportunity emerge. Blacks had the right to be treated as individuals. However, given that "our population" (U.S. whites) was so "deeply saturated" with consciousness of categories, Boas doubted that education and socialization in liberal attitudes could lead whites to treat Blacks as individuals. "Even if, in the education of the young, the importance of individual differences were emphasized so that an intelligent understanding could be attained of the irrationality of the assumption that all Negroes are inferior, we should not overcome that general human tendency of forming groups that in the mind of the outsider are held together by his emotional attachments towards them" (79). This tendency was buttressed by his sense that among nations populated by "descendants of the Teutonic peoples of Northern Europe," race consciousness was particularly acute (78). In the U.S., white consciousness of categorical blackness was, for Boas, largely inextricable from invidious evaluation. He suggested that the prospects for the realization of a white liberal stance toward the Negro were dim: "there is no great hope that the Negro problem will find even a half-way satisfactory solution in our day. We may, perhaps, expect that an increasing number of strong minds will free themselves from race prejudice and see in every person a man entitled to be judged on his merits. The weak-minded will not follow their example" (80). Education in racial tolerance could help cultivate "strong minds," but it was not sufficient to overcome the "Negro problem" as a problem of white racial consciousness.

Boas thereby reiterated his earlier faith in miscegenation: "the greatest hope for the immediate future lies in a lessening of the contrast between Negroes and whites" (80). If Blacks could come to appear more like whites, the diminution of the visible contrast would lead whites to be less conscious of the differences between the social groups and thus better able to recognize individuals as individuals. "If conditions were ever such that it could be doubtful whether a person were of Negro descent or not, the consciousness of race would necessarily be much weakened. In a race of octoroons, living among Whites, the color question would probably disappear" (80). Boas concluded with the provocation with which I began this chapter: "Thus it would seem that man being what he is, the Negro problem will not disappear in America until the Negro blood has been so much diluted that it will no longer be recognized just as anti-Semitism will not disappear until the last vestige of the Jew as a Jew has disappeared" (81).

We are now in a position to explore the paradoxes and tensions within Boas' imagination of discrimination and its overcoming. It is important to recognize that Boas did not view miscegenation as the ultimate solution to racism based on ideas of innate Black inferiority or a vision of racial-biological improvement of the Black population. Rather, he developed this position in relation to what he saw as (most) whites' culturally cultivated incapacity to see beyond racial type, a particular social manifestation of what he saw as the universal tendency to stereotype. His logic led him to paradoxical conclusions. Most generally, Boas proposed a *biological solution* to what he clearly articulated as a *social problem*. Though he argued that the creation of social categories/groups did not necessarily depend on racial differences, he posited the diminishing of racial differences as key to the reduction of prejudice. But why would the lightening of African Americans—even into a "race of octoroons"—necessarily entail the reduction of prejudice, especially considering that in the U.S. Blacks had long been categorized and defined via the "one drop rule" (any identifiable Black ancestry resulted in the classification of an individual as Black) and that Blacks were, as Boas noted, already substantially racially "mixed" as a population? Boas suggested that the problem came down to one of visible recognition by phenotypical appearance; insofar as a person could be readily identified with a stigmatized social category/group, then he or she would be typecast. For this reason, he saw the lightening of the Black population as necessary for the attenuation of that difference. This position, however, still relied on the rather dubious assumption—voiced prominently in his earlier essay—that as social *groups* became physically/biologically similar the social tensions between them diminished.

The gendered dimensions of Boas' understanding of interracial sex and its regulation are crucial and have been ignored even in critical discussions of his work. Boas was, as noted earlier, not only suggesting that a key factor in the reduction of racial tension would be the creation of lighter generations of Black children, but that these children, raised as Black in Black communities, would be fathered by white men. Boas was keen to depict miscegenation as producing a lighter Black population rather than a merging of populations. He noted a contrast between the U.S. and Mexico, where equal mixture between white men and Indian women and white women and Indian men led to a "mixed type in which both lines are equally represented" (1945, 77). In the U.S., racial mixture led to the lightening of Blacks because of a historically rooted social pattern of miscegenation almost exclusively between Black women and white men. Boas encouraged (or at least accepted) this pattern, introducing the question of interracial marriage after promoting miscegenation:

It would seem, therefore, to be in the interest of society to permit rather than to restrain marriages between white men and Negro women. It would be futile to expect that our people would tolerate intermarriages in the opposite direction, although no scientific reason can be given that would prove them to be detrimental to the individual. (80)

Accepting as invariable the white social taboo against sexual relations between white women and Black men, he imagined the lessening of physical contrast between Black and white races as possible only through the transmission of white "blood" through Black mothers. Of the conditions of interracial sexual relations between white men and Black women in slavery and beyond—almost always occurring outside of legal marriage, typically involving patriarchal violence of some kind, and certainly implicated in systematic inequality—he had nothing to say.[8] I will elaborate further on these issues in my discussion of an alternative account of miscegenation produced by George Schuyler in a later section. What is particularly noteworthy here is that Boas deferred serious attention to past and present Black-white social relations to an effort to imagine the conditions of a liberal future where whites might treat Blacks as individuals.

That effort nonetheless merits attention precisely because it called the very possibility of a fully realized American liberalism into question. Michel-Rolph Trouillot casts the problem of liberalism in the Boasian tradition as follows:

Liberalism wishes into existence a world of free willing individual subjects barely encumbered by the structural trappings of power. The dubious proposition follows that if enlightened individuals could indeed get together within their enlightened space, they could recast "culture" or "race" and, in turn, discharge other free willing individuals of their collective delusions. (2003, 111)

Boas may have embraced the ideal of a world where enlightened individuals could cast off their collective delusions, but he hardly imagined the U.S. as a place where such a world could come into existence in any near future. Trouillot's account skips over a key tension within Boasian thought between its liberal emphasis on individual choice and its view of culture as largely molding the perspectives, consciousness, and choices of individuals; the question of how cultural patterns might be changed to facilitate the equality and freedom of individuals was a persistent preoccupation. In a statement of his credo as an anthropologist, Boas famously said "my whole outlook upon social life is determined by the question: how can we recognize the shackles that tradition has laid upon us? For when we recognize them, we are also able to break them" (1938, 202). As we have seen, however, Boas was not always sanguine about the possibilities of breaking the shackles of tradition. Nowhere did he more acutely express this tension than in his evaluation of white Americans' racial consciousness, particularly with regards to blackness. In *The Mind of Primitive Man* (both editions) he spoke of the "race instinct" of whites to highlight how "social conditions" can become "so deeply ingrained in us that they assume a strong emotional value" (1911a, 274). In "The Problem of the American Negro" he identified white racial consciousness as inhibiting recognition of Blacks as individuals. The conflation of racial distinction with social categories in the U.S. almost ensured that whites would refuse liberal recognition to Blacks. As Trouillot contends, Boas did not theorize race/racism in terms of the structural dynamics of power relations; he also overtly rejected economic explanations of racial conflict and discrimination on the basis that such explanations presupposed the fundamental issue—social categorization of groups based on race. His white Americans were, however, certainly encumbered by culture.

These considerations lead me to a different proposition concerning Boas' liberalism. Boas' discussion of white Americans' race consciousness, particularly with regard to Blacks, is a moment where his liberalism faced a contradiction. This was a contradiction between his liberal impulses—his desires for individuals to be evaluated as individuals and for individuals to make rational choices over emotive responses—and his sense of the power that cultural conventions and social conditions exert on human emotion and thought. The whole reasoning behind his promotion of miscegenation rested on a pessimism concerning the possibilities of American whites actually being or becoming liberal subjects—able to exercise reason over emotion and judge individuals as individuals—as long as membership in social categories was readily apprehensible. The result of this crucial tension in his thought makes it worthy of attention: Boas' faith in liberalism faltered at the color line.

Boas' understanding of the so-called Negro problem as a white problem provides a resource to critically rethink anthropological liberalism. But rather than interrogate either liberalism or racial categories and face head-on the tensions between liberalism and the social life of race/racism, he turned to the possibilities of miscegenation, acceding to normative strictures on sex between Black men and white women—shackles of tradition too entrenched to suggest breaking. Without an alternative account of how racial consciousness might be transformed, without an orientation toward the transformation of social relations between socially defined groups, refusing any possibility of the oppressed transforming those relations via social struggle, and operating with a sense of racial consciousness as overdetermined by physical difference, the only solution left him was the long-term transformation of the physical makeup of the oppressed.

George Stocking suggests that by the time Boas wrote *Anthropology and Modern Life*—originally published in 1928 and revised in 1932—he had "undercut his assumption that the ultimate solution of the race problem would be biological" (1979, 43). The motivation lay in the physiological and genealogical study of African Americans by Boas' student Melville Herskovits. Herskovits argued that the African American population demonstrated significant white and Indian ancestry and represented a distinctive biological "type" (not a race). Most importantly for the issue at hand, Herskovits contended that sexual relations between white Americans and Black Americans had diminished considerably since slavery and speculated that the Black American population would become physically darker over time as a result of marriage patterns among Black Americans; Black women proportionally married men darker than themselves while the lightest of Black men passed into the white population.[9] Accepting Herskovits' logic, the lesson for Boas was clear: the contrast between Black and white in the U.S. was increasing rather than decreasing (Boas 1928, 72–74). He could no longer assume that the Black population would invariably become physically whiter over time. "Biological assimilation having for the moment failed him, he was forced to rely on the hope that by the conscious control of the cultural process itself mankind might eliminate racial prejudice" (Stocking 1979, 43). Specifically, Boas hoped that "instinctive race antipathy" could be overcome "if we succeed in creating among young children social groups that are not divided according to the principle of race and which have principles of cohesion that weld the group into a whole" (Boas 1928, 76). He thus resorted to a version of socialization via education that he had previously identified as insufficient; if the emphasis here was on the creation of racially integrated social groups among children it remained unclear how such groups would ultimately subvert the racial order of the society as a whole.

Moreover, Boas did not ultimately abandon or even significantly alter the logic of his overall thought concerning the "Negro problem" and miscegenation. In *Anthropology and Modern Life* he retained the position that when social divisions correlated with racial distinctions "the degree of difference between racial forms is an important element in establishing racial groupings and in accentuating racial conflicts." He thus identified the darkening of African Americans as a "most undesirable" tendency (1928, 74).[10] He also reiterated his previous view: "Looking forward towards a lessening of the intensity of race feeling an increase of unions between White men and colored women would be desirable. The present policy of many of the Southern States [outlawing miscegenation] tends to accentuate the lack of homogeneity of our nation" (75). If the lightening of the Black population was less likely than Boas presumed, it was no less important in his estimation of the intransigence of the "Negro problem." The effort to create integrated social groups among children would, he suggested, meet with strong resistance from "the pressure of present popular feeling" (76). Having moderated his hopes for physical whitening, Boas also moderated his pessimism that education and socialization could liberalize the racial consciousness of whites. He did not, as far as I can tell, change his position opposing the cultivation of racial solidarity and struggle among Blacks or members of other socially stigmatized categories, presumably because he continued to view such efforts as accentuating rather than diminishing group differences and thereby reinforcing the group consciousness and antipathy of whites. The "real race problem"—whites' socially cultivated illiberal perception of non-whites—remained a quandary for cultivating a liberal future.

Anthropology and Modern Life provides further insight into the logic of Boas' imagination of the relationships between miscegenation, race, and nation. Boas used comparison between the United States and Latin American societies to illustrate the social variance of racial prejudice and discrimination.

> Race feeling between Whites, Negroes, and Indians in Brazil seems to be quite different from what it is among ourselves. . . . The discrimination between these three races is very much less than it is among ourselves, and the social obstacles for race mixture or for social advancement are not marked. Similar conditions prevail on the island of Santo Domingo between Spaniards and Negroes. Perhaps it would be too much to claim that in these cases race consciousness is nonexistent; it is certainly less pronounced than among ourselves. (1928, 64)

In these countries, the "socially coherent groups are racially not uniform. Hence the assignment of an individual to a racial group does not develop as easily" (70). In the 1932 edition Boas developed this position further with regard to its implication for national belonging. He asserted that in Mexico—"where the intermingling of Indian and White has produced a numerous mixed population which is not permanently separated by social barriers"—distinctions between Indian, Mestizo and Spanish were "weak." Individuals belonging to these groups were "not only members of the Mexican nation, but also of Mexican nationality, provided they participate in the social and political life of the country" (1962, 90). Histories of race mixture in the former Portuguese and Spanish colonies had produced conditions where, unlike in the U.S. and northern Europe, racial differences did not correlate to distinct social groups and thus did not provide a ready marker of social group belonging implicated in invidious stereotyping of individuals. Boas thus drew at least an implicit association between the prevalence of race mixing and the relatively weak development of racial consciousness and discrimination.[11] Conversely, in the U.S. race consciousness was particularly pernicious because racial differences and social groups coincided.

These considerations informed his account of race and national belonging. Boas used the term "nation" to refer to a political unit or state and "nationality" to "designate groups the same in culture and speech without reference to political affiliation" (1962, 82).[12] Race, however, troubled his conceptualization of nationality. On the one hand, Boas argued against theories that identified cultural belonging with racial origins and particular races as "true bearers of national culture" (84). These were the views of the racialist ideologues of exclusionary nationalism. On the other hand, Boas had to contend precisely with the racial exclusions of group belonging associated with nationality as a lived social phenomenon. He recognized that in practice nationality could hinge on racial distinctions, as was the case in the U.S.:

> Racial descent has significance in determining nationality in those countries in which fundamentally distinct races live side by side. Everybody will agree that American Whites, Negroes and native-born Asiatics are members of the same nation, but they would hardly be called members of the same nationality, because of the social barriers between these groups and the consciousness that they are derived from races that continue to be distinct. They are separated by divergences in bodily form which causes, at least for the time being, permanent segregation. (89–90)

In the U.S. nationality thus involved more than Boas' initial definition of the concept as "groups the same in culture and speech." The divisions of nationality between whites, Blacks, and native-born Asians were not derived from fundamental cultural differences—elsewhere in the text Boas refers to the "northern Negro city dweller" as "to all intents and purposes like his White neighbor"

(136) and "the anomalous position of American-born children of Japanese parents who have become completely Americanized and who nevertheless have no place in the White Community" (65). Rather, participation in a common nationality was impeded by social barriers and racial consciousness that created the conditions for perpetual segregation. Nationality as a lived phenomenon was a racial phenomenon.

This insight points to another crucial paradox in Boas' thought. Boas recognized a distinction between the position of whites and non-whites vis-à-vis American nationality, yet he modeled the solution to the racism facing non-whites on the situation of European immigrants and the possibility of their assimilation into American nationality. Boas perceived that race—to be specific, the "fundamentally distinct" races of whites, Asians, and Blacks—defined the parameters of American nationality. The European immigrant could, in principle, assimilate by abandoning any outward markers of difference, changing his or her dress, habits, and name. For individuals understood as non-white, their physical difference made a social difference; they could never become white and thus could not share a nationality with whites. American nationality, a sense of belonging to a unified cultural and speech community, was fractured at the color line. However, rather than pursue this insight to fully interrogate the relationship between American nationality and whiteness and question whether American nationality itself was a generative source of the "race problem," Boas analogized the situation of non-white natives to European immigrants. Miscegenation proved key to his thinking in part because it secured the analogy: if Blacks as a group became light enough that whites could not readily type them then they would be in a position similar to that of European immigrants able to choose their own relationship to American culture and nationality. This of course meant that Blacks could assimilate only by becoming biologically more white; they could not assimilate *as* Blacks. Boas never resolved the conundrum that the power of the color line represented for a liberal American future even as his own accounts of white racial consciousness and the racial constitution of American nationality pointed to the real race problem as the imbrication of America with whiteness.

A number of scholars contend that Boas' views on anti-racism and assimilation had their roots in nineteenth-century Jewish German confrontations with anti-Semitism.[13] The two decades following Boas' birth (in 1858) were a period of heightened nationalist fervor accompanying unification and the formation of the German empire. They witnessed both the "emancipation" of Jews—the abolishing of restrictions on civic rights on the basis of religion—and a reactionary anti-Semitic discourse that racialized Jews and denied them belonging to German nationality. Non-Jewish Germans with liberal politics understood Jewish belonging to necessarily entail the complete abandonment of distinctive customs and attachment to Judaism. Under these conditions, Jewish efforts to insist on their national identity, rights, and loyalty as Germans were difficult to reconcile with public affirmation of Jewish identity. According to Glick, "Boas was in many respects a typical representative of late-nineteenth-century Jewry who had in effect abandoned the struggle to integrate Jewish identity with German nationality and had opted for an all-out effort to assimilate themselves out of existence" (1982, 546). After becoming a U.S. citizen, his own public identification was as German-American though he continued to be interpellated as a "German Jew" by intellectual and political enemies. His own experiences with anti-Semitism in Germany and the U.S. surely informed his critical stance on racism, his sympathy with those denied national belonging and individual recognition, and his liberalism.

We should, however, be careful not to reduce Boas' thought to his background. Marshall Hyatt suggests that Boas' interest in Blacks and critiques of anti-black biological determinism ultimately served as "camouflage" to address his primary interest—defending Jews from anti-Semitism (1990, 33–34). Such a position merely presumes anti-Semitism as Boas' principal motivation, providing a ready alibi for evidentiary support in his texts by recourse to his Jewish background.[14] Attention to the intellectual and personal influences of his German Jewish background need not devolve into reductive identity claims.

Boas tended to equate full national belonging with complete assimilation. That position, it appears, was informed by the history of German Jewish struggles for national belonging in the late nineteenth century. In the 1932 edition of *Anthropology and Modern Life* Boas asserted:

> When the Jew is separated from the rest of the people among whom he lives by endogamy within the Jewish community, by habits, occupation and appearance, he is not entirely a member of the nationality, although a member of the nation, for he participates in part only in the interests of the community and endogamy keeps him permanently separated. When he is completely assimilated he is a member of the nationality. This appears most clearly in those North European countries in which the number of Jews is small and intermarriage and assimilation is correspondingly rapid. (1962, 90)

Boas' position here helps us understand his contention that anti-Semitism could only disappear when the possibility of ready identification of the Jew as Jew had disappeared. That position, of course, was not shared by all those of Jewish background. To cite one prominent example: Horace Kallen, a man of Jewish German heritage who moved to the U.S. as a child, promoted a form of cultural pluralism that emphasized the compatibility of ethnic diversity and national belonging, resisting an assimilationist position (Goldstein 2006, 178–183). The issue was not that Boas was speaking from some generic Jewish position or wrote about Blacks as a cover for a struggle against anti-Semitism but rather that his understanding of the overcoming of anti-Semitism vis-à-vis national belonging provided a model for his anti-racist imagination as applied to European immigrants, as well as Blacks and other peoples of color, in the United States.

However, a racial distinction between European immigrants (including Jews) and peoples of color (particularly Blacks) created a conundrum. Recall that for Boas, Blacks, like Asians, were, in racial terms, "fundamentally distinct" from American whites. He was clearly aware of the consequences of being classified as white and non-white. In 1925, he testified that Armenians were Caucasian in a court case assessing the racial eligibility of an Armenian for naturalization (Liss 2015, 302–303). Boas earlier noted that the contemporary African American "carries even more heavily the burden of his racial descent than did the Jew of an earlier period" (1911b, viii). Given that Boas viewed the reduction of racial tension as a question of the diminishing visibility of physical differences between groups, Blacks had a rather formidable additional step to take on the road to national belonging. Only when Blacks became more physically like European Jews, other European immigrants, and "old American" whites—whose physical differences, according to Boas, were quite minor compared with those of the "fundamentally distinct races"—could they overcome the typecasting associated with their category and become accepted individualized members of a national collective. Rather than see in this perspective a problem with a model of national belonging based on assimilation into American whiteness, Boas retained a sensibility that miscegenation between white men and Black women would be necessary for the resolution of racism.

George Schuyler's Alternative Vision of Racial Mixing

If Boas resorted to miscegenation as a result of his underlying premises concerning race, nation, liberalism, and discrimination, his contemporary George Schuyler was an active proponent of interracial *marriage* as the solution to the race problem. Schuyler's vision, based on distinctive premises concerning race and racism, provides another standpoint to reflect on Boas' anthropological imagination of the issue. Schuyler was an important writer (and critic) of the Harlem Renaissance. He later became notorious as a self-proclaimed Black conservative who joined the anti-communist John Birch Society and attacked the civil rights movement. In the 1920s and early 1930s, when he came to prominence as a columnist, journalist, novelist, and satirist, his politics leaned more to the left. Schuyler worked as office manager of *The Messenger* between 1922 and 1928, publishing a weekly column and other material for the magazine. *The Messenger*, founded by socialists A. Philip Randolph and Clyde Owen, was, along with *The Crisis* and *Opportunity*, one of the most important periodicals associated with the Harlem Renaissance. Schuyler also published a weekly editorial in the *Pittsburgh Courier*, which became the most popular newspaper among African Americans. His work was widely read and appeared in journals where Boasians also published, such as *The Nation* and *American Mercury*.[15]

The question of miscegenation appeared frequently in Schuyler's writings during the late 1920s and early 1930s. It was a personal subject; in 1928 he married Josephine Cogdell, a white Texan from a wealthy family. In his reflections on interracial marriage, Schuyler was keen to note the historic prevalence of interracial sex in the United States and to suggest that contemporary interracial marriage was more prevalent than assumed. The theme also figured in his satiric novel *Black No More* (1971 [1931]), which he dedicated to "all Caucasians in the great republic who can trace their ancestry back ten generations and confidently assert that there are no Black leaves, twigs, limbs or branches on their family tree." His pamphlet *Racial Intermarriage in the United States* (1929a) tried to debunk myths concerning the taboo subject, namely that racial aversion was natural and that interracial marriages were rare, only occurred in the lower classes, and were doomed to failure. On the question of a "natural aversion" to interracial sex, Schuyler cited the scientific authority of Boas and Herskovits. He quoted Boas on the futility of anti-miscegenation laws and cited Herskovits on the racially mixed character of the African American population; Herskovits contended that only 20 percent of the American Negro population could be identified as having no Indian or white ancestry, refuting census figures which reported that 85 percent of that population was "pure Negro" (Schuyler 1929a, 10). Schuyler identified Herskovits and Boas as allies. He corresponded with Herskovits, praising his article "When Is a Jew a Jew," which argued against any common, essential biological or cultural basis of Jew-ish identity (Herskovits 1927).[16] Herskovits later arranged for Schuyler to give a talk on Liberia at Northwestern.[17] Schuyler gave Boas a position of honor in his fictional send-up of two corrupt Black newspaper men running for president, who curry favor with whites by complying with their demands to hand over "such anti-Nordics as Franz Boas, J. A. Rogers, and A. A. Goldenweiser" (Fer-guson 2005, 87).[18] Like many other Black intellectuals, Schuyler appreciated the Boasian intervention against scientific racism.

Although Schuyler would invoke academic authority he could also critique academics as a parasitic class loathe to rattle the status quo. In an article titled "When Black Weds White," he again cited Boas and Herskovits but chided, "So far none of the professors has waxed bold enough to speculate publicly on the percentage of whites whose family trees cannot be scrutinized too closely else an Uncle Tom be disclosed" (1934, 12). He was right. Their investigations of racial intermixture were investigations of American Blacks, not American whites. More generally, Schuyler offered a very different account of racial in-termixture and intermarriage than Boasians. He selectively deployed Boasian arguments, ignoring others; to foreground the "influence" of Boasians on his thinking would be to miss the various ways his thinking departed from theirs, particularly his attention to the sexual politics of race and his effort to subvert U.S. racial categories.

Schuyler understood the regulation of interracial sex between whites and Blacks in terms of the reproduction of white supremacy, noting, "the bogey of interracial marriage looms very big, and probably with justice, before the ad-vocates of Nordic supremacy. This is doubtless due to the fact that no student of the color problem in the United States can long fail to see that it is basically sexual" (1929a, 30). The distinction between interracial sexual relations and interracial marriage figures explicitly in his account, in contrast to its muted significance in Boas' writings. In "When Black Weds White," Schuyler identified the structural underpinnings of legal prohibitions against Black-white mar-riage: "Without the ban on such marriages, it is impossible to maintain the system of exploitation based on color which exists almost everywhere in this country" (1934, 12). For Schuyler, the regulation of marriage and sex involved a systematic control of Black men, Black women, and white women central to the reproduction of white male supremacy and the color line in the U.S. politi-cal economy.

Especially must the Negro male be isolated sexually and kept from the white woman who, by her sexual isolation, remains the foundation of the entire color caste system of exploitation, since the pure white exploiting group can only be perpetuated through the white woman. . . . Sex freedom for the white male and the Negro female does not disturb the status quo and so it is tolerated. But in order to prevent the Negro woman from getting any wealth by marrying a white man or a Negro man from escaping the black proletariat by marrying a white woman with money, every Southern state has passed laws forbidding marriage between the races. (1929b, 361)

Schuyler underscored the crucial distinction between "clandestine affairs" (1934, 12) and marriage within the political economy of interracial sex. The prohibition on interracial marriage and the taboo against any sexual relations between white women and Black men were foundational to the "color caste system." For Schuyler, interracial marriage subverted that system because it subverted racial purity and broke down the racial lines of wealth of inheritance; thus he promoted it.

Boas and Schuyler each understood interracial mixing as key to the overcoming of racism in the U.S., but they understood racism in distinct ways and effectively imagined different solutions. Boas envisioned *sex* between white men and Black women as producing a lighter Black population. *Marriage* appears in his expositions as a secondary consideration. The lessening of the physical contrast between Black and white was the primary preoccupation; lifting the prohibitions on interracial marriage would facilitate that process. Schuyler, on the other hand, promoted interracial marriage as an end in itself, placing particular emphasis on marriages between white women and Black men as a means to subvert the color caste system and its political economy. Schuyler suggested that "clandestine" interracial sex between white men and Black women was tolerated because it did not undermine the color caste system. As Boas knew, the children of such unions were classified as Black and became part of the Black community. Boas was also clearly cognizant of the particularly charged white taboo prohibiting sexual relations between white women and Black men but did not inquire into the role it played in a racialized social structure based on white male supremacy. In effect, by ceding to that taboo in his imagination of the future, he tacitly made a concession to white male supremacy. Subordinating other considerations to the necessity of Black lightening—a condition for white recognition of individuality in Boas' logic—facilitated this lacuna.

In delineating the difference between Boas and Schuyler in such stark terms I would, as a counterpoint, highlight that Schuyler, like Boas, was compelled by a vision of social implications of the diminution of the physical distinction between Black and white implied by the proliferation of children of mixed racial ancestry. Projecting forward from Herskovits' calculations of the mixed ancestry of American Blacks, Schuyler claimed: "By 2000 A.D. a full-blooded American Negro may be rare enough to get a job in a museum, and a century from now our American social leaders may be as tanned naturally as they are now striving to become artificially" (1930, 220). He thus suggested that U.S. Blacks were "destined to disappear through amalgamation with the surrounding Caucasians" (1930, 212). Yet on this question too Schuyler departed from Boas. Given his attention to relations between white women and Black men, he viewed racial intermarriage not merely as implying the lightening of the Black population, but the darkening of the white population; amalgamation implied the transformation of both. Moreover, Schuyler reveled in highlighting the ambiguity and ultimate absurdity of U.S. racial categories in ways that went beyond the Boasians.

Intellectual biographies of Schuyler characterize his project of highlighting and promoting racial intermixture as "challenging and denaturalizing 'race' as a stable governing concept" (Favor 1999, 133). We see this in *Black No More* (1971), Schuyler's comedic novel of what happens when a Black scientist and entrepreneur invents a way to turn Black physiognomy into white physiognomy. Blacks rush in droves to lose their stigmata of disadvantage, white supremacists freak out and obsess over the problem of their daughters marrying unrecognizable Blacks, and the leaders of Black organizations are beside themselves as they lose both their cause and their supporters. Schuyler's critiques of Black leadership and, more generally, of efforts to assert pride in Black identity and culture were a consistent feature of his writing at the time. Most notoriously, he mocked the artistic and intellectual project of the New Negro movement in "The Negro-Art Hokum" (1926), referring to Blacks as "lampblacked Anglo-Saxons," that is, as culturally indistinguishable from whites.

Yet *Black No More* mocked more than Black pretensions. As the plot progresses, it lampoons white supremacy and the stability of whiteness itself. The main character, the first to get the treatment, wiles his way into second-in-command of a white supremacist organization, marrying the daughter of its dull-witted leader. Meanwhile, another, more august organization attempts to use genealogy to identify genuine whites only to discover that, by the application of their one drop rule rendering anyone with a fraction of Black ancestry Black, nearly all whites are actually Black. Without delving further into the details of the plot, suffice it to say that mayhem ensues, identity confusions abound, and, in the end, not only is "Black no more, but neither is white" (Favor 1999, 135). When everyone becomes white, no one is white; if one drop of Black blood makes one Black, the discovery that most whites have Black ancestry makes a mockery of the biological classifications of the color line.

Schuyler undermined racial-color categories in his non-fictional writing as well. In his very use of terminology, Schuyler mocked it. In the span of a single piece, "Our White Folks" (1927)—a send-up of white supremacy—he used the following terms to refer to whites: "white," "Nordic," "pork-skinned friends of Southern derivation," "pale neighbors," "peckerwood," "cracker," "townsfolk of paler hue," "red-necked comrades," and "Caucasian." Some of these terms had class and regional connotations, but in this piece and elsewhere Schuyler evinced little respect for propriety in racial terminology, now using a capital-ized term like Nordic (to refer to all whites, not to a specific sub-set of Cau-casians), now terms like "pork skinned" or "ofay." He did the same with terms referring to Blacks, which include "Negro," "Black," "Ethiop," "Senegambian," "Sambo," "Aframerican," "Sons of Ham," "dark brothers," "moke," and "Uncle Tom." Schuyler showed little concern for using proper or scientific language, underscoring the injury trafficked across the color line by engaging in it himself.

Schuyler continually highlighted the absurdity of how racial identity was reckoned in the United States, especially through the one drop rule—"that dis-tinctive American contribution to the science of anthropology which lists as Negroes all people having the remotest Negro ancestry, despite the fact that they may be, and often are, indistinguishable from the purest Nordic" (1927, 389). Racial integrity laws resulted in white children being barred from white schools because genealogists but no one else thought they were Black. Blacks, Schuyler mocked, should hope that racial integrity laws could be passed every-where so that the Black population would quadruple. Just as absurd, a judge had fined a woman legally classified as Black for marrying a Black man because she appeared "too white" (1929a, 18–19). Melville Herskovits argued that the use of the term "Negro" in denoting the U.S. Black population was, because of mixed ancestry, "without justification from a biological point of view"; he nonetheless used the term "American Negro" as a sociological ascription and portrayed the American Negro as a distinct biological "type" (1930, 2). Schuyler on occasion referred to "so-called Negros" (1934, 12) to call attention to racial ascription as social convention. By mocking the absurdities resulting from U.S. conventions of racial classification, Schuyler underscored the social artifice underlying the color line.

In calling attention to the subversive dimensions of Schuyler's understanding of race and race mixture, I do not mean to endorse his suggestion that interracial marriage would ultimately resolve racism. Rather, his writings provide a source for reflective juxtaposition with the work of Boas in a shared field of progressive, New York–based intellectual production. Schuyler's attention to the structural dynamics of power posed the question of racism in different terms than Boas, who cast the problem in terms of a contest between liberal individualism and social convention. Whereas Boas suggested that racial-social groups and economic classes were analogous types of categories, Schuyler suggested that they were intertwined in a "color caste system." Whereas Boas saw interracial sex as necessary for blurring perceptions of difference, Schuyler highlighted how the regulation of interracial sex and marriage was crucial to racial classification itself. Whereas Boas held Blacks and whites to be the most divergent types of mankind, Schuyler refused to respect the integrity of race as a scientific concept as he mocked the absurdity of American classificatory conventions.

As a final word on Boas and Schuyler, it bears noting that their positions on African American identity and miscegenation ran against a prominent current in the Harlem Renaissance—the effort to identify, promote, and enhance a distinctive Black cultural presence. Boas published "The Problem of the American Negro" in 1921, at a moment when *The Messenger* was identifying "New Negros" asserting themselves collectively (Randolph and Owen 1920). Schuyler explicitly rejected the New Negro movement, and Boas appears to have ignored it, maintaining his position that Blacks should minimize their social distinctiveness and eschew a politics of racial solidarity. For both, integration into America ultimately required the dilution of blackness. In contrast, as discussed in the prior chapter, many Harlem Renaissance intellectuals sought to render Black identity and culture as both distinctive and resolutely American, refusing the opposition between Black and America implied in assimilationist discourses. Although many of them could claim a mixed heritage and mulatto identity, they increasingly embraced the term Negro themselves (Williamson 1980, 151–152).

Conclusion

This chapter has provided an account of Boas' imagination of the resolution of anti-Black racism as a window into his thought concerning the social life of racial distinctions and the social nature of prejudice and discrimination. I have argued that his identification of miscegenation as key to the long-term resolution of racism involved a train of reasoning based on his liberalism, his understanding of racial difference and national belonging, and a pessimism concerning the ability of whites to recognize non-whites as individuals, to become the sort of free individuals he championed. The conceptual kernel of the "real race problem" Boas identified—the racial consciousness of the dominant group as socially acquired yet deeply entrenched—remains crucial for the critical analysis of racism, however problematic, contradictory, and distasteful the solution he envisioned. Racial consciousness, discrimination, and prejudice were not, for Boas, phenomena that could be simply eliminated by education in the facts of race. In other words, racism was not merely "a delusion about race" (Trouillot 2003, 111). Race, for Boas, was made socially salient by particular forms of social classification that rendered social group identity and identification on the basis of physical difference coterminous. Such conditions did not prevail everywhere, but where they did—as in the U.S.—racial consciousness implied a social perception of biological difference that was extremely difficult to dislodge. Boas thus called attention to the power of socially cultivated racial perception and interpellation in everyday life.

That he did not pursue this issue further than he did perhaps reflects his understanding of racial difference as ontologically real, despite his various criticisms of the use and abuse of the race concept. Boas was fully aware that American whites were responsible for creating and sustaining segregation and the barriers to participation in a common nationality. Yet he presented the production of racial exclusions of nationality in striking naturalized terms, as a product of the tripartite division of "fundamentally distinct races" with Negros and Caucasians as the most "divergent" stocks of mankind. If Boas continuously cast doubt on the presumption that such differences entailed innate white superiority and Black inferiority, he also viewed the physical differences between them as having a kind of causal impact on the white psyche: "the consciousness that the Negro belongs to a class by himself is kept alive by the contrast presented by his physical appearance with that of the whites" (1945, 78). To be sure, Boas also emphasized that social formations produced variable forms and degrees of racial consciousness in their members, as the Latin American cases illustrated; but in those cases the underlying historic dynamic he identified was that race mixture had produced gradations of physical difference. Boas' account of the social significance of race co-existed with a fetishization of phenotype. This should hardly come as a surprise given the late nineteenth- and early twentieth-century fascination with biological difference and physical type, but the consequences bear noting: his identification of physical differences as having causal efficacy in maintaining social distinctions and segregation appears to have attenuated further inquiry into the social and political production of racial classification and white domination. An additional underlying issue here—how can analysis of race/racism attend to the social significance of phenotypical variations without reifying and fetishizing them?—remains an important problem for anthropology.

Finally, we can return to Boas' account of race, racism, and American nationality to raise troubling questions. Boas perceived that race—to be specific, the "fundamentally distinct" races of whites, Asians, and Blacks—defined the parameters of American nationality. American nationality, a sense of belonging to a unified cultural and speech community, was fractured at the color line. Here was a potential point of departure for a thoroughgoing critical examination of American nationality as constituted through white domination and exclusion. Did white Americans deny Blacks and Asians belonging to American nationality precisely because such belonging was defined in racial terms, as the exclusive provenance of whites? Could a liberal world be fashioned within a nationality configured by racial exclusion? Was the equation between whiteness and America key to the race problem? Was American nationality itself—and not just imperialist nationalism—a key source of racism and the denial of individual recognition? Such questions were not ones Boas raised himself: he embraced the value of nationality as a community necessary for individual development and took the whiteness of American nationality largely for granted. Still, his pessimistic evaluation of whites' racial consciousness suggested that white racism was not simply an aberration from American ideals of freedom and democracy but a pervasive feature of whites' social existence in the U.S. It is no small irony, then, that his student Ruth Benedict would take up his antiracist mantle with an appeal to "America" as a *culture* founded on democracy and assimilation.

3 Ruth Benedict, "American" Culture, and the Color Line

RUTH BENEDICT DID AS MUCH and perhaps more than any cultural anthropologist to develop and disseminate the Boasian intervention on race and racism. Benedict's work on race, however, has received little attention; only recently have scholars focusing on the history of anthropological discourse on race begun to acknowledge its importance (Burkholder 2011; Teslow 2014). The omission is particularly noteworthy given that Benedict is among the most famous of U.S. anthropologists. Her books *Patterns of Culture* (1934) and *The Chrysanthemum and the Sword* (1946) are considered classics and still circulate widely. The book she wrote in between, *Race: Science and Politics* (1940), is today largely unknown. The irony is that during her own lifetime it was her work on race—especially the controversial pamphlet *The Races of Mankind* (Benedict and Weltfish 1943)—that brought her to the attention of the media and a mass readership. *Patterns of Culture* was, to be sure, well known to an academic audience from its date of original publication, but only after it came out in a trade edition in 1946 did it begin its ascendance to one of the best-selling anthropology books ever (Caffrey 1989, 214).

Benedict's writings on race have been neglected largely because of a perception that they were a form of public anthropology produced out of loyalty to Boas and derivative of his thought, offering little in the way of novel insight or theory. Her biographers damn *Race: Science and Politics* with faint praise. Caffrey calls it "a summary of information clearly and stylistically presented" (1989, 293) while Modell evaluates it as "an accomplishment of a certain sort" (1983, 253). They follow the tone set by Margaret Mead, who says that Benedict worked on the book "without delight as if in payment of a moral debt which anthropologists owed a world threatened by Nazism" (1959, 350). Benedict herself wrote to Mead after finishing the book: "I feel I've done my good works and my Christian duty for the rest of my natural life and shan't ever have to again" (Young 2005, 85). But Benedict perhaps remained too much a Christian, and certainly was too dedicated an anti-racist liberal, to simply leave the good works behind. She continued to write and lecture extensively on race until her death eight years later, publishing academic articles, pamphlets, and even a children's book. At a moment of intensified nationalism resulting from World War II, she sought to wed Boasian anti-racism to an affirmation of American democratic values. If any single figure exemplifies a core argument of this book that U.S. anthropologists instructed an (white) American audience in how to reconcile liberal principles with racial differences, it is she. Examining her thought can teach us something not only about the history of anthropology but about the paradoxes of U.S. liberal anti-racisms that speak in the name of America.

This chapter provides a (re)reading of Ruth Benedict's work on race and racism, paying particular attention to her efforts to think through the relationships between racial discrimination and liberal democracy. I focus first on *Race: Science and Politics* and then subsequent articles and other works geared toward the general public. On the one hand, I argue that Benedict's thought on race and racism was more original than presumed. She did not merely reproduce and popularize key Boasian claims but addressed a set of issues raised but not resolved within Boasian thought concerning the origins and overcoming of racism. She sought to theorize, from a cultural anthropological perspective, the nature and history of racism, as well as its dissolution. Working from Boas' insight that racial prejudice, consciousness, and conflict were not universals but culturally generated evaluations of human difference, she developed a historical account of racism as a recent product of Western modernity. Benedict also offered solutions to "race problems" in the United States that went beyond prescriptions of debunking scientific racism and promoting tolerance. She held no illusions that a critique of scientific racism was sufficient to solve "race problems"; the "social fact" of racial conflict required social intervention (1941, 74). In *Race: Science and Politics* she advocated state-sponsored social engineering to diminish social and economic inequalities, which she viewed as the motor of discrimination. Despite her own comments that race was "a field where all my knowledge is second-hand,"[1] Benedict theorized "racism" in her own fashion, contributing to the Boasian intervention.

On the other hand, this chapter identifies paradoxes and tensions within her work, particularly in its treatment of racial discrimination and cultural patterns in the U.S. Understanding these paradoxes requires unpacking not only her constructs of race but also her constructs of "America" (the people) and American culture. Benedict, like fellow Boasians, critiqued discriminatory uses of the race concept and the labeling of European/white nationalities as races yet affirmed the racial categories of Mongoloid, Negroid, and Caucasoid as biological stocks of humanity. She acknowledged that U.S. non-whites faced specific forms of discrimination yet modeled the solution to "race problems" on the assimilation of European immigrants into "American" culture and citizenship. Moreover, Benedict recognized and critiqued racial discrimination in the U.S. yet developed a construct of "America" as a society with a history and culture of assimilative inclusion. She found new ways to mediate and defer the tensions between liberalism, American nationhood, and racism.

As we have seen, immigrant analogies loomed large in Boasian thought. Boasians modeled the overcoming of racism suffered by Blacks and other non-whites on the perceived situation of those they deemed, in racial terms, to be white. In the prior chapter we saw the crucial role the immigrant analogy played in Boas' imagination of the overcoming of anti-Black racism in the U.S. Benedict also modeled the overcoming of racism in the U.S. on the figure of the European immigrant, but her writings tend to present a more hopeful view of American (white) culture than her mentor's. Whereas Boas had worried whether white Americans could become true liberals when it came to race, Benedict suggested that they inherited a culture that, in its foundations, was liberal. Her analysis of racism largely elided the differential effects of the color line on the possibilities of national inclusion while rendering American racism distinct from American culture. It also contributed to the reproduction of the deep association between America and whiteness while ignoring the social power of that equivalence. This equation became most pronounced in the visual imagery of popular media designed to instruct (white) Americans in knowledge of racial distinctions and tolerance of cultural difference. Benedict's authorial voice as an Anglo-Saxon liberal American affirming egalitarianism and assimilationism at the core of U.S. culture produced a version of American exceptionalism that contradicted the more radical possibilities of her cultural history of racism. In a nutshell, I argue that Benedict's anti-racism accentuated racial distinctions in its construction of biological race, minimized the sociocultural consequences of racial distinctions in the U.S. body politic, and reproduced a normative relationship between whiteness and America.

Ruth Fulton Benedict

Unlike many of Boas' students, Ruth Benedict (née Fulton) came from a family with deep roots in North America. Her mother's side traced their lineage to Pilgrims who landed on the Mayflower, and she had several ancestors who fought in the Revolutionary War (Caffrey 1989, 21). Benedict shared a family pride in her forebears, writing as an adult: "My own grandparents were Puritans, and no better stock was ever reared in any country that I know of" (quoted in Caffrey 1989, 22). Benedict's mother received a college degree in an era in which it was uncommon for women to attend university. She worked as a teacher, principal, and librarian to support the family after her husband died in 1888, when Ruth was less than two years old. Ruth and her sister were able to attend Vassar College on scholarships secured through their exceptional abilities and family connections.

Benedict's college years (1905–1909) nurtured her feminist desire for self-cultivation and independence, her intellectual versatility, and her considerable writing talents. After graduation and a year traveling in Europe, she had unsatisfying stints as a social worker and teacher—two of the limited job prospects for university-educated women. She married a physician in 1914 but could not abide living a life confined to the role of wife and worked on a biography of three feminist writers.[2] She decided to return to the university in 1918, enrolling at Columbia to study under the educational philosopher and prominent liberal John Dewey. With Dewey on sabbatical the following year, she attended courses taught by Elsie Clews Parsons and Alexander Goldenweiser, close associates of Boas, at the recently established New School. Caffrey notes the liberal values Benedict shared with the Boasian circle—"belief in freedom of choice, an almost fanatical tolerance of differences, and a dislike of the tyranny of convention"—as well as a shared ability to view "America with an outsider's eye" (1989, 97–98). In the spring of 1921 she became an anthropology graduate student at Colombia, completing her library-based dissertation "The Concept of the Guardian Spirit in North America" a mere three semesters later.

Despite early recognition of her talents—her first published anthropological article was the lead piece in the *American Anthropologist* (Benedict 1922)—Benedict struggled to achieve secure professional employment in the years after obtaining her PhD. Her career is a study in how even the most successful of women were denied their standing via institutional sexism. She conducted fieldwork among the Serrano in California in 1922 and worked as an assistant to Elsie Clews Parsons on Southwest mythology, doing summer fieldwork among the Zuni, Cochiti, and Pima peoples in the mid-1920s. She was unable to fund her work with government and foundation grants; in the case of the National Research Council her application was denied because she was too old (Caffrey 1989, 111). She succeeded Boas as editor of the *Journal of American Folklore* and was given temporary teaching assignments at Columbia but did not have regular employment with a steady salary. For several years Boas attempted to secure her a full-time position, but the sexism of the Colombia administration prevented the appointment until 1931, when Benedict was named assistant professor. A year later a group of twenty anthropologists selected her as one of the top five anthropologists in the country for *Science* magazine, and in 1934 she was selected by *American Men of Science* as one of the three leading women scientists in the U.S. (270). Despite the increased stature she would achieve, Columbia would pass her over as the logical successor to Boas as department chair and only appoint her full professor in 1948, the year she died.

Fully discussing the body of her work up to the point she wrote *Race: Science and Politics* is beyond this scope of this chapter, but a few remarks on her conceptualization of cultural patterns and her efforts to make Americans "culture-conscious" (Benedict 1929, 648) provide important orientation. These leitmotifs are at the heart of *Patterns of Culture*, an eloquent exposition of culture not only as the key concept to understand primitive societies but "ourselves" in the modern U.S. Benedict used the notion of pattern to highlight how the culture of a group of people was given form and orientation by an underlying configuration of key values and foci. Each culture, over a long history, had developed its own pattern out of the almost infinite combination of human possibilities. She illustrated the striking contrasts in cultural patterns by comparing three peoples—the Kwakiutl of the Pacific Northwest, the Zuni of the Southwest, and the Dobu of the Pacific islands. All were strikingly different and all bore some resemblance to modern Americans, the aggressive and suspicious Dobu appearing almost as a caricature of competitive individualism, the Kwakiutl obsession with wealth "in many ways a parody on our own economic arrangements" (Benedict 1934, 188). The wide appeal of *Patterns of Culture* derived less from its contributions to anthropological theories of culture than its efforts to make readers aware of how their own taken-for-granted cultural lenses filtered how they saw the world and lived within it. Since "we" could not perceive our own cultural lenses directly, the study of primitive cultures could provide us with a perspective to relativize our taken-for-granted orientations. In the process, we could begin to liberate ourselves from the dogmas of convention that produced rigid constructs of the normal and abnormal and created unnecessary suffering for those who deviated from convention. The oppressive treatment of homosexuality served as a prime example of the need for cultural reform in U.S. society. Benedict's writings reveal that she was acutely aware of the individual turmoil produced by the disciplinary normalization of sexuality, an awareness surely informed by her non-normative sexuality. *Patterns of Culture* revealed her talent for making anthropological insights relevant to a general audience of educated Americans. This would prove both a boon and a problem in her work on race and racism.

Benedict's Cultural History of Racism

The project resulting in *Race: Science and Politics* emerged when Modern Age Books approached Benedict to write an accessible book on race to promote tolerance (Caffrey 1989, 292). Benedict had mentioned race and racial prejudice at several points in *Patterns of Culture*, articulating the Boasian distinction between inherited biological traits and acquired cultural patterns while chiding Anglo-Saxons both for their prejudices and their failure to see prejudices as social products. "Racial differences and prestige prerogatives have so merged among Anglo-Saxon peoples that we fail to separate biological racial matters from our most socially conditioned prejudices" (1934, 44). In much of her writing, Benedict was fond of using "we," speaking as an insider to a readership she sought to influence, in this case (Anglo-Saxon) white Americans. It was precisely this identity that made her an appealing choice for the editors of Modern Age Books. According to Caffrey, they recruited her "because of her Anglo-Saxon background, her Revolutionary War ancestors, her descent from the Pilgrims on the *Mayflower*. These, combined with her reputation as a scientist and an anthropologist, gave her words an authority few other writers could command" (1989, 292).

Benedict agreed to the project, working on the book she wanted to call "Race and Racism" through most of 1939. The publishers asked her to change the title, noting that "racism" was not a commonly known term. In arguing for her original title Benedict noted, "The special point of the book, as compared with other discussions of Race, is its complete separation of Race from Racism and its 'propaganda analysis' of racism."[3] Benedict began by emphasizing the contrast between race and racism.

> I suppose every anthropologist has had the same experience. When his lecture is over and he has shown that racism has no scientific basis for its claims of congenital superiority for any one race or nation, some listener gets to his feet and says, "But the Negroes"—or the Japanese, or the Indians—"are *not* Whites." Then the anthropologist, who has probably spent years of his life patiently investigating racial differences, has to say again that to recognize Race does not mean to recognize Racism. (1940, v)

Benedict affirmed that races exist; notice that she did not challenge audience members' categorical assertions that Negroes, Japanese, and Indians "are not whites." She held fast to the idea of the three major racial "stocks" and "anatomical specializations" of Negroid, Mongoloid, and Caucasoid (50–53). Her point was that racialist claims of the innate superiority of some races have no validity. Accordingly, *Race: Science and Politics* was divided into two sections, "Race" and "Racism." The first provided an interpretation of racial science that summarized Boasian critiques of biological determinism, of the equation between race, language, culture, and nation, of the idea of "pure races," and of the notion that civilizations were products of racial genius. The second was the most original, providing a history of racism, an explanation of racial prejudice, and suggestions for advancing racial equality.

Benedict identified racism as a product of modernity, a "modern superstition" (153) that fully flowered only in the twentieth century. Her "natural history of racism" (151–219) reads less as a clearly delineated series of processes than as a genealogical account identifying multiple, overlaying points of origin. Her object was not a history of "races" or the race concept. Rather, Benedict sought to explain the development of racism, understood as a philosophy, belief, or dogma of group hierarchies based on biological differences: "Racism is the dogma that one ethnic group is condemned by nature to congenital inferiority and another group is destined to congenital superiority. . . . Racism is not, like Race, a subject the content of which can be scientifically investigated. *It is, like a religion, a belief which can be studied only historically*" (153, emphasis added). For Benedict, race was a viable field of scientific study "of genetic relationships of human groups" (151). Racism turned the race concept into a "dogma" of superiority-inferiority backed by false science. She noted that science, "a word to conjure with in this century," had acquired a kind of magical authority: "The slogan of 'science' will sell most things today, and it sells perse-cution as easily as it sells rouge" (232). Benedict used the authority of science to disprove racism, but she posited that understanding racism required examin-ing a belief that was not universal or ahistorical, but culturally and historically particular. In this sense, her "natural history" of racism was a cultural history of a modern idea.

Benedict echoed Boas' assertions that racial antipathy, prejudice, and con-sciousness were not natural, universal characteristics. However, she did not merely compare societies to relativize racism but traced racism's historical formation, suggesting that its seeds were planted in the decline of European feudalism and the colonization of the Americas. With the decline of feudalism, antagonisms between classes and nations intensified, creating "an uncongenial home for the doctrine that God had made of one clay all the peoples of the earth," and setting the stage for "a doctrine which taught that in the struggle of rival interests which was the rule of the day, their favored group was made of special clay" (166). In the pamphlet *Race and Cultural Relations*, Benedict identified racism as a theory of innate inequality produced out of particular historical circumstances:

> racism proper is the doctrine of the *biological* superiority of one group over an-other—and out-group antagonism up to now had obviously been based not on "blood" or difference of inherited physical characteristics but on considerations possibly more basic in terms of the given situation, such as clash of economic interests or religious beliefs. For a "racial" point of view to arise, western Europe had to become more conscious of the separation of peoples in the purely physi-cal sense. (Benedict and Ellis 1942, 34–35)

This attention to transformations in European understandings of difference—the rise of biology as a key mode of imagining human difference and inequal-ity—prefigured recent work on the epistemological underpinnings of racial thinking in modernity (Seth 2010).[4] For Benedict, these transformations were initiated within the colonies of the New World.

Benedict dedicated a section to "Racism and European Expansion Over-seas," suggesting that Europeans came to view natives as "outside the pale of humanity, without religion, law or morals." This was not originally a product of racism; it was "a consequence of the fact that they were not Christians, not of the fact that they belonged to the darker races" (1940, 168). In much of the New World, especially the colonial dominions of the Spanish and Portuguese empires, Christian missionaries mitigated colonial exploitation of natives. Over time, however, contradictions between efforts to convert colonial subjects and exploit native land and labor created the need for new rationalizations of subjection.

> The time was ripe for a new theory of superiority and inferiority, and people began to talk of natives as sub-human, as related to apes rather than to civilized man. After all, color was the most conspicuous difference, and it set off the opposing parties on the frontier as religion often no longer did. But the shift from one basis for the white man's superiority to the other was gradual and was not formulated. It was an inevitable response to social conditions and was practical rather than intellectualized. (171)

From the start, the English settlers of North America took a "highly secular attitude toward natives" and were preoccupied first and foremost with acquiring Indian land. "The early royal grants of land in the New World had made no mention of the natives already living there; they read as if no human being occupied the territories. The dearest wish of the settlers was to achieve this happy condition as soon as possible" (172–173). They did so via extermination or removal of Indians, practices that persisted after U.S. independence.

Although Benedict wondered "whether the doctrine [racism] would have been proposed at all . . . if the basis for it had not been laid in the violent experience of racial prejudice on the frontier," she argued that full-fledged racism did not develop within the colonies but within Europe itself. European colonialism "set the stage for racist dogmas and gave violent early expression to racial antipathies without propounding racism as a philosophy. Racism did not get its currency in modern thought until it was applied to conflicts within Europe" (174). Benedict thus left the Americas behind in her genealogical account of racism, a move I will consider later in a discussion of her treatment of racism in the U.S.

Benedict argued that racism as a systematic ideology of biological superiority/inferiority first emerged as an expression of class conflict within Europe. She identified the earliest expression of racist thought in the eighteenth-century writings of the Norman Count de Boulainvilliers, who invoked the blood of nobles as the birthright of the aristocracy to superior rank and rule in conflicts with both monarchy and populace. Racist doctrine did not achieve prominence, however, until the mid-nineteenth century with the publication of

Count Joseph Arthur de Gobineau's influential *Essay on the Inequality of Races.* Gobineau was responding to the revolutions of 1848 and the challenges liberal and socialist politics posed to the established order. The essay was a political tract against liberalism that denied the demands of the masses and justified the perpetuation of inequality on the basis of racial inheritance. Benedict argued that Gobineau's racism was not nationalist but aristocratic in orientation and involved a reactionary defense of the old order.

> These aristocrats, who had reigned in all countries, were now threatened by the degeneracy of democracy and by claims of equality. When he divided the races of the world into White, Yellow, and Black, his application of the matter was that the Alpines were of Yellow extraction and the Mediterraneans of Black extraction; his Whites were represented, therefore, in Europe only by the group which is today called Nordic. They were the only ones on whom the hope of civilization could be pinned. (1940, 180–181)

Gobineau's influence was widespread, and by the early twentieth century, racist doctrine had become hitched to nationalisms across Europe. This was the contemporary form of racism that plagued the world. Racist claims served as "camouflage" (217) for self-interested aggressions and alliances, serving both to rally the populace against rival nations and, especially in the case of anti-Semitism, to provide scapegoats within the nation. Here, Benedict focused particular attention on German Nazism and, as I will discuss in a later section, anti-immigrant campaigns in the U.S.

It is important to note here some of the tacit implications of Benedict's genealogy of modern racism. First, in identifying Gobineau as essentially the father of racism, Benedict identified racism itself as primarily a reaction to political democracy and the liberal tradition. The possibility of intimate ties between liberalism and racism in the history of Western thought lay beyond her conceptual schema. Second, her account of nineteenth-century European racism said nothing about the relationship between European states and their colonies (old and new), populated predominately by "Black" and "Yellow" subjects. This was, after all, a century of colonial expansion for European powers. Unlike her contemporary Hannah Arendt (1944), she drew no link between forms of racist thought internal to Europe and expanding European imperial power, despite her aforementioned attention to earlier phases of colonialism. Rather, for Benedict racism as such was essentially a product of illiberal aristocratic elitism wed to European nationalisms. The significance of this perspective for her understanding of racism in the U.S. will become apparent as we move forward.

Solving Racism

In the final chapter of *Race: Science and Politics,* Benedict advocated social solutions to racial prejudice and discrimination that reflected her overall effort to explain racism. She argued that racism, like religion, could only be understood historically, as a product of culture; it had to be treated as a belief. In so doing, she produced a secular account of racism in a double sense, treating both religion and racism as modes of affective thinking and identifying the secular origins of racism as the successor to religious persecution and conflict. In her effort to explain the genesis of racism as belief, she developed the race-religion analogy to argue that race succeeded religion as the key modality of justifying oppression in the nineteenth and twentieth centuries. "Racial slogans serve the same purpose in the present century that religious slogans served before, that is, they are used to justify persecution in the interests of some class or nation" (1940, 232). Racial discourse provided the key idiom of contemporary persecution for two principal reasons. First, racism bore the stamp of scientific authority and science possessed unmatched legitimacy. Second, racial dogmas defending "purity" emerged because modernity had placed "ethnic groups" in intimate contact. While racial persecution represented a historically novel mode of oppression and "the ism of the modern world" (3), Benedict held that understanding and combating the problem ultimately required looking beyond "race" to dynamics underlying oppression that, she asserted, were not "racial" in character. We see this position enunciated in various ways: "in order to understand race persecution, we do not need to investigate race; we need to investigate *persecution*" (230–231); "For the friction is not primarily racial. We all know what the galling frictions are in the world today: nationalistic rivalries, desperate defense of the status quo by the haves, desperate attacks by the have-nots, poverty, unemployment, and war" (237–238); "To minimize racial persecution, therefore, it is necessary to minimize conditions which lead to persecution; it is not necessary to minimize race" (244–245).

These perspectives require unpacking. Recall that for Benedict the concept "race" offered a scientific, neutral descriptor of biological differences that was abused by racists. The source of tension between groups lay not in their "racial" differences but in their social relations. The investigation of race—biological differences—was therefore largely irrelevant to understanding the sources of conflict and discrimination, sources with roots in social conditions.

> Race is not in itself the source of the conflict. Conflict arises whenever any group—in this case, a race—is forged into a class by discriminations practiced against it; the race then becomes a minority which is denied rights to protection before the law, rights to livelihood and to participation in the common life. The social problem does not differ whether such a group is racially distinguished or whether it is not; in either case the healthy social objective is to do away with minority discriminations. (245)

The elimination of such discriminations would necessarily involve both protection of minorities' civil and human rights and the transformation of the social conditions that produced inequality. The state was to play a key role. Drawing from the New Deal, Benedict promoted state intervention and social engineering in the U.S. to create greater economic opportunity and ensure the health and welfare of the entire populace. The state, in fact, was the only institution capable of minimizing "economic discrimination" and ensuring civil liberties (248–249). Benedict tied this socioeconomic prescription to an appeal to U.S. democracy, concluding with the line: "Our Founding Fathers believed that a nation could be administered without creating victims. It is for us to prove that they were not mistaken" (256).

Benedict's cultural-historical account of racism and discrimination in *Race: Science and Politics* pushed the Boasian intervention beyond scientific critiques of racial science and prescriptions for socialization into tolerance of difference. She highlighted the ideological power of scientific discourse in modernity while invoking that same power. She articulated the limitations of truth-revelation, myth-busting, and educational reform in overcoming prejudice and discrimination, which, in her diagnosis, arose from social inequalities and power relations. Racial distinctions did not "naturally" translate into social differences and discriminations. They mattered only as biology acquired social significance in modernity and as they came to be filled with cultural meaning as ideological weapons for the powerful to ensure their rule, create scapegoats, and exploit the weak. Recourse to race as a weapon could thus diminish only when the unequal conditions promoting social warfare were leveled. The critique of racial science could strike a blow against racism, but Benedict argued it was insufficient; more sweeping state-sponsored social reforms were necessary to undermine the social frictions driving discrimination.

Benedict's account suggested that political-economic conditions under-pinned racial divisions in Western modernity, but this account was not be-holden to a Marxian theoretical perspective. While Benedict identified racism essentially as an ideological product of social division and inequality justified by the powerful, she eschewed an attention to capitalism found within Marxist approaches. Oliver Cox, one of the few social scientists to substantively engage *Race: Science and Politics*, critiqued her work from a Marxian analytic (1944).[5] Cox lauded Benedict's observation that racism was a recent European develop-ment that emerged as a result of European colonialism. But he rejected her presumption—common to other Boasians—that race antagonism grew out of ethnocentrism common to all societies. Ethnocentrism was merely a term to describe a feeling of social unity in reaction to a stranger; it "does not become anything else" (461). Similarly, he rejected her contention that race prejudice and religious persecution were variants of essentially equivalent social process of oppression, an association that implied that racism was, at root, a form of intolerance. For Cox, the dynamics generative of racism did not lie in intoler-ance of difference but in relations of labor exploitation under capitalism. He suggested, contra Benedict, that the historical emergence of racial domination represented more than a change in the ideological instrument of oppression; it reflected a transformation in the order of oppression itself.

Benedict conceived racism as a belief system particular to modernity and amenable to cultural analysis, but she also precluded the need for such anal-ysis in treating racial oppression as one manifestation of social persecution and conflict conceived in universal, abstract terms. In this sense, according to Visweswaran, she treated the racial dimensions of oppression as "epiphe-nomenal" (1998, 73), a charge often applied to Marxist approaches to racism.[6] That is, Benedict understood racial oppression as a "social fact" yet cast the "racial" dimension of racial oppression as derivative of and secondary to the "real" problem, oppression, conceived in abstraction from any particular social formation. She extended a core Boasian proposition—that race, as biological difference, did not itself generate discrimination—to the more objectionable contention that racial oppression should not be treated as analytically distinct from any other mode of oppression. Benedict thus eschewed the need for fur-ther historical and ethnographic inquiry into the social-cultural life of race and racism. The limitations of such a perspective are particularly evident in her treatment of racism in the U.S.

American Cultural Patterns and the Color Line

In her chapter "The Natural History of Racism" in *Race: Science and Politics*, Benedict dedicated several pages to racism in the twentieth-century U.S. (1940, 191–199). Her principal focus was racism against immigrants from southern and eastern Europe, and her prime example of American racist theory was *The Passing of the Great Race* by Madison Grant (1916), who held that a nation's vigor depended upon the amount of "Nordic blood" it contained (Benedict 1940, 192–193). Noting the lack of attention to "our great national problem, the Negro" in this scholarship, she suggested that "racism in America turned out to be no more than the spectacle of immigrants of one decade condemning to everlasting inferiority the immigrants of a later decade" (198–199).

Benedict herself had difficulty developing an analytic frame that could adequately incorporate discrimination against European immigrants and discrimination against non-whites, whether native or immigrant. Her discussion of racism in the nineteenth- and twentieth-century U.S. demonstrated a notable selectiveness. As noted previously, she glossed over racism in the nineteenth-century U.S. Her account thus ignored the racial science practiced in the U.S., as well as the racialized slavery it justified. Just as she ignored the relationship between nineteenth-century European colonialism and racism, so too she ignored U.S. imperialism and the role of racial discourse in western territorial expansion and deployment of military power beyond the continent.[7] To be sure, Benedict recognized that non-Europeans, especially Blacks, were targets of particularly virulent forms of racial discrimination. She accounted for the relative lack of attention to Blacks in the work of Grant and other racist theorists of the 1910s and 1920s by noting "our treatment of the Negro conforms so closely to the predilections of these authors that they doubtless had little to suggest" (198). Yet those same authors had, by the 1920s, increasingly devoted attention to what Leopold Stoddard called the "rising tide of color" threatening to swamp white civilization (Guterl 2001, 51–55). Benedict's tendency to gloss over racism as applied to peoples of color in her historical account of U.S. racism after the eighteenth century—that is, after U.S. independence—facilitated a framework that opposed racism to American liberal democracy. That is, it allowed her to narrate a history of "America" as a country with democratic and egalitarian principles that had become violated by racism. Most notably, Benedict asserted that recent immigration restrictions represented an aberration from a previous era of acceptance. "The American temper had changed since the days when our motto was 'No distinctions of race, creed, or color' and we offered an 'asylum for the oppressed' and wrote enthusiastically about 'the Melting Pot'" (1940, 196). As Jacobson wryly notes, "And when, we ought to ask, was *that*?" (1998, 133). As we saw in Chapter 1, from the early days of the republic the ability of immigrants to become citizens depended on racial distinctions. The 1924 immigration law condemned by Benedict not only restricted European immigration but excluded Asian immigrants precisely on the grounds that they were ineligible for citizenship (Ngai 2004, 7). Acceptance of immigrants (and natives) as "American" was always coded by race and color.

A year after publishing *Race: Science and Politics*, Benedict published the article "Race Problems in America" (1941). Benedict asked: "What can alleviate racial conflict in America?" (74). She approached the question indirectly, noting that during World War I efforts to "'Americanize' aliens" through sudden, forced assimilation failed, sowing resentment among minorities. Likewise, contemporary programs designed to celebrate cultural plurality were doomed to fail. Such programs contradicted an "American cultural pattern" that facilitated the rapid abandonment of traditional customs, "a cultural pattern fostered by American labor mobility, the schools, and the culturally conditioned lessening of parental authority over children. This cultural pattern is no respecter of persons; it involves segregated native populations as well as immigrants." The promotion of cultural diversity thus ran against a "cultural current" toward the "desired elimination of imported caste and cultural distinctions" (76). If the U.S. pattern fostered the elimination of such distinctions, what then reproduced racial conflict? "What interferes with this cultural current in America is overwhelmingly the defensive attitudes of longer established Americans who are chary of sharing prestige and opportunities with newcomers" (76). In other words, "Old Americans"—whites who claimed an Anglo-Saxon heritage for themselves and the nation—resisted the American cultural pattern of minority assimilation. Solutions to the race problem, therefore, lay in encouraging the predominant pattern, "to capitalize on the aliens' will-to-function as an American" (77). This would entail eliminating "disadvantageous circumstances which confront the alien" and incorporating immigrants into all state programs of educational, health, or civic improvement (78).

Benedict's account of American culture affirmed a tradition of inclusiveness and implicitly rendered discrimination against minorities as "un-American." Similar efforts to position racism in terms of the conflicts between American principles of inclusion and practices of discrimination can be found in the contemporaneous work of Mead (1942), Myrdal (1944), and in liberal, nationalist political discourses unto the present. If Boas had suggested that (white) American cultural configurations rendered racial perception an almost intractable problem, Benedict provided a more optimistic account by asserting the tendency of American cultural patterns to foster assimilation. She thus echoed the exceptionalism of her historical account of American racism while glossing over the problem of the color line—the different positioning of whites and non-whites—in the U.S., equating the conditions of immigrants and "segregated native populations." This uneasy equivalence is reflected in the title of an article that focuses almost exclusively on European immigrants ("Race Problems in America"). All her examples of immigrant groups were drawn from Europe; only once did she name a "segregated native population" (Blacks). Whether immigrants or natives, other non-Europeans—Chinese, Japanese, East Indians, Native American peoples, Filipinos, Jamaicans, and others—were absent. When Benedict addressed the situation of Blacks, she could cast them as analogous to European immigrants. In a lecture delivered at Bryn Mawr College in 1941, Benedict objected to forms of intercultural education requiring minority students to perform folkloric difference. "So in our schools we put on assembly programs where the Negro children sing their spirituals and the Balkan children dress in their native costume—and wonder why they don't like it. But in America, aliens want more than anything else to be American" (quoted in Burkholder 2011, 70). That Blacks, with American roots as deep or deeper than whites, were rejected as American may have made them similar to European immigrants—as "aliens" within the nation—but that very condition should have given Benedict pause and in some moments did give her pause. In the *Race and Cultural Relations* pamphlet, Benedict noted that Blacks, Asians, and Jews faced distinctive types of race prejudice in the U.S. (Benedict and Ellis 1942, 8–12). This recognition, however, was rarely incorporated into her theorization of race relations or her assessment of American cultural patterns.

Benedict's reflections on the "race problem" in the U.S. reveal tensions not only in her theorization of racism but in her imagination of "America" and American culture. Benedict is often (justifiably) considered a cultural critic of U.S. society (Geertz 1988, 102–128; Handler 1990). Geertz identifies the power of her classic books in their satirical perspectives on "us" (a U.S. us, as Geertz points out) held up against the mirror of a "not-us"—for example, the Zuni (a people within the U.S. nation-state), the Dobu, or the Japanese. Her writings on race, however, reveal the ambiguity of that U.S. "us." As I have suggested,

Benedict often wrote not only as an American to Americans but as a white (Anglo-Saxon and "Old") American to white Americans. In a short piece called "We Can't Afford Race Prejudice," Benedict could say, "America must prove that we are not backing our own version of a master race. We must convince our own minorities and the peoples of Asia and Africa of this" (1942a, 2). In such phrasing, "our own minorities" (a marked category) were both rendered part of America and positioned outside the subject America (and its unmarked whiteness).

The issue at stake here is not simply the play of marked and unmarked categories in her representation of America (the people) but her representation of American culture. Her critical analysis of many aspects of American culture notwithstanding, Benedict affirmed individualism and egalitarianism as quintessentially American values.

> Equality is the highest, most moral American basis for hopes for a better world. It means to us freedom from tyranny, from interference, and from unwanted impositions. It means equality before the law and the right to better one's condition in life. It is the basis for the rights of man as they are organized in the world we know. We uphold the virtue of equality even when we violate it and we fight hierarchy with a righteous indignation. It has been so ever since America was a nation at all. Jefferson wrote it into the Declaration of Independence, and the Bill of Rights incorporated in the Constitution is based on it. These formal phases of the public documents of a new nation were important just because *they reflected a way of life that was taking shape in the daily living of men and women on this continent.* (1946, 45, emphasis added)

This passage from *The Chrysanthemum and the Sword* serves to distinguish "an individualistic, egalitarian culture [the U.S.] and a hierarchical, holistic culture" [Japan] (Handler 1990, 257). I quote it at length because it highlights a view of American egalitarianism as emergent out of a "way of life" produced from a European settler colony. However plausibly an egalitarian worldview and daily life might describe relations among Europeans in the formation of what became U.S. society, it surely cannot describe the history of relations between those who came to be classified as whites and non-whites. Benedict, of course, acknowledged a distinction between an ideal and reality, making reference to violations of the American ideals of equality with racism likely in mind. The key point I want to make is that Benedict nonetheless produced an account of American culture as based on liberal precepts, rendering non-egalitarian impositions on individual liberty and practices of discrimination violations of a core principle.[8]

Benedict's discussion of the history of racial prejudice in the U.S. in *Race: Science and Politics* followed the same trajectory, representing prejudice, discrimination, and exclusion as aberrations from founding cultural principles of inclusion. So did her identification of a pattern of cultural assimilation violated by the defensive attitudes of Old Americans in "Race Problems in America." In each instance, Benedict represented American culture as inclusive and egalitarian. By way of contrast, she did not represent racial hierarchies and everyday discriminations, codified in slavery, Jim Crow segregation, and immigration law, as emergent from an American "way of life." Burkholder notes "Benedict emphasized the value of the anthropological concept of culture, by which she meant American national culture . . . to promote social equality in America" (2011, 82). Whereas Boas worried whether white Americans could become true liberals when it came to race, Benedict presumed they inherited a culture that was liberal in its foundations. The resolution to the race problem for her lay in the actualization of American cultural principles. White Americans already had the cultural resources to be their better selves. Benedict's commitment to American equality, as a moral value and ideal, drives the passion of much of her writings on racism. As a *description* of American culture, however, that commitment rendered racism as distinct from American cultural patterns, separating the analysis of American culture from a critical analysis of race and racism. Perhaps that is the ultimate paradox of her work on race and racism.

A certain coda is in order. Benedict provided a different account of American racial culture in "Postwar Race Prejudice" (1959), an article written in 1947 but published posthumously. Assessing the U.S. in the post-war era, she identified a resurgence of racial prejudice and identified aspects of American culture as part of the problem. Benedict related a story circulating among African Americans about two U.S. Black soldiers serving in WWI in France. One soldier said that when he returned to the U.S. he would walk up Sixth Avenue and "get me a drink in every white man's joint." His companion responded that he would walk behind his coffin. Benedict says of the latter: "He knew that when the war was over, and they were back in America, they would be subject to the same taboos they had known before the war. The old pattern would powerfully reassert itself, and that old pattern vigorously denies social equality to many racial and ethnic groups" (363). Here, Benedict identified an enduring pattern of inequality and exclusion as part of American culture, suggesting that racial prejudice was part of the American cultural fabric. "Only a miracle would enthrone ethnic equality as a daily practice in the United States. However much we hesitate to acknowledge it, race prejudice is deeply entrenched in our routine life and probably, measured by any objective standards, only South Africa goes further in segregation, discrimination, and humiliation" (367).

American exceptionalism, in this formulation, takes on a more critical guise than in Benedict's earlier iterations. To be sure, Benedict also mentioned assets of American culture: a faith in nurture over nature; the absence of an aristocratic society's notion that biological inheritance determined personal destiny; increasing knowledge of the facts of race. On the whole, then, Benedict here suggested multiple, conflicting tendencies in American cultural patterns. Racial prejudice, in this account, was no longer epiphenomenal to American culture. Benedict never abandoned an American "we" implicitly coded as (Anglo-Saxon) white, but she did forgo some of the optimism and elisions pegged to the use of the European immigrant as the model figure for understanding and transcending American racism. Indeed, it is likely no coincidence that she developed some of her most critical comments on American culture by invoking a narrative of racial exclusion and violence derived from U.S. Black popular culture. It is also significant that they remained unpublished in her lifetime.

That Benedict held an ambivalent position on American culture as assimilationist and egalitarian is evident in other unpublished work. In the written version of a lecture (date unknown) called "America's Racial Myth" she directly identified that myth—a folk belief in white superiority—as "a part of our American culture."[9] In the draft of an essay on intercultural education programs titled "American Melting Pot, 1941 Model," she noted that Blacks and Asians did not have the same opportunities as European immigrants for assimilative social mobility and that an individual's standing was contingent in part to the degree to which "in color and features they approximate white characteristics."[10] Interestingly, the published version omitted the reference to Asians and the reference to physical whiteness as a factor in the perception of individuals but retained a comment on the need to confront the specificity of anti-Black discrimination: "An intercultural program which does not face our Negro problem fairly would be about on a par with a German program which omitted Nazi treatment of the Jews. . . . In our schools we must be truthful about Negro discrimination. We cannot gloss over the disabilities enforced by law and custom" (1942b, 18). In these moments, Benedict hinted at the cultural power of the color line in shaping the conditions facing non-white peoples. She also noted that anti-Jewish prejudice, like anti-Black and anti-Asian prejudice, persisted no matter how long Jews resided in the country (19). She knew that assimilation was not a cure-all for American racism.

How might we reconcile Benedict's insights here with her tendency to extol the virtues of American culture and model the overcoming of "race problems" on the assimilation of European immigrants? Did she cast her arguments in terms she deemed most effective in reaching a white American audience? This appears likely. Identifying liberal moral precepts such as individualism and egalitarianism *with* American culture rendered the struggle against prejudice a moral duty of citizenship grounded *in* American identity. Being a good American meant being a racial liberal. A rhetorical strategy emphasizing the democratic tradition of America was an appeal to white moral consciousness intertwined with an appeal to patriotism. Conversely, identifying racism as an equally characteristic feature of American cultural patterns would have compromised such an appeal. The conundrum here is the contradiction facing those who would combat racism through appeals to nationalism. If, as in the U.S., national identities have been produced along racially exclusionary lines, a critical confrontation with national identity formation is required to combat racism. Yet to call critical attention to the nation as constitutively oppressive and racially fractured is to undermine the appeal to national identity as the grounds for anti-racism. In any event, if we assume that an appeal to the nation and patriotism circumscribed what Benedict could say—or felt she could say—about American culture and racism, we must nonetheless confront the power of nationalist discourse in shaping her public intervention. Whatever her motivations, Benedict ultimately participated in a discourse of American exceptionalism that identified American cultural patterns of assimilative inclusiveness as a basis for minority integration, rendered racism as an aberration of those core patterns, and modeled the overcoming of racism on the possibility of inclusion open to white immigrants.

Popularizing Anti-Racism

Benedict and other Boasians worked hard to bring their perspectives on race and racism to the U.S. public in the war era, participating in efforts to reform how U.S. schools taught children about race and culture and to create accessible media for a mass audience. *Race: Science and Politics* turned out to be a larger book than Benedict and her publishers initially imagined, but its core arguments were synthesized in the pamphlet *The Races of Mankind* (Benedict and Weltfish 1943), co-written with Gene Weltfish, Benedict's colleague in the Columbia anthropology department.[11] *The Races of Mankind* in turn spawned an animated film sponsored by the United Auto Workers, a traveling exhibition created by the Cranbrook Institute of Science, and a children's book about a white, middle-class American who learns to confront the "green devils" of prejudice and embrace liberal principles through the facts of science (Benedict and Weltfish 1948; Teslow 2014, 246–251).[12]

The Races of Mankind distilled Boasian refutations of biological determinism in favor of cultural explanations of human differences, encapsulated in such section titles as "Customs Not Racial," "Character Not Inborn," and "Civilization Not Caused by Race." Other sections identified racial mixture as a historical norm and intelligence testing results as a product of opportunity and environment rather than racial endowment. In "Race Prejudice Not Inevitable" the authors identified the roots of prejudice in fear and scapegoating and noted the government's role in protecting individuals from discrimination. Benedict and Weltfish avoided the stance of promoting state policies to reduce economic inequalities found in *Race: Science and Politics*, emphasizing instead the role of individual action: "But at best the government can act only as a policeman, finding a wrongdoer here and there. Only the people themselves can really end racial discrimination, through understanding, sympathy and public action" (1943, 30). The authors did, interestingly, invoke Russia as a country with a recent record of racial progressivism at the risk of facing the red-baiting that contributed to divisions among liberal-left organizations with which Boasians were affiliated (Kuznick 1987, 208–226). Benedict and Weltfish ended, as would be expected, with an evocation of the promise of American democracy in its confrontation with fascism.

> With America's great tradition of democracy, the United States should clean its own house and get ready for a better twenty-first century. Then it could stand unashamed before the Nazis and condemn, without confusion, their doctrines of a Master Race. Then it could put its hand to the building of the United Nations, sure of support from all the yellow and the black races where the war is being fought, sure that victory in this war will be in the name . . . of the universal Human Race. (1943, 31)

This final appeal reflected a growing Americanist concern that domestic racisms would compromise U.S. leadership in world affairs in the post-war era.

The Races of Mankind circulated widely, with one million copies sold within a decade of its appearance. It was adopted by a number of school districts and advertised on radio programs to average citizens. It was, in fact, originally written at the request of the United Service Organizations for use by the U.S. military but was not distributed to servicemen because of opposition from Southern politicians. Of particular objection was the presentation of government-sponsored World War I intelligence test data indicating that Blacks from select Northern states scored higher than whites from select Southern states. Kentucky Republican Andrew May, chairman of the House Military Affairs Committee, led the campaign against the pamphlet, deeming it subversive communist propaganda. Among his supporters was the avowed white supremacist Senator Theodore Bilbo, who held a long-standing grudge against Boas and contended the pamphlet was part of a communist plot to repeal immigration law and foster miscegenation (Teslow 2014, 253–262).

If *The Races of Mankind* represented a threat to segregationists, it also represented a liberal account of racial equipotentiality and a critique of racial prejudice that refashioned rather than completely subverted an American racial order founded on normalized whiteness. The pamphlet contributed to the popularization of racial classification as reduced to the tripartite division between Negroid, Mongoloid, and Caucasoid such that European immigrants were not composed of distinct races but were members of the same race with different nationalities or religious persuasions (1943, 10–11). As we saw earlier, Boasians were long involved in this project of remaking racial classification, even if they expressed a certain tentativeness about it. In 1935, Otto Klineberg said of racial categories:

> The classification which is in fairly general use, and which, with one modification or another, has the sanction of a great many anthropologists . . . is by no means free from this inevitable arbitrariness, but is presented here as a convenient starting point for further discussion. It describes three main races: the Negroid or "black," the Mongoloid or "yellow-brown," and the Caucasian or "white." (1935, 22–23)

Even Ashley Montagu (1945)—known for his arguments against the *term* race as irretrievably compromised by its association with social myths of biological determinism and inequality—held to the general classification scheme. He suggested the term "divisions" for denoting major human branches—Negroid,

Australoid, Caucasian, Mongolian—and the use of the term "ethnic group" for "minor" distinctions (Jacobson 1998, 101; Teslow 2014, 293–305). Though Boasians differed in their treatment of "race," all agreed that human physiological and biological diversity could be divided into a small number of categories of ancestral distinctions, and most used the term race to denote them.

We can identify a certain tension in Boasian thought on the politics of racial classification. On the one hand, of course, Boasians sought to minimize race as an explanation of human differences; whatever the classification system, group biological differences meant little relative to cultural differences. On the other hand, Boasians were keen to revise racial classification and naming practices— what kinds of groups counted as "races"—to ensure the term race would not be used to denote ethnicities or nationalities. They implicitly recognized that the act of racial classification itself carried political significance. In the late 1930s, the issue retained pressing significance for Boasians with the Nazi persecution of Jews and enduring anti-Semitism and anti-immigrant agitation in the U.S. It is, however, important to recognize that the Boasian intervention operated differently with respect to those they classified as whites and non-white, scientifically cast as Caucasians and non-Caucasians. In the U.S., where citizenship and belonging had long been associated with whiteness, the argument that European immigrants from Irish to Jews were not discrete races but (Caucasian) nationalities and/or ethnicities brought them closer both to whiteness and Americanness. In *Patterns of Culture*, Benedict lamented: "We have come to the point where we entertain race prejudice against our blood brothers the Irish, and where Norway and Sweden speak of their enmity as if they too represented different blood" (1934, 11). If her rhetorical point was to call attention to the absurdity of racial prejudice in general, its force relied on the supposition of a fundamental similarity between different groups of Caucasians in implicit contrast with differences across the categories recognized by anthropological science—Caucasian, Negroid, and Mongolian (Jacobson 1998, 106). In other words, it relied on the presumption that "we" Americans were white.

Matthew Frye Jacobson, in his important work on the changing position of European immigrants from "races" to white ethnics and/or (white) Americans in the twentieth century, identifies Benedict as "among the chief popularizers of the new racial geography" (1998, 109), an argument elaborated further by Teslow (2014) and Burkholder (2010; 2011). The illustrations accompanying *The Races of Mankind* and related media provided a visual distillation not only of global racial classification schemes but of an American identity presumed as white.

The map of the Eastern Hemisphere in Figure 2 identifies the Caucasian Race (A) with northern Europe, the Mongoloid Race (B) with eastern Asia, and the Negroid Race (C) with central-west Africa. The text also identified subdivisions of Caucasians (Nordics, Alpines, and Mediterraneans) and noted that native Australians are sometimes called a "fourth primary race" (Benedict and Weltfish 1943, 11). If the text emphasized that most people in the world were of intermediate appearance between the "primary" races, the illustration visually emphasizes a tripartite racial division of humanity.[13] Notice also that from the western direction a suited white man peers at this diversity. This figure reappears two pages later, scratching his head at a range of men of various hues and appearance, though one of them looks identical to himself (see Figure 3). The caption reads: "There is no Jewish 'Race'" (1943, 11).

The white American character recurs throughout the text, first as a white man in juxtaposition to other global races and then simply as an "American" (1943, 15). In Figures 2 and 3, the reader is invited to share his subject position as an observer of human racial (and cultural) diversity. This position is

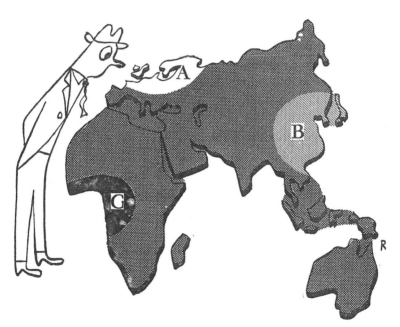

MOST PEOPLE IN THE WORLD HAVE IN-BETWEEN-COLOR SKIN.

Figure 2 Illustration from *The Races of Mankind*.
Source: Benedict and Weltfish (1943, 9). Published with permission.

THERE IS NO JEWISH "RACE."

Figure 3 Illustration from *The Races of Mankind.*
Source: Benedict and Weltfish (1943, 11). Published with permission.

reinforced in two other drawings that illustrate the contributions of various peoples of the world to civilization and American culture. In one (Figure 4), the (white) American sits at a table surrounded by a group of standing men of color wearing native garb and offering a bounty of foods that contribute to the American diet (1943, 24).

The point that American gastronomic culture was a product of many peoples and traditions was thus made through a representation of consumptive practices that figures a white man as representative of that culture. He is, in fact, the only one equipped to eat. A similar scene was re-created in the Races of Mankind Exhibition by the Cranbrook Institute in photographic version, where the visual disparity between half-naked and exotically costumed non-whites and suited white man is striking (Teslow 2014, 268–271). As Teslow observes, the reiterated presence of exoticized non-whites in *The Races of Mankind* and its offshoots visually subverted the Boasian insistence on distinguishing racial difference and cultural difference while reinforcing the equation between Americanness and whiteness (265–283). The dissemination of the Boasian intervention through popular media associated with *The Races of Mankind*— necessarily requiring simplification and dilution—accentuated its tendencies toward a certain reification of racial categories and normalization of whiteness.

According to Zoë Burkholder (2010; 2011), the Boasian intervention on race had a profound impact on educational discourses in the 1940s. As early as

OUR FOOD COMES FROM MANY PEOPLES.

Figure 4 Illustration from *The Races of Mankind*.
Source: Benedict and Weltfish (1943, 24). Published with permission.

1937, Benedict had begun participating in education committees oriented toward reducing racial prejudice, urging programs of intercultural education to move away from folkloric celebrations of cultural differences in favor of treating "minorities" as Americans. In addition to producing *The Races of Mankind*, she co-authored a pamphlet for teachers on race and published on intercultural education and racial prejudice in educational journals. Boas, in response to a resurgence of anti-immigrant sentiment connected to political battles over school funding in 1939, led a team of Columbia students in analysis of racial discourse in high school and college texts, finding that 20 percent taught racial superiority in ways similar to Nazi discourses while 66 percent confused race with nationality (Burkholder 2011, 58). He then coordinated the publication of a pamphlet called *Can You Name Them?*, the cover of which featured photographs of six middle-aged white men and asked the reader to guess their nationality—French? German? Australian? American? (59). Boasian critiques of racism provided teachers not only with intellectual tools but the armature of science to instill liberal values in their charges. The accompanying transformations in educational discourse were equally important:

> An historical analysis of the dominant educational discourse on race demonstrates that teachers consolidated white racialized minorities into an overarching category of "Caucasian" by 1945. At the same time, teachers developed a new way of speaking about racial minorities that emphasized the culture concept so that teachers in the postwar era were likely to refer to African Americans and Asian Americans not as "racial" minorities but instead as "cultural" minorities. In part, this reflected teachers' willingness to embrace the colorblind ideal. (Burkholder 2010, 357)

Boasians, of course, did not engender these transformations alone, but the accounts of race and prejudice they developed played no small role in the consolidation of liberal racial discourses that simultaneously minimized, maintained, and accentuated racial distinctions across the color line, enacted an incomplete substitution of race with culture, and aspired toward an ideal of a color-blind America while reproducing its dominant whiteness.

Conclusion

In the 1940s, Ruth Benedict was arguably the most prominent public anthropological voice on race and racism in the United States. Her effort to theorize and historicize racism is striking when juxtaposed against the writings of other Boasians, who worked diligently to scientifically disprove racial prejudice yet developed little in the way of a theory to explain it. Boas and his students had reworked the concepts of race and culture to challenge biological determinist and racialist explanations of human differences and inequalities. They did not, however, pursue in a sustained fashion the historical problem of the emergence of racism and how and why race became a key mode of social differentiation and prejudice. Benedict took up that problem in the context of a book intended to synthesize a liberal, scientific critique of racism, providing an account of racism as an ideological product of modernity, a new mode of oppression that rendered socially produced differences into ostensibly stable hierarchies of innate, biological differences. Her attention to racism as a cultural product of modernity, building from Boas' arguments that race consciousness, prejudice, and conflict were products of particular cultures rather than human universals, suggested the potential of a cultural analytics of racism emergent from the Boasian tradition.

Benedict, keenly aware not only of the role of science in promoting racism but of the ideological power of science in modernity, argued that the critique of scientific racism alone could not overcome racial oppression and advocated state intervention to protect civil rights and promote socioeconomic equality. Sidney Mintz, a former student of Benedict and one of the few anthropologists to highlight the originality of her work on racism, noted to an audience of anthropologists in the early 1980s: "I find it nothing less than remarkable that Benedict should have called attention more than thirty years ago to the fact that the most important force for the elimination of institutionalized racism in America was the United States government. . . . Who among us has been more outspoken on the issue of racism than she; who has done as much to use his or her professional stature to impel our country toward social justice?" (1981, 150–151).

Taking Benedict seriously as a scholar of race and racism, however, requires that we move beyond venerations of a disciplinary ancestor to critically examine the paradoxes in her work. Benedict largely modeled "race problems" in the U.S. on the question of European immigration while providing a construct of "America" as a culture imbued with egalitarian values, thereby deferring both the problem of the color line—the distinctive forms of racial oppression confronted by non-whites—and the question of whether racial oppression was endemic to (white) American culture. As we have seen, Benedict's positions resulted both from certain legacies of the Boasian tradition and from her own commitment to America and what she saw as its cultural ideals. If Stocking is correct in asserting that Boasian anthropology "was able to speak to Americans as the voice of science on all matters of race, culture, and evolution" (1968, 307), then we need to also reflect on how Boasians addressed Americans, whom they addressed as Americans, and how they conceptualized America.

Benedict, more than any other Boasian besides Margaret Mead, explicitly wrote as an American to Americans. Implicitly, she often spoke to white Americans as a white American. Perhaps her voice achieved the prominence it did precisely because it simultaneously articulated a commitment to anti-racism and a commitment to America that (re)produced an image of a tacitly white nation built on virtuous foundations. Appealing to democratic traditions as essential features of an American culture derived from the descendants of European settlers, Benedict implicitly rendered non-Europeans as others to the making of America, others whom, to be sure, she hoped to include in the American body politic. The Boasian intervention on the race concept had itself produced a similar paradoxical effect, rendering certain heretofore racialized, minoritized groups of (suspect) whites as racial Caucasians while reconstructing "race" to mean the biological stocks of Negroid, Caucasoid, and Mongolian. In the context of a U.S. nation-state where America was heavily identified with whiteness, this reconfiguration of racial categories reinforced the crucial distinction between whites and non-whites even as Boasians argued against biological determinism. Boasians accentuated the paradox by modeling the overcoming of racism against non-whites on the situation of assimilating Europeans. Their efforts to rethink race left the color line intact while their efforts to understand and overcome racism never came to terms with the importance of the color line in the American social body and their own racial imagination. As a result, the anti-racism associated with anthropology participated in the making of a liberal Americanist tradition on race with enduring contradictions.

4 Post–World War II Anthropology and the Social Life of Race and Racism

IN 1951, African American social anthropologist St. Clair Drake published an article in the *Journal of Negro Education* analyzing race relations in the post-war era. He began by highlighting the global disparity across the color line. "There is a world-wide cleavage between 'white' and 'colored'" that reflected four hundred years of European political domination (1951, 261). Changes, however, were afoot. The war against fascism had impelled states "which incorporated racist dogma in their own legal codes and social structures" to proclaim opposition to racism (263). At the same time, the war galvanized anti-colonial nationalism, pan-African and pan-Asian movements, and rising resentment against white supremacy in the non-white world. The Soviet Union and its allies were all too ready to exploit Western racism to court the peoples of Asia and Africa. The United States government, along with most Western nations and the newly created United Nations, were thus politically compelled to confront racism as a "weakness of American democracy" and had begun to take tentative measures toward promoting "progressive change in the actual structure of race relations" (266). Drake recognized that "institutionalized segregation and discrimination" (265) would not disappear overnight. His implicit message was that as the West was being forced to confront racism, new opportunities for political action were emerging. He also sounded a cautionary note, speculating that growing acceptance of Black participation in the mainstream of U.S. life might depend on whether the "popular mind" could dissociate campaigns for Black civil rights from communism (269).

Drake's overview reflected key dimensions of Cold War racial politics crucial for understanding anthropological engagements with race and racism in

the post-war era.¹ This short chapter provides a bridge from my account of
Boasian anthropology as a liberal Americanist project to chapters on the post-
war comparative study of social race by Wagley and Harris and the racial implications of critiques of anthropology that emerged in the late 1960s and early
1970s. I first provide a broad overview of developments in U.S. anthropology
in the post-war context of formal decolonization abroad, domestic civil rights
mobilization, and the ascendance of the U.S. as a global power. Rather than
focus on anthropological theory, I highlight the institutional expansion and
transformation of the discipline and examine the situation of Black anthropologists in a white-dominant academy confronting challenges to racial exclusion
in the civil rights and Black power eras. I then briefly discuss anthropological
contributions to the civil rights movement and engagements with race as a
social phenomenon, qualifying a common argument that cultural anthropologists abandoned the analysis of race and racism.

Anthropology in the Post-War Era

Before World War II, much of Asia and the Caribbean and almost all of Africa
were under the direct administrative control of an imperial power. By the early
1970s, the vast majority of former colonial territories were formally independent states. India gained formal independence in 1947, Ghana in 1957, and
Jamaica in 1962. In Africa alone, there were thirty-three "new nations" by 1963
(Gerstle 2001, 271). The United States emerged from World War II the preemi-
nent global power and prime architect of the order of nation-states represented
by the creation of the United Nations and international financial institutions
(e.g., the International Monetary Fund, the World Bank) (Kelly and Kaplan
2001, 15–17). U.S. foreign policy was driven by a dual concern for securing
favorable conditions for American business and military power and ensuring
that newly independent governments endorsed U.S.-led capitalism rather than
communism in the (new and old) "underdeveloped" nation-states of the "Third
World." The U.S. government exerted power through a variety of mechanisms,
from violence (war, military intervention, CIA sponsorship of coups and political assassinations), to economic intervention in the name of modernization
and development, to the ideological influence of knowledge production.

Racism, as Drake suggested, represented an embarrassing contradiction to
U.S. claims to support freedom, equality, and democracy across the globe. Recognition of that contradiction within the U.S. government contributed to the
(limited) racial reforms of the early Cold War period. For example, improving

the racial image of the nation abroad was a key consideration in passage of the McCarran-Walter Act, the first major immigration legislation since 1924, which lifted the ban on Asian immigration and permitted Asian immigrants to naturalize (Gerstle 2001, 256–266). Likewise, the executive branch was motivated by international image concerns to support the plaintiffs in *Brown v. Board of Education*, the 1954 case in which the Supreme Court rejected the "separate but equal" doctrine upholding racial segregation (Dudziak 2004). Liberal antiracist discourse, wed to the pragmatics of U.S. nationalism and imperialism, was in ascendance. Of course, it was ultimately the civil rights movement, led by Black churches, that forced the executive branch to enact legislation such as the Civil Rights Act (1964) and the Voting Rights Act (1965). Operating within the strictures of U.S. Cold War anti-communism, many civil rights activists, including Martin Luther King, drew on a discourse of civic nationalism that affirmed the rights of all citizens, regardless of race, to share in the American dream of freedom, individualism, and equality of opportunity (Gerstle 2001, 273–274). Even so, right-wing political figures and the repressive agencies of the U.S. government viewed efforts to combat white supremacy as subversive and drew equivalences between anti-racist activism and "un-American" sympathies. David Price, in his account of Cold War surveillance and persecution of anthropologists, notes: "Perhaps the only thing that fanned the FBI's paranoia more than advocacy of racial equality was the advancement of international political positions that either ignored or ridiculed American Cold War positions" (2004, 283).[2] Drake had good reason to think that the U.S. government and white American public would support Black civil rights only if they could be dissociated from communism.

Anthropology underwent major changes in the post-war era. Native Americans were no longer the main subjects of ethnographic attention. As the U.S. became a global hegemon, anthropologists "invaded in force all the major areas of the world not closed to them by hostile powers" (Wolf 1974, 8). This global expansion was facilitated by the perceived need for knowledge of the societies and cultures of the "second" and "third" worlds, reflected in government and private foundation support for the creation of university-based Area Studies and a boom in research funding. One major initiative was the Coordinated Investigation of Micronesian Anthropology, funded by the Office of Naval Research with additional support from the Wenner-Gren Foundation, which sent forty-two anthropologists to study conditions in the islands of Micronesia in the years following the war (Price 2016, 46–51). At Columbia, Ruth Benedict secured a large grant from the Office of Naval Research to found the Research in Contemporary Cultures project, building on the national character studies developed during the war, retooled for the Cold War context (Price 2016, 100–102). Julian Steward led a project on modernization in the U.S. dependency of Puerto Rico funded by the Rockefeller Foundation and Puerto Rican government (Steward et al. 1956). Such projects provided a significant source of funding for dissertation projects. Area research training fellowships—sponsored by government organizations such as the Social Science Research Council and American Council of Learned Societies and private foundations such as the Ford Foundation (which had CIA connections)—provided additional sources of funding. We need not reduce anthropologists to lackeys of U.S. Cold War interests to recognize the importance of government and private funding in influencing the direction of anthropological knowledge production (Price 2016).

As anthropology expanded geographically it diversified conceptually and theoretically. There is no space here to discuss the various trends from the late 1940 to the 1960s—national character studies, cultural ecology, structuralism, symbolic anthropology, among others—except to highlight that in some quarters Boasian approaches to culture not only fell out of favor as the perceived price of scientific progress but were directly attacked as retrogressive.[3] This was nowhere more the case than in the institutional home of Boas and Benedict, where a post-war generation of graduate students influenced by Leslie White and Julian Steward developed materialist approaches to culture and society. White and Steward—the latter a faculty member at Columbia in the late 1940s—argued that Boas and his followers had preemptively dismissed evolutionary theory, accusing them of abandoning a scientific approach to culture and eschewing nomothetic explanation. A number of Columbia graduate students—among them Stanley Diamond, Morton Fried, Marvin Harris, Eleanor Leacock, Anthony Leeds, Sidney Mintz, Sally Falk Moore, Robert Murphy, Marshall Sahlins, Elman Service, and Eric Wolf—developed a variety of materialist theoretical perspectives for anthropology. Leeds later referred to Columbia as the "generating milieu of the major works in Marxist Anthropology since World War II" (quoted in Sieber 1994, 8), although explicit annunciation of Marxist approaches was too dangerous to voice until the mid-1960s (Leacock 1982). With a turn toward materialist theory, the Boasian heritage in anthropology became identified with power-avoidant liberalism (Wolf 1969a) or with anti-scientific eclecticism (Harris 1968). The Boasian legacy of anti-racism, however, persisted among this influential cohort, many of whom remained vigilant in condemning reworked expressions of biological determinism over the following decades. Moreover, in theory the stage was set for the development of a critical, structural, materialist analysis of race and racism from this same cohort but, as I argue in the following chapter, this potential was only partially realized.

A final consideration for understanding anthropology in the quarter century after the war was that anthropology, like the academy in general, grew exponentially while diversifying in uneven ways. Morton Fried noted in the early seventies that within the lifetime of then middle-aged faculty, the profession had been "tiny," consisting of a small, interpersonal community in which senior anthropologists either knew each other or had friends in common (1972, 223). Between 1941 and 1964 the membership of the American Anthropological Association increased by twenty-fold (Wolf 1974, 8). Over the course of the 1960s, the number of departments offering a BA or higher degree increased from 87 to 217 and the number of PhDs awarded quadrupled (di Leonardo 1998, 236). To get a sense of the change, consider that in the mid-1950s, nearly half of the anthropology PhDs awarded in the U.S. came out of Columbia, Harvard, and the University of Chicago, and almost 80 percent came from those three institutions plus Yale, Cornell, and the University of California, Berkeley. By the late 1960s, Columbia, Harvard, and Chicago accounted for roughly one-quarter of anthropology PhDs.[4] The diversification of PhDs would not be reflected in faculty numbers until later due to the historic dominance and continued prominence of the elite programs. Of the full-time faculty in the largest fifteen departments in the country in the 1968–1969 academic year, 58 percent held their highest degrees from just four programs (Harvard, University of Chicago, UC Berkeley, and Columbia) (Fried 1972, 175).

The expansion of anthropology reflected the dramatic growth of university education, initially fueled by the GI bill, other state funding, and the economic boom in the post-war period. The growth rate peaked in the 1960s and included an increasing number of students who were women and/or people of color, who demanded changes in the discipline to reflect their presence. Anthropologists influenced by feminist and anti-racist struggles of the 1960s called attention to the predominance of white men within the discipline. Fried calculated that women held 13.3 percent of full-time teaching positions, with lower rates of tenure and department leadership than men and higher rates of part-time positions (1972, 218–220). The number of anthropologists of color grew in absolute terms in the 1950s and 1960s but remained a tiny fraction of the discipline. In the early 1970s, the Committee on Minorities of the American Anthropological Association identified 122 minority professionals (categorized as Asian, Black, Native American, or of Spanish-speaking origins) out of a total of approximately 4,000, that is, 3 percent (Hsu et al. 1973).[5] That such a committee existed at all reflected the organizing efforts of anthropologists of color in the American Anthropological Association (AAA) in the late 1960s and early 1970s.

A brief overview of the history of African American anthropologists and university employment provides fodder for reflection. Until the mid-1950s, most of the small number of Black anthropologists worked outside of the university or taught at Black colleges and had an ambiguous and ambivalent relationship to the discipline.[6] Before the U.S. entry into World War II, no African American scholar in any discipline held a full-time position outside a Black college. During the late 1940s and early 1950s such opportunities remained severely limited by racial discrimination. Anthropologist Allison Davis was the first African American hired by a white dominant institution, in the Department of Education at the University of Chicago (where he received his PhD), in 1942. In 1946, St. Clair Drake was appointed to the faculty at Roosevelt College, a new university established on integrationist premises. Hugh Smythe (PhD, Northwestern, 1945) eventually secured a position at Brooklyn College in 1953 after years of frustrated searching. As I discuss elsewhere, one prospective employer in a sociology department asked letter-writer Melville Herskovits to send a picture of Smythe, asserting that since he would be the "first appointment of a Negro to our staff" his physical appearance was "of some importance" (quoted in Anderson, forthcoming). This incident highlights the exceptional challenges faced by Black scholars in securing employment, as well as the co-existence of institutional racism and emergent efforts toward faculty integration.

In the late 1970s, Drake reflected that the handful of Black intellectuals who studied anthropology in the pre-war era "believed the discipline had relevance to the liberation of black people from the devastating consequences of over four centuries of white racism" (1978, 86). Black intellectuals, however, gravitated in greater numbers to the fields of history, literature, and sociology. Indeed, Drake and Smythe—who published in the field of race relations— were typically identified as sociologists and rarely published in anthropological journals. Post-war transformations in domestic racial politics and the civil rights movement created new conditions and opportunities for Black anthropologists within the confines of enduring white supremacy. With the expansion of access to university education, a still small but growing number of Black graduate students entered the discipline. Like existing PhDs such as Drake and Smythe, a number of them conducted fieldwork in new or emerging states in Africa.[7] Black anthropologists also worked in other world regions.[8] The employment situation also improved as the most prestigious universities began to hire Black faculty. UCLA hired Councill Taylor (who studied under Mintz at Yale) in 1955. Elliott Skinner was employed as a visiting assistant professor by Columbia (1957–1959), where he returned in 1963 with tenure after working at New York University. As the pressures for desegregation grew and the university system expanded, teaching/research jobs for Black scholars in white-dominant universities became a viable if trying career option. Demand for Black faculty would accelerate with the development of the Black Studies movement and creation of Black Studies programs, some of which became headed by Black anthropologists.

A comparison of three graduate students at Columbia in the early 1950s—William Willis, Elliott Skinner, and Jerome Rauch—exemplifies the divergent career paths of Black scholars in the complex era of racial integration, racist recalcitrance, and Cold War politics. By conventional standards, Elliott Skinner was the success story. Skinner conducted fieldwork in British Guiana and the Upper Volta, became a tenured professor at Columbia and, in the late 1960s, was named U.S. ambassador to Upper Volta. He returned to the academy after his ambassadorship, pursuing a highly productive career at Columbia, where he became the first Black chair of a department at any Ivy League university in 1972 (Matory 2015, 82). In contrast, Jerome Rauch was displaced from the profession. He never completed his dissertation, leaving academia on advice of his advisor Julian Steward after publishing a critique of Area Studies as the product of U.S. geopolitical interests, one of the earliest of its kind (Rauch 1955). Rauch wrote from a critical, anti-colonial, anti-imperialist tradition associated with Du Bois—with whom he subsequently worked—but his perspective was lost to anthropology and the academy as he was deemed by Steward to be "unemployable" after his article appeared (Price 2004, 346–347). Finally, William Willis began his graduate studies in 1946, completing a dissertation on the ethnohistory of southeastern Indians in 1955 and then working on the history of Black-Indian relations. Willis could not secure regular university employment until 1965, when he became the first Black faculty member hired at Southern Methodist University, where he resigned in 1972 in protest of the treatment he received from his department. As detailed in Chapter 6, his experiences of racial integration in a Southern university in the midst of the Black Power and Black Studies movements led him to a highly critical evaluation of anthropology as the study of peoples of color for the benefit of white-dominated societies. Post-war scholars of color occupied, in varying degrees and circumstances, marginal spaces within an ambivalently integrating academy; it was they, along with an increasingly militant cohort of students, who would bring critiques of racism to the academy itself and help force a reevaluation of anthropology as a discipline.[9]

Anthropology, Civil Rights, and the Cultural Study of Race and Racism

What role did anthropology play in the civil rights movement? Lee Baker has shown that the National Association for the Advancement of Colored People used Boasian arguments against biological determinism in its desegregation cases, including *Brown v. Board of Education* (Baker 1998, 188–207). In the decade following *Brown*, the AAA helped oppose "a well-financed campaign to reignite scientific arguments that racial inferiority and, hence, racial segregation, had a basis in science," affirming and publicizing a scientific consensus that segregation had no scientific justification (Baker 2016, 377). As an index of the significance of the Boasian legacy of anti-racism in the public sphere, Baker shows how white nationalist supremacists cast it (to this day) as a Jewish conspiracy to destroy the white race (2010, 156–219; 2016). Beyond the continued assault on scientific racism, however, there was "no institutionalized effort by the AAA to end racial discrimination against the people who were the primary subject of anthropology" (Hutchinson 2012, 37). This likely reflected an effort to maintain a distinction between science and politics that has been a hallmark of dominant visions of the social and biological sciences (Reardon 2005), a division that was overtly challenged in the latter half of the 1960s (see Chapter 6). Public pronouncements against scientific racism were reactive correctives to the use of biological science to support racism. Active participation in the civil rights movement or other forms of political struggle was left up to individuals.

As far as I know, a full accounting of anthropologists' involvement—or lack thereof—in the civil rights movement has yet to be undertaken. Some white anthropologists were involved in various capacities. For example, Robert Redfield served as an expert witness in desegregation cases (Baker 1998, 202); he was also director of the American Council on Race Relations from 1947 to 1950. Philleo Nash helped found that organization and worked on the Commission on Civil Rights in the Truman administration, helping draft legislation integrating the armed forces; Senator Joseph McCarthy attacked him as a communist (Price 2004, 263–277). Black anthropologists such as Hugh Smythe and St. Clair Drake were actively involved in various ways. Drake, for example, led an organization attempting to prevent the University of Chicago from displacing Black residents in the late 1950s and worked with the Student Non- Violent Coordinating Committee (SNCC) in the 1960s. He was present at the 1966 march in Mississippi when Stokely Carmichael and Willie Ricks voiced the "Black Power" slogan (Drake 1978, 98–100). The main contribution anthropologists made toward promoting racial equality likely came through teaching. Reflecting on the post-war period, Drake suggested that Boasian principles directed those interventions:

> I think that most anthropologists ... were convinced that college students could be made "more tolerant" through substitution of fact for error, through criticism of stereotypes, through comparative studies that led to an appreciation of differences, and through equal-status contacts involving shared experiences. The pedagogical procedures were referred to as education for better "intergroup relations" through "intercultural education." However, few anthropologists studied what we now call "institutional racism" or asked searching questions about the extent of racial and ethnic participation within the profession itself. This was a weakness not rectified until the late sixties. (1978, 88)

How then, did anthropologists engage the social life of race and racism in research and theory?

In the 1990s, anthropologists advocating greater attention to the critical analysis of race and racism in the discipline argued that the cultural anthropologists who succeeded the Boasians abandoned it. Micaela di Leonardo lauded the anti-racist work of Benedict to then assert: "The real narrative on race in American anthropology, though, shifted in the postwar years to the realm of international abstractions and to the subdiscipline of physical anthropology" (1998, 201). Eugenia Shanklin (1998) argued that the success of the Boasian critique of biological determinism led to anthropology becoming a "profession of the color blind" that failed to explore race as a "folk ideology." The lesson anthropologists derived from the Boasians was that if racial differences were biologically insignificant "then racism was an irrelevant response to skin-color differences, one doomed by its own (scientific) inexactitude to fade away. This proposition helped to ensure that American anthropology won the battle and lost the war" (670). Kamala Visweswaran (1998) argued further that the Boasian distinction between race (as biology) and culture precluded an anthropological inquiry into race as a cultural phenomena made salient by racism. Other scholars contended that in the wake of the critique of scientific racism, "many sociocultural anthropologists assumed that race was not useful for understanding social distinctions" and therefore remained silent on structural racism (Harrison 2008a).

These arguments require significant qualification. On the one hand, they rely on the noteworthy omission of anthropologists who, in the late 1960s and early 1970s, argued that anthropology was itself complicit with racism and colonialism. As I show in Chapter 6, some of these scholars not only promoted structural analytics of racism; they developed some of the very critical tools and historical perspectives employed in later critiques of the discipline. On the other hand, in the 1950s and early to mid-1960s not all anthropologists simply ceded race to biological science or ignored the social import of race and racism in their scholarship.

Some cultural anthropologists explicitly refused to allow biological science the authority to assess race. For example, Manning Nash, in an article titled "Race and the Ideology of Race," said: "no amount of sober scientific refutation ever stills the controversy on the meanings of race differences. The interpretation of physical and biological differences between populations is a social phenomenon, and the understanding of how that interpretation is reached and codified is a problem in social and cultural dynamics" (1962, 285). Stanley Diamond asserted in stronger terms, "I do not believe that the specialized biological scientists are, by virtue of their training, necessarily in a position to evaluate or understand cultural behavior, and the problem of making judgments about 'racial' capacity is, technically defined, precisely a problem of recognizing and interpreting cultural behavior" (1964, 108; see also Diamond 1962; 1963).[10] To my knowledge neither Diamond nor Nash developed a systematic program to study the social and cultural dynamics of race and racism; their arguments were squarely in the tradition of refuting biological determinism from a cultural point of view. My point in citing them is simply to illustrate that the race-culture distinction and refutation of biological determinism did not *logically*, *necessarily*, or *invariably* relegate race to the biological sciences or impede a social-cultural approach to race and racism. In the early 1960s, Marvin Harris could note that it is by now widely agreed, that even if a sound evolutionary taxonomy of racial types is eventually produced, the folk or vernacular categories must continue to be accepted as the principal framework for race-relations studies in the behavioral sciences. For these disciplines there are as many hereditary groups as people say there are, regardless of the objective genetic facts. (1962, 28)

Regardless of what the biological sciences said about race, it was a viable topic for social and cultural analysis. The question is not whether cultural anthropologists ignored race but what they did with it.

Anthropological engagements with the social life of race and racism in the post-war era were more extensive and varied than has generally been recognized. Schooling and socialization was one arena of investigation.[11] Mary Ellen Goodman studied the formation of racial attitudes among young U.S. children (1946; 1952). The Boasian-trained Ruth Landes and Jules Henry did critical ethnographic studies of U.S. schools in the 1960s that included analysis of the negative effects of the imposition of white middle-class norms on students of color (Handler 2006).[12] Eleanor Leacock later elaborated a powerful intersectional analysis of race and class that identified schooling practices as not simply reproducing inequality but denying "being" to lower-class Black children (1969).

With the rapid expansion of U.S. anthropologists across various parts of the globe, comparative analysis involving the race concept emerged. For example, comparisons between caste and race took on new dimensions as anthropologists reflected on the relationship between caste and race based on fieldwork in India, Japan, and elsewhere. French anthropologist Louis Dumont produced the most famous work on caste of the day, but UC Berkeley anthropologists Gerald Berreman and George De Vos also published on caste and race. Berreman compared systems of power, hierarchy, and inequality in the U.S. South and India, arguing that lower-caste Indians, like African Americans, resented and resisted their caste oppression (1960; 1967). De Vos compared the condition of the pariah caste Burakumin in Japan with U.S. African Americans (De Vos and Wagatsuma 1966), a comparison that Hugh Smythe had made earlier (Anderson, forthcoming). De Vos initiated a symposium on comparative approaches to caste and race that included U.S. anthropologists Berreman and Sidney Mintz (de Reuck and Knight 1967).

Anthropologists also generated accounts of the social life of race in Latin America and the Caribbean, often in implicit comparison with the U.S. The most theoretically expansive effort along these lines was the work of Harris and Wagley, but they were not alone. Ralph Beals wrote a synthetic essay on "Indian-Mestizo-White Relations in Spanish America" (1955) that revealed considerable interest among anthropologists in questions of discrimination. Beals vacillated on the existence of "real racial discrimination"—by which he appears to have meant discrimination based on biological distinctions alone—ultimately concluding that discrimination was based on cultural and class distinctions. He thereby downplayed evidence of discrimination involving perceptions of racial descent as well as evidence of the reproduction of white exclusivity and domination. Such an analysis ultimately minimized the social force of racism and whiteness, but it was not the product of a color-blind stance that ignored race. It is worth noting here that some anthropologists did call attention to racial discrimination in Latin America. For example, Morris Seigel (1953) produced an ethnographic report documenting everyday, informal forms of anti-Black prejudice and discrimination in Puerto Rico, arguing that while Puerto Rico did not have the forms of virulent racism characteristic of the United States and South Africa, race consciousness and discrimination could not be explained away—as many Puerto Ricans did—as class discrimination. In the late 1960s, Norman Whitten (1969) revisited his previous research in northwest coastal Ecuador to highlight increased mestizo racism and Black disenfranchisement resulting from political economic transformations in the region. Angela Gilliam (1992) provided a forceful critique of the denial of Brazilian racism. The turn toward a more critical appraisal of the social dynamics of race in Latin America by U.S. intellectuals was very much tied up with the retheorizing of racism prompted by the Black Power movement.

Rather than further belabor the point that cultural anthropologists did not completely abandon the study of the social life of race and racism in the 1950s and 1960s, I would clarify that these engagements did not amount to a project of a cultural anthropology of race and racism promoted in later years (Harrison 1995; Mullings 2005). "Race relations" in the U.S. was a field occupied primarily by sociologists and historians, and the cultural and social analysis of race was by no means a central focus of the discipline. The felt need for cultural studies of racism would be truncated as long as scholars understood the problematic primarily in terms of an invidious ideology of biological superiority and inferiority. Anthropological engagements did, however, amount to more than silence on race and racism. Fully reckoning with anthropological discourse on race and racism in the 1950s and 1960s is beyond the scope of this chapter and, frankly, my own knowledge. At minimum, it would require not only close readings of such works as noted above but also an analysis of the extent to which anthropological discourse framed under such auspices as "ethnic group" relations, "minority-majority" relations, and "acculturation" avoided, engaged, illuminated, and/or occluded the social life of race. My contribution can be found in the following chapter on Wagley and Harris, who aspired to go beyond Boasian critiques of racial determinism to theorize the social life of race and the relationship between social structure and racial discrimination.

A final word of contextualization, however, is in order. Anthropological engagements with race sometimes betrayed a U.S.-centric orientation clearly beholden to Cold War dichotomies and U.S. nationalism. A prominent example is the textbook *Racial and Cultural Minorities* (Simpson and Yinger 1958), first published in 1953. The authors, anthropologist George Eaton Simpson and sociologist J. Milton Yinger, instructed their readers in how to think about global race relations from the standpoint of a first-world power.

> The student of race relations is confronted with a rapidly changing situation, both as to the facts of prejudice and discrimination and as to our knowledge of the meaning of those facts. In the enormous international struggles of our time, with their power and ideological aspects, the role of minority groups inevitably became tremendously important. How maintain national unity? How win or preserve the cooperation of colonial or former colonial peoples? How adjust to the rising literacy, power, and demands of minority groups everywhere? How preserve and extend a democratic ideology in the face of its obvious violations in almost every land? Such questions might, perhaps, have been treated casually a generation ago; they have leaped, now, to the forefront of international attention and cannot be disregarded. The result is a ferment in minority-majority relations of greater importance than the modern world has witnessed before. (1958, 7–8)

These questions framed race relations in terms of the problems they posed for Western nation-states: potentially fracturing "national unity" and providing the Soviet Union with ideological fodder in the decolonizing world. The interests of "colonial or former colonial peoples" in liberation, integration, autonomy, and/or equality were ignored, subordinate to the imperatives promoting democratic ideology and securing the global position of the U.S. The authors succinctly captured key elements of the U.S. State Department's post-war orientation. However, failing to annunciate a critical or even distanced perspective from it, they reproduced it. Accordingly, their discussion of African American relationships to socialism, communism, and Black Nationalist movements was titled "Deviant Political Action and the Negro" (1958, 472–478) and invited readers to imagine Black radicalism and domestic race relations in terms of their threat to American liberal democracy. *Racial and Cultural Minorities* was, according to Marvin Harris, "widely accepted as the most intensive introduction" to the field of race relations (1962, 28), appearing in multiple editions after its initial appearance in 1953.

The most compelling anthropologists writing in the field of race and racism—including Harris—did not succumb so readily to Cold War logics but, as I show in the chapter that follows, it behooves us to explore the more subtle ways Americanist attachments and liberal outlooks also informed their work. If the Boasian intervention on race and racism was part of a liberal Americanist project, U.S. anthropological thought in the post-war era on race continued to bear an Americanist imprint. Overall, until the late 1960s U.S. cultural anthropologists remained unable or unwilling to fully address white supremacy and the role of racial differentiation along the color line in the constitution of power within and beyond U.S. society. It was *only* with the crisis of anthropology catalyzed by the political events of the mid to late 1960s that U.S. anthropologists began to pose direct and sustained challenges to the racial worldview of a discipline all too comfortable in its liberal progressivism and its largely taken-for-granted Americanism. This part of the story is taken up in Chapter 6. First, we shall explore in detail how two Columbia-based anthropologists sought to expand the study of the social life of race.

5 Charles Wagley, Marvin Harris, and the Comparative Study of Race

IN THE AFTERMATH OF WORLD WAR II, race was a major preoccupation of the United Nations Educational, Scientific and Cultural Organization (UNESCO). Boasian networks figured prominently in UNESCO's race work. As is well known, in 1950 UNESCO issued a "Statement on Race" (UNESCO 1969), drafted by Ashley Montagu, that drew on the Boasian critique of racial determinism and suggested that the term race itself should be abandoned in public discourse: "For all practical social purposes 'race' is not so much a biological phenomenon as a social myth" (UNESCO 1969, 33).[1] At the same moment, UNESCO's Division for the Study of Racial Problems developed a research agenda for the study of race contacts in Latin America, focusing on Brazil (Maio 2001). The head of the division was Swiss-U.S. anthropologist Alfred Métraux and his main assistant was Ruy Coelho, a Brazilian anthropologist who received his PhD under Melville Herskovits. The goal of the Brazil project was to determine the factors "favorable or unfavorable to the existence of harmonious relations between race and ethnic groups" (quoted in Maio 2001, 119). The emphasis on racial harmony reflected UNESCO's U.S.-led approach to anti-racism through promoting cultural understanding and economic modernization (Hazard 2012, 169).[2]

In the early 1950s, Brazil was widely viewed as a society with high levels of miscegenation and minimal racial conflict. As we saw in Chapter 2, Boas invoked Latin America to exemplify the social variability of racial consciousness, highlighting miscegenation as blurring categorical ascriptions based on race. The favorable image of race relations in Brazil was reinforced by the respected scholarship of Gilberto Freyre (1946), Frank Tannenbaum (1946), and Donald

Pierson (1942). There were dissenting voices. W. E. B. Du Bois, like many other African Americans, had once painted a favorable contrast between Latin American and U.S. race relations, but by the 1940s he sounded a cautionary note.

> In South America we have long pretended to see a possible solution in the gradual amalgamation of whites, Indians, and blacks. But this amalgamation does not envisage any decrease of power and prestige among whites as compared with Indians, Negroes, and mixed bloods; but rather an inclusion within the so-called white group of a considerable infiltration of dark blood, while at the same time maintaining the social bar, economic exploitation and political disenfranchisement of dark blood as such. (Du Bois 1992, 118–119)

Latin American societies, he suggested, had their own versions of the color line that maintained white supremacy, not in the form of a racially "pure" white population but in the superior status of whiteness and "disenfranchisement" of blackness. This was not the perspective that motivated UNESCO's interest in Latin American race relations. Métraux explained:

> Latin America, among others, is a continent in which, until a few years ago at least, racial feeling was not strongly developed and antagonism between people of different colour was far from exhibiting that brutal character exemplified by several English-speaking countries. What better argument can be opposed to race prejudice than a demonstration that harmonious race relations are possible? . . . The aim is to explain all the various factors that in South America have created a spirit of tolerance contrasting sharply with the morbid intransigence obtaining in other social and cultural surroundings. (1950, 388)

Métraux admitted the possibility that the study of race in Brazil would uncover subtle forms of racial prejudice and discrimination. Ultimately, tensions between efforts to identify prejudice, theorize discrimination, and affirm "harmonious race relations" would become manifest in the studies undertaken in Brazil, including those conducted by U.S. anthropologists.[3]

This chapter focuses on two of those anthropologists, Charles Wagley and Marvin Harris, and their comparative analysis of racial classification and discrimination in the Americas. Beginning with their participation in the UNESCO Brazil project, they developed the most extensive body of work on the social life of race produced by prominent white U.S. cultural anthropologists in the 1950s and 1960s. I provide an account of this work, focusing on its novel contributions, liberal paradoxes, and frustrated potential.

Wagley and Harris were among the early post-Boasian anthropologists trained at Columbia who strove to develop a materialist orientation for the discipline. In 1950, Wagley was a tenured professor at Columbia University. He had received his BA (1936) and PhD (1941) from the same institution, studying under Franz Boas, Ruth Benedict, Ruth Bunzel, and Ralph Linton. His dissertation research was on the economics of a Mayan village in Guatemala, and in the early 1940s he began the first of several studies of Indian communities in the Amazon. During World War II he worked on health and sanitation projects in Brazil (Kottack 2000). He returned to Columbia as a faculty member in 1946. At the time the UNESCO study of race in Brazil was being formulated, Wagley was directing a research project in the northeast state of Bahia with the Brazilian anthropologist Thales de Azevedo, funded by Columbia University and the state of Bahia. This research was originally modeled on a post-war study of Puerto Rico by a team of anthropologists from Columbia directed by Julian Steward (Steward et al. 1956). Wagley proposed the incorporation of the Bahia project into the UNESCO initiative. He, along with Thales de Azevedo and Luiz de Aguiar Costa Pinto, directed the part of the UNESCO project focused on northeast and central Brazil.[4] Wagley oversaw community studies conducted by three anthropology graduate students from Columbia University—Marvin Harris, Harry Hutchinson, and Ben Zimmerman—and collected them in *Race and Class in Rural Brazil* (Wagley 1952). Wagley's interest in race in Latin America endured after this project, as reflected in a book on comparative minority relations in the Americas co-written with Harris for UNESCO (Wagley and Harris 1958) and an influential essay on "social race" in the Americas (Wagley 1965).

Marvin Harris likewise developed an enduring engagement with the social life of race. He was born in Brooklyn and raised in a working-class family of Jewish Russian provenance. He received his PhD from Columbia University in 1953 (and his BA in 1948), where he was hired, received tenure, and remained until relocating to the University of Florida in 1980. Today, Harris is best known for his particular brand of cultural evolutionism known as cultural materialism, a theoretical approach that emphasizes the ecological, economic, and demographic determinants of social relations and cultural practices. Harris opposed this approach to what he considered the atheoretical "eclecticism" (1968, 284–285) of Boasian perspectives on culture and rejection of evolutionary theory. His massive history of anthropology tried to recuperate a materialist, evolutionary agenda for the discipline, drawing on Marxist theory while rejecting political Marxism (Harris 1968). His later popular works exemplified his core thesis by identifying the origins of dietary customs in material conditions. But in the formative years of his career in the 1950s and early 1960s Harris was known as a scholar who worked on race relations, and he published extensively on the topic. In a 1962 letter requesting a summer grant from Columbia to work on a book theorizing race and ethnic relations, he characterized his research trips to Brazil (in 1950–1951), Mozambique (1956–1957), and Ecuador (1960) as the empirical basis for such a project.[5] Although he never published that book, Harris did elaborate a cultural materialist account of social race in *Patterns of Race in the Americas* (1964a).

This chapter is divided into three sections. I begin with a discussion of the different accounts Harris and Wagley provided of race, class, and discrimination in *Race and Class in Rural Brazil* (1952). Both anthropologists struggled to reconcile the existence of racial prejudice in Brazil with the absence of racial conflict, extensive racial miscegenation, and the absence of racially defined ("caste-like") social groups. The problem boiled down to the question: did racial discrimination exist in Brazil? Harris, in his ethnographic analysis of race-class relations in a Brazilian town, suggested it did, insofar as whiteness and blackness operated as social values that helped define social status and class position. Wagley, by contrast, affirmed Brazil as a "racial democracy" (Wagley 1952, 7) characterized by a system of social differentiation/discrimination based on class rather than race. This position minimized white hegemony in Brazil and reflected a liberal faith that, in the absence of corporate races, economic development would advance racial equality.

The second section of this chapter focuses on the book *Minorities in the New World* co-authored by Wagley and Harris (1958), also written for UNESCO. This work compared six loosely defined "minorities" conceptualized along racial lines—Indians of Brazil, Indians of Mexico, U.S. Blacks, Blacks in Martinique, French Canadians, and U.S. Jews—in order to generate an anthropological approach to minority-majority relations. The book was deeply flawed and Harris would soon disavow it as he articulated his materialist perspective. My critical lens focuses primarily on its comparative framework that relied on notions of "competition" and "cultural adaptability" to explain the positions of various white, Black, and Indian peoples in the Americas. Although Wagley and Harris were clearly aware of the role of racism in structuring opportunities for minorities, they downplayed the implications of the color line—the crucial distinction between white and non-white—in their evaluation of Blacks, Indians, and minorities who could claim a white/European racial identity. They reproduced problematic immigrant analogies common to Boasian anthropology and suggested that the subordinate position of Blacks and Indians derived in good measure from their cultures.

The final section of this chapter provides a reading of Harris's "cultural materialist" historical explanation of racial classification systems in *Patterns of Race in the Americas* (1964a). According to Harris, the creation of "caste-like" corporate racial groups in the United States and highland Latin America and the absence of such groups in lowland "plantation" Latin America emerged out of distinct demographic, ecological, and labor histories and in accordance with the differing imperatives of white elite domination. This approach suggested the possibility of a comparative structural analysis of racial discrimination and white power (and the power of whiteness) across the Americas. This possibility, however, remained latent as Harris contended that the absence of caste-like corporate groups prevented "systematic racial discrimination" in Brazil. Ironically, he abandoned key insights of his own earlier ethnography, in which he suggested racial valuation played a key role in social stratification and discrimination in a Brazilian town. Harris thereby foreclosed analysis of the power of social race in the Brazilian social structure and of whiteness as a social value and enduring *material* problem throughout the Americas. Indeed, he ultimately resorted to another version of the immigrant analogy, identifying European immigrants to Latin America in the nineteenth and twentieth centuries as a vital ingredient in modernization in contrast with a culturally backward, largely non-white, peasantry. The potential of his comparative analysis to illuminate the structural dynamics of racism was compromised by a reduction of systemic racism to caste-like segregation and by a conflation between whiteness and modernization.

Overall, I argue that a certain U.S.-centric perspective on race and racism informed the comparative projects of Wagley and Harris. That race in Brazil appeared less problematic than in the U.S. derived from the implicit understanding that rigid caste-like divisions associated with segregation, strictures against interracial marriage, and pervasive racial discrimination represented a maximal form of racial oppression. Insofar as that maximal form of racial oppression appeared absent in Brazil, the country could be seen as having a minimal race "problem." Brazil offered a hopeful image of a society formed out of conquest and slavery that had largely transcended racial divisions. The alternative lesson of the studies undertaken in Brazil—that varying social systems

of racial classification and class configuration might entail different but pernicious forms of racism—was not readily apparent to U.S. scholars operating
with a caste model of race relations.

The Complexities of Race and Class in Minas Velhas

Harris' first published essay was an account of race and class in Minas Velhas,
the county seat of what was once an important mining region reliant upon
slave labor. Like the other graduate students working for the UNESCO project, Harris incorporated an investigation of race relations into a larger project
on modernization in the community. He initially classified the population of
Minas Velhas (1,500 people) into four categories based on "anthropological
descriptions of racial phenotypes": white (Caucasoid), Negro, mulatto (mixture of white and Negro), and *caboclo* (mixture of white and Indian). Sam-
pling one hundred households, he identified the distribution of these types as:
white 42.5 percent, Negro 28.2 percent, mulatto 26 percent, *caboclo* 3.3 percent
(1952, 50). Harris held that there were no significant cultural differences between these types, which did not constitute social groups. He was well aware
that his observed "anthropological" classification of racial types differed from
local classification practices. Indeed, it was merely the starting point for a consideration of social ascriptions in which phenotypical differences did not, by
themselves, determine social identities. "The socially derived 'racial' classification, which alone has dynamic import, is related to physical characteristics in a
flexible and subjective fashion" (49).

If racial classification was socially derived, flexible, and subjective, racial
identity and physical appearance had social import. Explicitly contesting assumptions that Brazilian society lacked racial prejudice, Harris devoted several
pages to local discourses of white superiority and Black inferiority. From school
textbooks to regional folklore, the Negro as "abstract type" was a subject of
derision and slander, deemed stupid, lazy, and ugly, fit only for menial labor.
"No amount of wishful thinking about the lack of 'race prejudice' in Brazil can
alter these facts about Minas Velhas: 1) Racial stereotypes are well-developed.
2) The stereotypes are graded and arranged in ascending-descending order.
3) The Negro occupies the lowest level. 4) The white occupies the highest level"
(56). This was confirmed by a survey Harris conducted asking respondents to
evaluate portraits of whites, mulattoes, and Negroes along a "racial value gradient" of six characteristics: intelligence, beauty, wealth, religiosity, honesty, and

"best worker" (57–62). The abstract Negro represented not just a physical type but a category of social abjection.

In lived social practice, however, stereotypical racial abstractions did not translate directly into discrete social categories and identities. On the one hand, many individuals avoided self-identification as Negro. "Since the society recognizes a continuum of racial forms from most white to most Negro with a large array of intermediate types, the tendency is to flee from the crushing stigmata of the lowest type by taking advantage of either slight physical deviation or by emphasizing social rank achieved on the basis of non-racial criteria" (1952, 60). On the other hand, in practice whites sometimes contradicted sentiments of racial superiority. Many whites engaged in everyday acts of sociality that did not inferiorize Negroes, and lower-class whites often practiced social deference to Negroes with higher status accrued from wealth or education. As we will see, the distinction between prejudice and practice played a key role in arguments put forth by Wagley, and later Harris himself, that class, as opposed to race, was the source of discrimination in Brazil. It is thus worth emphasizing that in this early essay, Harris identified a direct relationship between racial prejudice and discriminatory practice: "Is there any connexion between how the white tries to think about the Negro and how the white actually behaves towards him? Are the slanderous stereotypes a factor in race relations? The answer is an emphatic 'yes'" (63).

Unpacking his interpretation requires exegesis. Harris insisted that in order to understand race in Minas Velhas "we must rid ourselves of the notion that the terms 'Negro' and 'white' denote clear-cut, readily identifiable physical groups for anybody but the anthropologist" (63). The "ideal stereotype" entailed the notion of groups with defined characteristics, but in everyday life individuals were identified as members of social classes rather than racial groups.

> In every real situation the fact that an individual manifests a particular set of physical characteristics does not by itself determine his status. There is no status-role for the Negro as a Negro, nor for the white as a white, except in the ideal culture. In Minas Velhas the one and only inclusive system by which actual rank is established is that of class. (63)

Physical appearance served as one criterion for assessing status, alongside and in relation to criteria of wealth, education, and occupation. Moreover, how an individual was labeled in racial-color terms depended not only on that individual's phenotype but also on the other criteria. The famous Brazilian adage "money whitens" reflected the variability of racial ascription.

> All four gradients considered together have the power of fixing an individual's position in the social hierarchy. In addition, the value of any one of the four may be modified or offset by the values of the other three. Wealth, occupation and education have, in other words, to a certain extent the power of defining race. It is owing to this fact that there are no socially important groups in Minas Velhas which are determined by purely physical characteristics. (63)

If wealth, occupation, and education affected the evaluation of an individual's racial position, did the evaluation of one's racial phenotype bear social significance and affect class position? Harris suggested that it did.

First, the achievement of relatively high-ranking class status by those with a Negro phenotype did not change the stereotypical evaluation of the "Negro" as abstract type. "High rank in other respects can only be achieved in spite of being, never because, one is black" (64). Moreover, the few high-ranking Blacks in Minas Velhas were subordinate in class status and social standing to whites of similar wealth, educational, and professional status.

> Much has been made of the expression which is heard in Minas Velhas, as well as other parts of Brazil, that 'money whitens.' The unstated corollaries: 'Whiteness is worth money' and 'Blackness cheapens' also need to be emphasized . . . the occasional Negro who rises to high social level cannot be used as an argument against the contention that race is one of the most important ranking principles in Brazilian culture. (64–65)

Harris thus identified *whiteness* and *blackness* as criteria of social evaluation and ranking, *even in the absence of "white" and "Black" as groups defined exclusively by racial criteria.* Whiteness operated as a form of social value and capital and blackness as a social deficit; racial meanings were thus important to and imbricated with social status and rank (class).

Harris elaborated on this relationship in a fascinating discussion of class in Minas Velhas. He began with a simple tripartite classification based on wealth and occupation, identifying an upper group of the wealthy (A) and a lower group characterized by extreme poverty (C). The majority of residents fell in a middle group (B). Harris showed that race played a role in social differentiation not only across but within these distinctions, as exemplified by the most prestigious social club in town. Although in principle any man could join the club (provided he had a suit and tie), in practice participation involved status distinctions where race played a key role. At club dances, dancers were almost exclusively white and mulatto, with the exception of the son of a wealthy Negro, who only danced with his white sisters-in-law.[6] Those excluded from the dances gathered outside, referring to the privileged insiders as "the rich" or "the whites," who in turn referred to the excluded as "the poor" or "the Negroes." Some of the onlookers were mulattoes and whites of low economic standing. The social club thus instantiated a dichotomous (class-race) structure divided between the "white-rich" and "Negro-poor." The actual composition of those strata was not racially exclusive, but whiteness and blackness played a key role in defining the strata. The white-rich strata consisted of: white and wealthy; white and of average wealth; white and poor; mulatto and wealthy; mulatto and of average wealth; Negro and wealthy. The Negro-poor strata consisted of: white and poverty-stricken; mulatto and poverty-stricken; mulatto and poor; Negro and poverty-stricken; Negro and poor; Negro and of average wealth. Given a strong correlation between wealth and race, Harris estimated that 90 percent of the Negroes, 50 percent of mulattoes, and 10 percent of whites could not dance at the club (72–73).

Harris further demonstrated that the very composition of the middle-status group (B) was stratified by racial criteria, once the broad cleavage between white-rich versus Negro-poor was taken into consideration. Harris modified his original tripartite class structure in Minas Velhas to consist of four classes (A, B1, B2, C), with racial evaluation playing a key role in the distinction within the middle strata. Individuals with middle-level educational, professional, or wealth values fell on the side of "Negro-poor" because of devalued racial blackness and were identified by Harris as members of the B2 group. Conversely, relatively poor (though not impoverished) whites occupied the B1 group and could qualify as "white-rich" in comparative status evaluations. Harris suggested the importance of race in the composition of class status, indeed of local class *categories*, noting that "its effect is sufficient to split the middle class in half and to create four classes where only three would otherwise exist" (73).

To be clear, Harris emphasized the primary importance of the "economic gradient" over the "racial gradient" in determining class status in Minas Velhas. In a summary moment, he asserted that "Race is secondary to economics as a diagnostic of rank" (79) and that class was the lived category of social group formation. However, he also documented efforts by those identified on the "Negro-poor" side of the social cleavage to contest social exclusions from the "white-rich" by creating parallel institutions and demanding better educational opportunities. Overall, his account showed how whiteness and blackness were social values that permeated evaluations of class status and affected social relations. Indeed, Harris argued against class reductivism.

> The Negroes in 'B2' seek not to destroy or level the class above them; they seek to enter it. They are prevented from doing this not because of an economic but because of a racial factor. What is at stake here is the relative importance of the racial ranking gradient. The whites tend to exaggerate it and the Negroes tend to minimize it. Hence there is no justification for dismissing racial discrimination as a chimerical side-effect of the class structure. (77)

He also left little doubt that racial discrimination existed in practice: "The socially-defined 'Negro-poor' is actually treated as an inferior, though for the most part the treatment might be dismissed (wrongly enough) as the mere expression of class differences" (80).

In sum, in this early essay Harris produced an ethnographic account of "race relations" in a Brazilian town where race alone did not define social groups but nonetheless mattered in the constitution of social differentiation and hierarchy.[7] He showed that race was itself an evaluative criterion of social status and classification such that the very composition of class status, divisions, and categories involved racial meanings, ascriptions, and evaluations. He thus identified racial distinctions as bound up with class differentiation and discrimination, without reducing the former to the latter. Ironically, he would later ignore the nuances of his own insights. So would Charles Wagley in his confirmation of Brazil as a "racial democracy."

Racial Democracy as Liberal Fantasy

As the senior anthropologist in charge of the Bahian project, Wagley wrote the introduction and conclusion to *Race and Class in Rural Brazil*. He began by affirming what the UNESCO sponsors presumed: "Brazil is renowned in the world for its racial democracy . . . race prejudice and discrimination are subdued as compared to the situation in many countries. In Brazil three racial stocks . . . have mingled and mixed to form a society in which racial tensions and conflicts are especially mild" (1952, 7).[8] Yet Wagley also presented evidence that Brazil was a racially stratified society (Warren 2000). He indicated pervasive anti-Black stereotyping and "well-known barriers to the social ascension of 'people of colour'" (Wagley 1952, 8). The upper class was almost entirely "Caucasian in appearance," and the middle class was predominately white (145–148). Among even the poorer classes, "racial type" was "a criterion for relative social rank within their class" (149). The Brazilian Congress had recently passed a law prohibiting racial discrimination because of its increase in São Paulo and Rio de Janeiro. How, then, could Wagley consider Brazil a racial democracy?

First, it is crucial to recognize that his conception of racial democracy rested on cross-national comparison. Forms of racial discrimination present in the United States, South Africa, and elsewhere appeared relatively absent in Brazil. Physical segregation, racial exclusion from voting, anti-miscegenation laws, and race-based violence did not exist there. Social organizations were not defined by race and no one was automatically disqualified from a position on the basis of race. In short, Brazil did not have Jim Crow or apartheid. The concept of racial democracy as deployed by Wagley was thus a negative concept, referring to a series of absences rather than the presence of racial equality.

Second, Wagley developed his argument through a selective account of which communities studied by the team of graduate fieldworkers should be considered representative of rural Brazil. The forms of discrimination and conflict found in Minas Velhas by Harris were, Wagley asserted, atypical. For him, the most representative of the rural Brazilian communities was Monte Serrat (studied by Zimmerman), which represented "a case of but mild racial prejudice and of relatively fluid social classes and *as such* is characteristic of numerous rural communities throughout north Brazil" (152, emphasis added). The selective bias here is evident. Rather than adjust an interpretation of race relations in rural Brazil according to the ethnographic data and variation across communities, Wagley identified the community characterized as having "mild prejudice" and "relatively fluid social classes" as representative of rural Brazil.

Third, Wagley minimized racial discrimination in Brazilian society by asserting a rigid distinction between prejudice and practice. "The expression of prejudice against the Negroes, the mesticos and people of Indian physical type is mainly manifested verbally and not in behavior. Other factors (wealth, occupation, education, etc.) are of greater importance in determining the actual patterns of inter-personal relations than race" (154). Wagley ignored the subtleties of Harris' effort to understand race in Minas Velhas, and his contention that racial stereotypes played a role in inter-personal relations. For Wagley, the argument that race was *one* of several criteria for determining class status meant that it was relatively unimportant as a social factor in Brazilian society.

Harris also emphasized economic criteria in defining class status, but his ethnographic account showed how evaluations of phenotypical whiteness and blackness affected the social status of individuals and membership in local class categories. Although race alone did not define social classification, understanding the composition and definition of social groupings divided along lines of "Negro-poor" and "white-rich" demanded attention to race as an eminently significant component of social life. Wagley, by contrast, worked to minimize the importance of race altogether, acknowledging extensive prejudice favoring whiteness over blackness and then dismissing it as largely irrelevant to social practice.

Wagley ultimately confirmed Donald Pierson's influential thesis that in Brazil racial distinctions did not inhibit social advancement because, there, race relations were not caste relations. Pierson inherited the caste concept from the University of Chicago, where he did his graduate training in sociology in the 1930s. As we saw earlier, the concept of caste was used to denote a stratified and hierarchical social division of races into endogamous groups with prescribed roles. For Pierson, the organization of Brazilian society was best characterized in contrasting terms as "a competitive order in which the individual finds his place on the basis of personal competence and individual achievement more than upon the basis of racial descent" (1942, 348). In other words Brazil was, with regards to race, a liberal society. Wagley largely embraced this view. To be sure, he suggested revisions to Pierson's thesis to acknowledge research findings that tempered an overly benign assessment of Brazilian racial democracy: pervasive anti-Black and anti-Indian prejudices; strong preferences for Caucasian physical features; and acute consciousness of "physical race" as expressed in numerous color-race categories. But here again Wagley asserted that race consciousness and prejudice were "not related to discrimination." Rather, race in Brazil was: "(a) a system by which individuals are described; (b) a way of diagnosing a person's probable social rank; and (c) a mechanism by which 'people of color' can avoid the stigma of being classed as Negroes" (1952, 154). Race, in this view, was merely a crude diagnostic of class position with minimal practical consequences. This position ignored the importance of whiteness and blackness as values in assessments of social rank discussed by Harris. For Harris, racial ascriptions were not merely diagnostics of class status; they were criteria of class status. Such ascriptions themselves involved forms of discrimination against individuals of color, operating as value gradients in assessments of status. Brazilian color terms and categories could only provide a partial means of avoiding the stigma of blackness, as long as race held social value. Harris had made this point clear, reminding readers that the adage "money whitens" entailed the social valuation of whiteness and devaluation of blackness. Wagley's effort to reconcile the idea of Brazilian racial harmony with persisting racial prejudice ultimately entailed a contradictory dismissal of racial discrimination.

He ended with an optimistic outlook for the Brazilian future. Racial democracy—the absence of a rigid color line and racial conflict relative to other nations or colonies—created a sound basis for progress.

> In most colonial areas, the intense and emotionally charged feelings of the native population (generally of Mongoloid or Negroid racial stock) toward the dominant European 'caste,' and the clash of economic interests between the racial castes, create numerous barriers to the improvement of social and economic conditions. (154)

In Brazil, by contrast, the absence of caste-like conditions implied the absence of such resentments and conflicts. With economic development, the educational and economic conditions of the lower strata should improve and "the people of darker skin colour now occupying the lower ranks should take their place in the middle ranks of society. There are no serious racial barriers to social and economic advance" (154). Wagley did identify potential threats to the realization of such progress. There were indications that tensions, prejudice, and discrimination were on the rise, particularly as Brazilians of color improved their standing and challenged the "dominant position of the white upper class" (155). The danger that race conflict and discrimination could assert themselves was real, especially if Western concepts of racism accompanied industrial modernization. The challenge for Brazil was to embrace Western industrialism, avoid Western racism, and maintain "its rich heritage of racial democracy" (155).

In these final passages, racism appeared as a foreign influence, even though Wagley described Brazil as a country having an almost entirely white upper class, with extensive (though "mild") racial prejudices that became activated when non-whites began to improve their economic and social status. These passages also betrayed the sentiment that non-white resentment against white domination was a "barrier" to progress. Wagley's optimism relied on the hope that economic transformation would loosen a rigid class structure that had the advantage of not being defined by caste-like corporate racial groups. In the absence of "conflict"—indeed, because of its absence—economic development might create greater racial equality, without whites having to do anything more than resist the siren call of (foreign-derived) racism. Brazil thus stood as a testament to a liberal hope that, despite racial prejudice, individual mobility could be achieved through economic development without social conflict. Here, conflict above all else—certainly above racial inequality and white supremacy—was the key concept in discerning the presence or absence of a "racial problem." Brazil held out the implicit promise that a peaceful liberal order could succeed the "caste" divisions inherited from colonialism and slavery, without social conflict. That was why Brazil was the focus of UNESCO attention in the first place.

Other scholars working on the UNESCO project in Brazil challenged that analysis and the comparisons that underwrote it. The starkest contrast emerged in the research coordinated by French sociologist Roger Bastide and Brazilian sociologist Florestan Fernandes on race relations in São Paulo.[9] Bastide (1957) provided a summary of this work in a comparative account of the various UNESCO projects on race relations in Brazil. The São Paulo studies combined historical, sociological, and social psychological approaches and established discussion groups with people of color from all social strata, including women and leaders of Black organizations. Rather than assess racial prejudice as "mild" or "harsh" in comparison with other countries, the researchers asked, "since prejudice exists only to the extent that it serves a purpose, how did it survive and what changes did it undergo with each alteration in the social structure of São Paulo?" (505). The conclusion they reached was that Blacks were integrated into the social hierarchy as dependent, subordinate citizens. Social patterns linking economic and racial stratification persisted despite miscegenation while competition from European immigrants relegated Blacks to the "lumpenproletariat," giving new impetus to stereotypes of Black inferiority. Although Negroes had entered the proletariat after World War II, working-class racial prejudice compromised class consciousness and "maintained the status quo against the rise of coloured people" (505).

This picture departed significantly from the racial democracy thesis and contested the comparative frame of the U.S. anthropologists working in Bahia. The differences were not merely the product of the different contexts of research (northeast vs. southeast Brazil, rural vs. urban) but in theoretical and political outlook.

> some were concerned with the racial situation in the United States of America and looked for differences, others with the Gestalt of the Brazilian situation in an attempt to discern the special forms that racial conflicts might take in Brazil.

The fact that what, for some, is a state of 'adjustment' is for others nothing but a crystallization of conflicts which have ended unsatisfactorily in the victory of the white and 'affective disarmament' of Negro resentment by a paternalistic code of behavior, is sufficient proof of how vitally important this difference of approach is in the study of this problem. (509, emphasis added)

From the point of view justifying the project and reinforced by Wagley, the relative absence of racial conflict in Brazil was evidence of a relatively healthy social condition. But from a perspective oriented toward understanding the specifics of Brazilian racial hierarchy and inequality, the absence of conflict represented the codification of white "victory" in the country's social structure and racial culture. From that perspective, purported "racial harmony" reflected a form of white racial hegemony. The U.S. anthropologists—at least as represented by Wagley—had effectively denied, even masked, white supremacy.

An Anthropology of Race as Minority Competition

Wagley and Harris engaged in a different kind of comparative project for UNESCO in their book *Minorities in the New World* (1958). Asked to prepare a report based on studies conducted in various countries, the authors took the opportunity to "make at least a beginning toward applying the comparative approach of social anthropology to minority problems" (xi). Focusing on the Americas, they selected six case studies: Indians in Brazil; Indians in Mexico; Blacks in Martinique; Blacks in the United States; French Canadians; and Jews in the United States. The chapters on these cases were divided into sections with the headings "The American Indian," "The Negro in the Americas," and "The European Immigrants." This structure invited comparisons within and across the three primary "racial stocks" (13) in the Americas, developed by the authors in a long concluding chapter. Wagley and Harris identified races not as discrete biological types but as social classifications or "social races" (xv; see Wagley 1965). Their principal analytical category, however, was minorities— "subordinate segments of complex state societies" differentiated from other kinds of social groups in that they "have special physical or cultural traits which are held in low esteem by the dominant segments" [the majority] and are "self-conscious units" (Wagley and Harris 1958, 10). Minority membership relied on "a rule of descent" which transmits membership "even in the absence of readily apparent special cultural or physical traits"; minorities tended to engage in endogamy, either by "choice or necessity" (10). As I argue below, the primary focus on the category minority invited problematic comparisons and obscured the role of race, particularly whiteness, in the structural positions of the groups under comparison.

The concluding analysis of *Minorities in the New World* relied heavily on the idea of "competition," a no less problematic focus than "conflict." For Wagley and Harris, minority-majority relations were characterized by competition for resources, power, and prestige within state societies. They identified two sets of "historical-cultural" factors that explained the competitive success of minorities: (1) "the adaptive capacity of the minority"—the cultural heritage of a minority group as a basis for success, adaptation, and protection in competition with a predatory majority; and (2) "the arena of competition"—the social and ideological context of competition, resources for which groups competed, the advantages the majority derived from minority subordination, and minority access to economic mobility (264). Although clearly connected, the authors separated these two sets of factors for analytical purposes.

The "adaptive capacity" thesis posited that minorities' relative success in adapting to their condition and achieving mobility depended significantly on their cultural endowments. Brazilian Indians, at one extreme, "began their career especially handicapped by their own cultural heritage," having no basis to adapt to European civilization (265–266). French Canadians and U.S. Jews, at the other extreme, "began their careers on a much better adaptive footing" than Indians and Blacks: "Their essentially European cultural traditions provided them with a basis for understanding their new social environment" (270). The authors' comparison of the "adaptive capacity" of various groups can be summarized as follows:

- Indians of Brazil: culturally maladaptive from colonial contact to the present.
- Indians of Mexico: civilizational history provided adaptive culture at contact with Spanish; the persistence of distinctive Indian cultures in modern, post-revolutionary Mexico was maladaptive to national ideals of progress.
- Blacks in U.S. and Martinique: "the slave culture" of these groups was maladaptive to requirements of modern society in the post-abolition era.
- French Canadians and U.S. Jews: adaptive cultures of European origin facilitated competitive success and social mobility. (265–273)

These comparisons are notable not simply for their evaluation of minority cultures solely in terms of a crudely assessed "adaptability" to Western civilization and Euro-American modernity. They also invited racial comparison. The only groups with "adaptive" cultures were European/white; the Indian and Black groups were all identified as culturally maladaptive. The subordinate position of Blacks and indigenous peoples within New World societies could thus be read as, in good measure, a result of their cultural shortcomings. We see here a clear example of how the concept of cultural difference can do inferiorizing and essentializing work akin to biological determinism (Abu-Lughod 1991). Indeed, Wagley and Harris speculated, "one might be tempted to state the general proposition that minority groups with the greater measure of cultural preparedness have been the ones least subject to extreme forms of hostility and exploitation" (1958, 272). This would suggest that Indian and Black minorities faced the most virulent oppression because of their lack of "cultural preparedness." Such were the flights of thought a certain neo-evolutionary approach to "minority" cultures could imply.

The authors complicated, but did not entirely repudiate, this perspective through their second set of explanatory factors, "the arena of competition." This concept called attention to the historical-cultural conditions beyond the control of minorities, the total sociocultural system that determined "whether the minority will be crushed and exploited, left alone to pursue its own course, or helped in its attempt to advance" (273). Here, Wagley and Harris identified differences in the situation of the European minorities and Blacks and Indians, their historical roles in colonial and national political economies, and the forms of discrimination they faced. Neither French Canadians nor U.S. Jews had lands coveted by majorities or were used for slave labor. French Canadians were European settlers who came under the political dominance of the English. U.S. Jews migrated in search of civil liberties and economic freedom.

> For the Jews or for the French Canadians the issue has never been whether they would be allowed to work as free men rather than as slaves or peons, but rather whether they would be allowed to enter certain occupations, professions, and commercial areas. Neither has the issue been, for these two minority groups, whether they be deprived of their lands and isolated on an Indian reservation or be forced into debt peonage.... Instead, the Jews in the United States have fought for the right to enter universities on an equal basis, and the French Canadians have struggled to maintain their right to their own educational system. (278–279)

These observations suggested that European minorities faced discrimination of a different order than Blacks and Indians. Wagley and Harris nonetheless attributed their comparative success in achieving social mobility to cultural experiences and skills acquired in Europe. They never addressed the possibility that their identity as European served as an advantage or that they occupied a racial status closer to normalized whiteness than Blacks or Indians in white dominant societies. *A crucial commonality across the various nation-states they considered—the superordinate position of whites and high evaluation of whiteness, evident in their own account—eluded their explanatory framework.*

That framework also betrayed the contradictions of using the (classically liberal) idea of "competition" to explain ethnoracial stratification as "minority-majority" relations. The concept of the "arena of competition" represented an effort to introduce power relations as a factor in explaining minority "success" or "failure." But that concept remained analytically removed from the dynamics of racial classification so clearly essential to group formation, structures of power, and thus "competition." How was one to assess the relative importance of the "cultural adaptability" of a group in "competing" with others as opposed to the repressive, exclusionary measures that shaped the "arena of competition"? If, as the authors argued, discrimination in the U.S. served to exclude Blacks from "full and equal participation in the American economy" (276), then it prevented them from "competing" on equal footing for middle-class status. How could the scholar assess the relative importance of an alleged lack of cultural adaptability when the ability to "compete" had been restricted? If, for example, Black culture was maladaptive to success in post-abolition U.S. society, why had whites prohibited Black competition? The effort to analyze New World race relations in terms of competitive majority-minority relations diluted the significance of racism across the Americas.

The resulting contradictions became evident in the authors' efforts to assess the future prospects of minority assimilation and pluralism in the U.S. They defined assimilation in terms of acculturation into majority norms and exogamy into a majority population; "complete assimilation" essentially implied "the absorption of one group by another" (288). Pluralism, by contrast, referred to the persistence of culturally adapted but distinct endogamous groups recognized by the majority. Assimilation and pluralism could be understood both as social processes and as social goals. Although the authors initially claimed to reserve judgment as to which goal was preferable, they later noted that "assimilation should in the long run provide a sounder base for a truly democratic society, for the presence of pluralistic minority groups in a society seems always to harbor the danger of conflict and subordination of one group by another" (294). This preference for assimilation—embraced previously by Boas, Benedict, and much of the mainstream sociology of race relations—sat awkwardly with Harris and Wagley's account of Blacks and Jews in the U.S. system of racial classification.

At various points in the text, Harris and Wagley noted that Blacks and Jews occupied different positions within the sociocultural system of racial classification, exogamy, and endogamy. In essence, within that system Jews were treated as racially white whereas Blacks were categorically and perpetually non-white. For Jews, exogamy and assimilation into the white majority represented a kind of choice unavailable to Blacks (except those that could pass for white). Jews faced pressures to assimilate into the white Christian majority yet also embraced a pluralistic orientation that facilitated endogamy. The maintenance of a distinct Jewish identity was thus largely a matter of Jewish agency. For Blacks, by contrast, pluralism was relentlessly forced upon them by strictures against intermarriage with whites and a "descent rule" that classified a child with any Black heritage as Black. Full assimilation in the sense of absorption into the white majority was a categorical impossibility: "not even miscegenation on a wide scale would lead to assimilation" (291). African Americans were "fated for at best a more satisfactory pluralistic adjustment within the larger society" (291), a condition that, the authors noted, organizations such as the NAACP had come to recognize in struggles for integration.

Yet Wagley and Harris suggested that assimilation was the basis for a truly democratic society. What were the implications, then, for thinking of the U.S. as a democratic society if a significant segment of its population could never assimilate? Was full democracy an unattainable possibility if there were categories of people who could never meld into the dominant majority? Did the sociocultural system of race classification in the U.S. compromise the possibilities of democracy? Was whiteness a principal barrier to democracy? Such questions were never broached by the authors as they struggled to reconcile the different positions of those classified as white and non-white with a comparative framework that treated them as analogous groups under the category minority.

A Materialist Comparison of Racial Classification and Discrimination in the Americas

Harris claimed that he was never satisfied with the theoretical framework of *Minorities in the New World*. In a letter to an admirer of the work, he wrote:

> I was always the reluctant partner in giving emphasis to ideological and value
> orientations as factors possessing long-range significance for the development
> of minority-majority situations . . . any theory that fails to stress the causal
> priority of ecological demographic and economic factors—in short, which fails
> to start with the material substratum of the "arena of conflict"—is doomed to
> failure.[10]

What was required was a thoroughgoing materialist account of race relations
as a sub-type of majority-minority relations. We can see hints of this perspective in a political tract he wrote on Mozambique (Harris 1958), published the
same year as *Minorities in the New World*. Harris conducted fieldwork in Mozambique in 1956–1957 to study cultural transformation and race relations
in Portuguese Africa, testing the theory that "the relative absence of serious
forms of racial antagonism in Brazil was the result of a distinctive Portuguese
cultural tradition or national character" (1958, 1). Gilberto Freyre, a foremost
proponent of such a theory, had extolled the virtues of the "luso-tropical" Portuguese empire in Africa and Asia purportedly characterized by harmonious
relations between white colonists and non-white natives (Harris 1958, 2). In
Mozambique, Harris found such an account "hopelessly unfounded" (2). What
existed—he detailed in a style far more fiery than in his other work—was a
coercive, legalized system of native subordination, racial discrimination, and
oppressive exploitation that "in practice is simply one of the several varieties
of apartheid which are to be found all over Southern Africa" (25). For Harris,
the contrast between the relatively "benevolent" interracial system of Brazil and
the apartheid conditions of Mozambique demonstrated that racism was not a
product of national culture but "a phenomenon which is produced in relation
to fairly well-defined circumstances of a socio-economic nature" (26). Though
never a Marxist in the political sense, Harris articulated a materialist perspective on racism as a product of colonial labor regimes.

This perspective emerged alongside an enduring interest in the social variation of racial classification in the Americas. Harris returned to Brazil in the
early 1960s, studying racial classification and identification in the fishing village
of Arembepe in Bahia. This study (1964b) not only confirmed the absence of a
descent rule in racial identification; it also highlighted considerable variation
and ambiguity in how individuals understood and employed racial categories.
Harris identified this ambiguity as precluding "systematic discrimination and
segregation" (28). Such ambiguity represented the inverse image of caste-like

race relations in the U.S., a comparison key to *Patterns of Race in the Americas* (1964a).[11]

That short but ambitious book sought to explain variation in racial classification systems and race relations in the Americas through a cultural materialist approach focusing on divergent histories of ecological adaptation, demographics, and labor systems. Harris adamantly opposed comparative approaches that identified cultural differences between the colonial powers—inculcating varying degrees of racial prejudice—as the source of differences in race relations. For him, it was differences in racial classification systems, not differences in racial prejudice, that required explanation. Why in some parts of the Americas was classification based on a descent rule and in other parts on physical criteria? Why were social groups defined by race in some areas and not others? Why did sharply defined and mutually exclusive racial identities emerge in some areas while ambiguous identities and a color continuum emerged in others?

Harris began with a distinction within Latin America between a "Highland Heritage" and a (lowland) "Plantation Heritage." In the highlands, pre-conquest societies were characterized by complex state formations and relatively dense and sedentary indigenous populations. Spanish colonization in these regions created mechanisms for exploitation of Indian labor through a bifurcation between Indian and non-Indian social categories that ensured a stable and subordinate workforce. Contests over control of Indians between Crown and elite within the colonies led to the end of Indian slavery and provided some measure of protection for Indians. Nonetheless, a succession of institutions (*encomienda, repartimiento*, debt peonage) ensured the availability of exploited Indian labor. The Catholic Church also played an important role here, striving to eliminate any indigenous religious features incompatible with the creation of a fiesta complex that would ensure Indian subordination and labor. By contrast, in the lowlands pre-colonial indigenous populations were small, dispersed, and mobile as a result of adaptations to tropical ecologies. These regions became the sites of colonial plantation complexes that typically focused on the intensive production of a single commodity (e.g., sugar) and required importation of labor, ultimately filled by large quantities of African slaves.

The highlands and lowlands came to differ not only in the composition of the population (Indian vs. Afrodescendant) but in forms of racial classification.

> The most important feature of Latin American lowland race relations since the abolition of slavery is the absence of sharply defined racial groupings. Unlike

> both the highlands and the United States, most of the former Latin American
> slave plantation areas lack racially derived caste-like divisions. The Negroes in
> the United States and the Indians in highland Latin America may be said to
> constitute separate social groups. Yet in much of the lowlands of Latin America
> one is obliged to conclude . . . that there is no such thing as a Negro group or
> white group. (Harris 1964a, 54)

Not surprisingly, Harris highlighted Brazil as exemplary of post-plantation systems. As his analysis developed, the contrast between Brazil and the United
States overshadowed the comparison between highland and lowland Latin
America. In the U.S., racial classification into the category Negro relied on the
principle of hypo-descent, the term Harris coined to identify the racial classification of individuals of mixed ancestry into the subordinate group "in
order to avoid the ambiguity of intermediate identity" (1964a, 56; see Harris
1964b). The "social lie" of hypo-descent facilitated the perpetuation of distinct,
racially defined social groups. In Brazil, by contrast, where hypo-descent did
not emerge as a form of racial classification, social groups were not defined
(primarily or exclusively) in racial terms. This contrast was crucial for his comparison of race relations and discrimination. According to Harris, the pattern
of racial relations in Brazil—resulting in the absence of corporate groups—did
not imply an absence of racial prejudice. Brazil was not, he insisted, a racial
democracy. But it did entail the absence of what he called "systematic racial
segregation and discrimination" (1964a, 61).

Harris relied on two types of arguments elaborating this crucial and, I argue, contradictory position. First, he asserted a theoretical principle that "systematic discrimination" required the presence of "separate social groups" or
"caste-like divisions."

> without a method for clearly distinguishing between one group and another,
> systematic discrimination cannot be practiced. The *sine qua non* of any thor-
> oughgoing minority system is a foolproof method for separating population
> into respective superordinate and subordinate groups. In order to prevent the
> members of a certain group from freely choosing their jobs, voting, enrolling in
> a school, or joining a club, it is absolutely indispensable that there be a reliable
> way of knowing who is a member of the group to be segregated and who is a
> member of the group that is to do the segregating. (1964a, 54)

In this view, the classificatory ambiguity in racial status found in Brazil made
systematic discrimination—equated here with practices of segregation—

impossible. Yet in his earlier ethnography of Minas Velhas, Harris had offered a more complicated picture. Ironically, he had identified the most important social club in Minas Velhas as an effectively segregated social space between people identified in local parlance as "white-rich" and "Negro-poor." These groupings did not rely exclusively on racial ascription but on a combination of evaluations of racial and economic status. Nonetheless, they represented acute social divisions based in part on racial ascription. Thus, in his own fieldwork Harris had identified a social-cultural system productive of forms of discrimination involving race (as one important, non-reducible criteria) that did not require a rule of hypo-descent or rigid status roles delineated exclusively in terms of race. Yet in *Patterns of Race in the Americas* Harris equated the idea of systematic racial discrimination exclusively with "caste-like" forms of racial categorization and segregation rather than explore the possibility that distinct forms of ("systematic") discrimination might have existed in Brazil.

Secondly, Harris resorted to a version of Wagley's argument in *Race and Class in Rural Brazil* that racial prejudice did not translate to discriminatory practice. Because individuals were always evaluated on the basis of multiple criteria, prejudice against the Negro as an abstract stereotype had little effect on how people treated one another: "these ideological phenomena do not seriously affect actual behavior" (1964a, 60). Thus, "extremely prejudiced Brazilians have been observed to behave with marked difference toward representatives of the very types whom they allege to be most inferior. Racial prejudice in Brazil, in other words, is not accompanied by systematic racial segregation and discrimination" (60–61). Like Wagley, Harris concluded that class was the socially salient, operative modality of distinction within Brazilian society, whereas race-color was of secondary importance. However, Harris also suggested that, from a materialist perspective, prejudice was a product of systematic oppression. "What we call prejudices are merely the rationalizations which we acquire in order to prove to ourselves that the human beings whom we harm are not worthy of better treatment" (68). Why then, from a materialist perspective, was *racial* prejudice not a reflection and rationalization of *racial* discrimination and oppression in Brazilian society? Harris did not confront the paradox generated by his own account, ultimately depicting enduring racial prejudice as unmoored from social practice and social relations.

I have dwelt on these contradictions because they suggest alternative possibilities in Harris' own work. The mutual imbrications of race and class he identified early in his career potentially opened the door to forms of analysis that might have complicated a ready prioritization of class over race. Ethnographic interpretation of Minas Velhas suggested the possibility that forms of racially informed "systematic discrimination" could develop even in the absence of race as the exclusive defining feature of social groups. In sum, sustained attention to the nuances and complexities of race, class, and discrimination originally identified by Harris could have provided a materialist analysis of racial classification attuned to variations in structural racism across the Americas. Instead, his comparative study of race in Brazil vis-à-vis the U.S. continued to downplay racism in Latin America by essentially defining systematic discrimination in terms of formalized segregation. Such a definition also suggested a rather restricted vision of racial discrimination and white supremacy in the U.S. that would be increasingly challenged in the latter half of the 1960s.

Still, Harris raised important questions. Why did a system embracing fluidity of racial identities along a color continuum blurring distinctions between Blacks and whites emerge in Brazil? Why did a system reifying those distinctions emerge in the United States? Why was hypo-descent characteristic of the U.S. but not of Brazil? These differences could be explained, according to Harris, by material conditions—the "natural, demographic and institutional" environment, especially labor systems and class relations. Spain and Portugal sent few colonists to the colonies, where large indigenous populations or African slaves fulfilled labor requirements. The North American colonies had smaller indigenous populations, and enclosures in England created a surplus population that settled in the New World. The result was an inverse proportion of whites to non-whites in the respective territories. Consequently, Brazilian planters were compelled to "create an intermediate free group of half-castes" to compensate for a shortage of necessary labor for "certain essential economic and military functions for which slave labor was useless," such as removing Indians from areas cleared for sugar plantations, capturing Indian slaves, destroying maroon (fugitive slave) communities, herding cattle, and supplying food (1964a, 86–87). In what became the United States, a white yeomanry filled these roles. This class of whites suffered a depressed standard of living due to slavery and represented a potential threat to the plantation class. Southern planters benefited from a descent rule that established rigid boundaries between whites and non-whites and fostered racial solidarity among whites that mitigated the potential of the white yeomanry to overturn the planter class. Despite their differences, the racial classification systems of Brazil and the United States both served to consolidate the power of the white elite.[12]

Harris (1970) briefly elaborated on this argument in a later essay published in the midst of the Black Power movement in the U.S., provocatively speculating that racial systems in both the U.S. and Brazil played a crucial role in undermining class solidarities in accordance with their divergent demographics. Whereas the rigidities of the U.S. system inhibited class solidarity by facilitating racial solidarity among whites, the ambiguity of the Brazilian system inhibited class solidarity by forestalling racial solidarity among Blacks.

> In the United States, racism and racial caste divisions have split and fragmented the lower class. In Brazil, racism and caste formation would unite the lower class. "Black power" in the United States lacks the revolutionary potential of the preponderant mass; "black power" in Brazil contains this potential. The ambiguity built into the Brazilian calculus of racial identity is thus, speculatively at least, as intelligible as the relative precision with which blacks and whites identify each other in the United States. (12)

In other words, if Brazil were to have developed a descent rule, then the large population of mixed descent in Brazil would be classified as Negro, creating the possibility of race unity as class solidarity. The ambiguities of race-color calculus prevented such unification and thus served to perpetuate the class order.

Left unexplored, but consistent with this argument, was the possibility that the Brazilian calculus of racial identity might also have entailed racial status differentiations (whiteness over blackness and indianness) that facilitated *a form of racial-color class hierarchy* in the absence of caste divisions. Once we reconsider the premise that racism (systematic racial discrimination) necessarily requires caste-like divisions associated with hypo-descent, we can pursue alternative formulations of racial hierarchy and discrimination in relation to class dynamics. Did the persistence of race prejudice in Brazil indicate that race-color differentiations continued to maintain a meaningful relation to the social dynamics of labor and power? If white identity could be leveraged to secure elite (white) power and capital in the United States, while also representing material advantages to the working strata who could claim that identity, what ideological role might whiteness have played in securing the social order in Brazil? What material benefits might have accrued to whiteness among the white elite *and* the "mixed" middle and lower strata of Brazilian society? Most fundamentally, did different classification systems in Brazil and the U.S. entail different forms of racism?

Full consideration of these issues in Harris' analysis was precluded not only by his premises that systematic discrimination required clear-cut categories

but by his final contention in *Patterns of Race in the Americas* that race relations were less conflictual in lowland (and highland) Latin America than in
the U.S. because opportunities for social mobility were limited by depressed
economies.

> The general economic stagnation which has been characteristic of lowland
> Latin America since the abolition of slavery . . . tends to reinforce the pattern
> of pacific relationships among the various racial groups on the lower-ranking
> levels of the social hierarchy. Not only were the poor whites outnumbered by
> the mulattoes and Negroes, but there was very little of a significant material
> nature to struggle over in view of the general static condition of the economy.
> (1964a, 96)

In contrast, rapid economic expansion in the U.S. fostered the growth of middle-class positions, "which the whites have sought to monopolize for themselves" (97). Harris then reached a depressing conclusion: "It thus appears that
the price which the underdeveloped countries or regions of Latin America have
paid for relative racial tranquility is economic stagnation" (98). Phrased in-
versely, the cost of economic vitality in the United States was intense racial
discrimination and strife.

What explained differences in economic dynamism across the region? Remarkably, Harris emphasized the presence or absence of European (white) immigrants as decisive. In both highland and lowland Latin America, "the labor
systems prevented the development early in colonial times of a white class of
small-scale European farmers" and the heritage of these systems crippled economic development (95). The only parts of Latin America that demonstrated
economic dynamism and industrialization were those that historically had a
sparse indigenous population and no plantation economies—the triangle between Rio de Janeiro, São Paulo, and Belo Horizonte in Brazil, and northern
Chile and Argentina. European migrants had been drawn to these regions since
the nineteenth century. For Harris, they

> added a new and vital ingredient to Latin America's melting pot, hitherto pre-
> cluded by the dominance of the slave systems and by debt peonage. Unlike the
> downtrodden slaves and the apathetic Indians, the nineteenth century Euro-
> pean migrants were animated by hope and a spirit of enterprise. . . . In the last
> twenty years remarkable strides toward industrialization have been registered in
> these more fortunate parts of Latin America. (97–98)

Harris sought to distance himself from any "racist" explanation identifying Indians and Africans as the cause of backwardness. After all, it was Europeans who introduced the labor systems that "doomed Latin America's chance for rapid economic development" (98). Yet he simultaneously could render the contemporary descendants of those exploited by the colonial world as "an inert peasant mass, psychologically, educationally and technologically ill-prepared for anything but the most rudimentary forms of subsistence agriculture" (98). The final lines of the book read:

> The backwardness of vast multitudes of the New World peasantry, illiterate, unskilled, cut off from the twentieth century and its brilliant technological advances, did not simply happen by itself. These millions, about whose welfare we have suddenly been obliged to concern ourselves, were trained to their role in world history by four centuries of physical and mental conditioning. They were deliberately bottled up. Now we must either pull the cork or watch the bottle explode. (99)

In these final passages, we see the return—in modified form—of some of the contradictions found in *Minorities in the New World*.

Whereas in that earlier work Harris and Wagley had identified the "cultural adaptability" of indigenous, Black, and white populations as key factors in their relative "success" as minority groups, the materialistic explanation of *Patterns of Race in the America*s foreground the role of exploitative labor regimes in constituting race relations, paying significant attention to how white elites created and reproduced racially stratified labor regimes to their own advantage. Yet, in the end, Harris reintroduced a culturally evaluative language identifying the Latin American (largely colored) masses as "backward" and conditioned to inertia by their suppression while figuring recent (white) European settlers as dynamic and industrious. It was they who were the dynamic agents of development. As in the earlier discussions of U.S. Jews and French Canadians, he never considered the possibility that European settlers achieved social mobility in Latin America at least in some measure because of their insertion as white populations into societies where whiteness reigned supreme as a dominant social value. After all, during the nineteenth and early twentieth centuries, Latin American states actively courted European immigrants, favoring whites as biologically and culturally superior to non-whites (Goebel 2016; Putnam 2010; Skidmore 1990; Stepan 1991). Rather, for Harris European migrants appeared as economic benefactors to the Latin American regions that were "fortunate" to attract them. The masses appeared as the downtrodden burden of societies in desperate need of more dynamic populations, a burden "we" (in the U.S.) must find a way to remedy or witness the apocalypse of social revolution. Once again, an anthropologist managed to conduct a study of the social life of race that ultimately explained away its significance while reinscribing tenets of white hegemony.

Conclusion

By way of conclusion, I would like to offer some final reflections on the work of Wagley and Harris in light of the arguments I developed in earlier chapters. Although the Boasians developed important anti-racist arguments, they never fully contended with the power of whiteness and the color line in the U.S. racial order, modeling the resolution of racism in the United States on the figure of the assimilating European immigrant. The European immigrant also played a crucial but undertheorized role in the work of Wagley and Harris. U.S. Jews appeared in *Minorities in the New World* as the exemplar of successful minority adaptation. In *Patterns of Race in the Americas*, European immigrants introduced dynamism into moribund Latin American economies. In both books, white immigrants served as the foil to culturally deficient non-white populations, rendered as either culturally maladaptive in origin or as culturally inert by subordination. The development of a structural perspective on race and racism was compromised by accounts of cultural adaptation that occluded the significance of whiteness as social value and power across the Americas.

As Seigel (2009) argues, images of race and racism in the post-emancipation U.S. and Brazil have long been co-produced via the comparisons between them. As we saw in Chapter 2, Boas embraced miscegenation as the long-term solution to the race problem in the U.S. in part because he saw the racially mixed societies of Latin America as lacking the virulent racial consciousness, prejudice, and discrimination of his adopted country. A similar comparison motivated UNESCO to study Brazil as a model of racial harmony. The studies themselves generated a more complicated picture. Wagley affirmed a view of Brazil as a racial democracy while Bastide and his Brazilian colleagues identified racial harmony as an effect of white hegemony. Harris would ultimately conclude that Brazil was a society that, owing to its racial classification system, lacked the "systematic racial discrimination" of the United States. For the U.S. anthropologists, Brazil thus represented a kind of inverse image of race relations in the U.S. This construct ignored the alternative possibility that racism—in the form of a practiced hierarchical valuation of whiteness and devaluation of blackness and indianness—was a pervasive feature of Brazilian society. It thus resisted the possibility of a comparative analysis of racisms in the comparative anthropology of race in the Americas.

The comparative analysis of racial classification in the Americas by Wagley and Harris in the Americas did, however, raise serious if muted questions about the possibilities of assimilation as the solution to race-based oppression in the U.S. Recognition of the importance of hypo-descent and enduring strictures against exogamy in the U.S. led to the recognition that assimilation into the white majority was a categorical impossibility for those perceived to be of African descent. Although Harris and Wagley persisted in the use of an immigrant analogy to assess the different position of white and non-white minorities, this insight implied a troubled image of American democracy as based on a contradictory assimilative politics of racial exclusion. Like the Boasians before them, they could not quite face the contradiction.

But the Black Power movement forced a certain reckoning. Harris, in an unpublished, undated draft essay probably written in the late 1960s, came to a position he found unsettling.

> A form of militant black pluralism has become inevitable. Verging on segregationism, it is accompanied for the first time by strong, overt, anti-white prejudice. Its objective power base lies in the densely packed, segregated neighborhood on [sic] the major cities. I reluctantly conclude that in this country, unlike Brazil, the best hope of the blacks for achieving parody [sic: parity] lies in further consolidation of this urban economic and political base and in the further enhancement of their sense of militant separateness.[13]

Like Boas in the early 1920s, Harris became haunted by a recognition that Blacks could not become fully American as long as being American meant being accepted as white. Yet he also recognized that hypo-descent implied that even massive miscegenation would not breach the categorical divide. Because the racial classification system in the U.S. categorically prevented Black assimilation into the white population, the U.S. was destined to remain a plural society. He thus came to conclude that organized struggle for power as a racial minority—a militant pluralism—was the most viable strategy in struggles for racial equality in the U.S. Perhaps his reluctance to embrace this position reflected an enduring attachment to the promise of an integrated liberal social order where race did not define social location. Black power discourses would, quite intentionally, unsettle core convictions of American liberalism by exposing systematic white supremacy in the wake of civil rights victories promoting integration. As I show in the next chapter, they would also play a role in transformative challenges to anthropology as a white discipline.

6 Black Studies and the Reinvention of Anthropology

WHEN THE U.S. POLITICAL order and American liberalism faced a crisis of authority in the 1960s, so too did U.S. anthropology. The discipline became politicized to an unprecedented degree as former colonial subjects challenged its authority, as the politics and ethics of knowledge production came under scrutiny, and as non-whites and women demanded transformations in anthropological theory and praxis. The intellectual and political ferment within anthropology during the 1960s and 1970s had enduring ramifications. The self-reflexive turn challenging objectivity and highlighting the perspectival nature of knowledge is often associated with the late 1970s and 1980s but has its origins in this era (Trencher 2000), as do many of the prescriptions for a revitalized, progressive, or even radical anthropology—"native" or "insider" anthropology (Jones 1970, Lewis 1973), "studying up" (Nader 1972), and activist scholarship (Moore 1971), to name a few. Capitalism and power now vied with kinship and ritual as subjects of attention. Most anthropologists did not become radical anti-imperialists, but the discipline could never be quite the same.

A comprehensive account of anthropology and the 1960s remains to be written.[1] Many of its critical and innovative intellectual contributions remain largely unexplored and under-acknowledged. Perhaps, as James Clifford suggests, the generation of scholars instrumental to the self-reflexive and critical turns of the 1980s were so deeply informed by the earlier critical turn that they failed to fully acknowledge it. Referring specifically to the collection *Reinventing Anthropology* (Hymes 1972), Clifford notes: "Everything in that book was part of our discourse, so much so that we sometimes forgot to reference it" (2003, 97). Ironically, one of the more sustained discussions of anthropology in the 1960s comes from someone who identifies the era as the moment when anthropology went astray (Lewis 2014, 27). Herbert Lewis documents the transformation by reviewing session and paper abstracts at the American Anthropological Association (AAA) annual meetings. Kathleen Gough first presented her "Anthropology and Imperialism" in 1967. The 1968 meeting included a session on a Black curriculum in anthropology and a paper titled "Savage Anthropologists and the Unvanishing Indians in the American Southwest." Within the next three years, sessions on women, Marxism, and racism appeared. A "Radical Caucus" put forth a series of resolutions, and a group led largely by Columbia anthropologists broke the AAA's standard protocol of producing leaders from within the existing board by nominating Gerald Berreman—a key figure in the critical reevaluation of anthropology—for president of the association. In 1972 there were five panels on anthropology and anti-imperialism (Lewis 2014, 32–46).

A full accounting of the period is beyond the scope of this chapter, though the question I pursue here is crucial for any such effort: How did the crisis in U.S. anthropology inform anthropological approaches to race and "America"? My central contention is that a number of anthropologists, most of them anthropologists of color, drew on the intellectual energies of popular mobilization—particularly the Black Power and Black Studies movements—to redefine the relationships between anthropology, race, and "America." I focus on key essays by William Willis ("Skeletons in the Anthropological Closet" [1972]), Diane Lewis ("Anthropology and Colonialism" [1973]), and Charles Valentine (*Black Studies and Anthropology* [1972]) to explore how they brought to anthropology new possibilities for theorizing and confronting racism and white supremacy, pushing beyond the critique of biological racism toward structural analysis of racism. Their interventions, largely unacknowledged today, contributed to a reevaluation of the discipline and provide resources for analyzing the intimate relationship between anthropology, race, and American liberalism. These authors identified racism as a constitutive feature of American society perpetuated within U.S. anthropology itself as a predominately white liberal discourse that essentialized difference across the color line, misrecognized the pervasiveness of racism, and perpetuated white imperial power. Echoing a disillusion with America found within Black Studies, they eschewed the liberal Americanism U.S. anthropology helped construct.

This chapter takes a different tone and involves a different mode of analysis than previous ones. I devote less attention to a critical reading of Willis, Lewis,

Valentine than I did in the chapters on Boas, Benedict, and Wagley and Harris, analyzing their work as an effort to subvert and break with the tradition of Americanist anti-racist liberalism associated with the Boasians and those who followed in its wake. I view this work as emerging out of collective struggles by anthropologists of color to promote what we might call a critical race turn within the discipline. These struggles were wrapped up in what I believe was the first collective and concerted effort to "decolonize" U.S. anthropology from within its ranks.[2] This chapter is a first foray into this neglected moment and movement. I focus on Willis, Lewis, and Valentine because they offered wide-ranging critical and programmatic statements on the discipline, implicating it in structures of white supremacy. Willis is of particular interest because he was trained at Columbia University in the 1940s and 1950s and explicitly identified ways in which Boasian anthropology—its critique of scientific racism notwithstanding—perpetuated white domination. Although I treat the authors sequentially, my aim is to tease out their critical race perspectives on anthropology as part of a wider effort to confront the contradictions of American anti-racist liberalism, as necessary today as it was fifty years ago.

U.S. Anthropology in "Crisis": Critical Turns

Diane Lewis began her article "Anthropology and Colonialism" by noting that "Anthropology is in a state of crisis," a common sentiment in the late 1960s and early 1970s. Lewis identified the sensibility as resulting from "the marked estrangement between anthropologists and the nonwhite people they have traditionally studied," an estrangement that extended from field to classroom (1973, 581). There were a number of early harbingers, typically from outside the U.S. The prominent French anthropologist Claude Levi-Strauss, in an oft-cited passage, raised doubts about the future of a discipline that was

> the outcome of a historical process which has made the larger part of mankind subservient to the other, and during which millions of innocent human beings have had their resources plundered and institutions and beliefs destroyed, whilst they themselves were ruthlessly killed, thrown into bondage, and contaminated by diseases they were unable to resist. Anthropology is daughter to this era of violence; its capacity to assess more objectively the facts pertaining to the human condition appropriately reflects, on the epistemological level, a state of affairs in which one part of mankind treated the other as an object. (1966, 126)[3]

Belgian anthropologist Jacques Maquet (1964) wrote an influential article which critiqued the notion of objective knowledge by highlighting the difficulties European anthropologists had in recognizing their complicity with colonial institutions and thought when confronted by African intellectuals. U.S. anthropologists began to reckon with critical perspectives from anthropologists from the Global South (e.g., Bonfil Batalla 1966; Magubane 1971; Stavenhagen 1971) and from scholars insisting that anthropology must study the "Third World" in relation to the dynamics of "First World" colonialism and imperialism (e.g., Balandier 1966; Worsley 1964).

Critiques of the relationship between anthropology and colonialism and/or imperialism emerged from various quarters. One catalyst in the U.S. academy was the revelation that the U.S. military was attempting to employ social scientists in a counter-insurgency project known as Project Camelot. Marshall Sahlins, credited with helping invent the "teach-in" as part of activism against the Vietnam War, denounced Project Camelot at the AAA meetings (Sahlins 1967). A similar scandal rocked the discipline and its professional organization when, in 1970, a student anti-war organization obtained illicitly copied files of an anthropologist that exposed the participation of social scientists in the development of U.S. counter-insurgency research in Thailand. The organization sent the documents to Eric Wolf and Joseph Jorgensen, anti-war members of the AAA Ethics Committee, and then published excerpts. Wolf and Jorgensen contacted the implicated anthropologist but were rebuked. The Ethics Committee then alerted the wider organization to the ethical-political problems of wedding scholarship to counter-insurgency programs designed to manipulate the subjects of research and neutralize protest. The AAA Executive Committee rebuked Wolf and Jorgensen for taking actions beyond the purview of the Committee; Jorgensen and Wolf responded by publishing an article (1970) in the *New York Review of Books*. Margaret Mead, in a report of an investigation on behalf of the AAA Executive Committee, "exonerated civilian anthropologists of complicity with United States military forces' counterinsurgency work but criticized Wolf's and Jorgensen's lapse of ethics in making their allegations public." When she read the report at the AAA meetings, Mead was "roundly and repeatedly hissed" and the membership voted to reject it (di Leonardo 1998, 239).[4]

Whereas in the 1940s anthropological involvement in World War II was largely accepted as a given, in the mid to late 1960s many anthropologists challenged the ethics and politics of producing knowledge for a state they viewed less as a defender of democracy than as an imperialist power. Dissent from abroad combined with polarization in the U.S. shook the political and epistemological foundations of knowledge production. An important hallmark of these developments was a 1968 forum in the journal *Current Anthropology*. The international journal, founded and edited by University of Chicago anthropologist Sol Tax, published many of the most important articles attempting to critique and reorient anthropology. The journal's unique format—numerous scholars responded to an article and the author provided a rejoinder—facilitated debate (Desai 2001, 72). The forum included articles by Gerald Berreman (1968), Kathleen Gough (1968), and Gutorm Gjessing (1968). Berreman and Gjessing drew on the burgeoning sociology of knowledge to contest the idea of "value-free" science, urging anthropologists to engage with public issues and responsibly use knowledge toward socially positive ends. Kathleen Gough went further. She provided a pointed indictment of anthropology as a "child of Western imperialism," wherein anthropologists had "commonly played roles characteristic of white liberals" (1968, 403). Using Marxist and world systems theories, she proposed a reorientation of the discipline toward the study of imperialism and revolution. The forum occasioned both vociferous opposition and welcome relief. Mexican anthropologist Daniel Cazes noted, "*Current Anthropology* has at last satisfied the need for an open and extended discussion of a theme that seems to many of us, especially those of us whose major interest is in 'underdeveloped'—superexploited—countries, to have been floating around since the beginnings of anthropology as a discipline" (Gough 1968, 408). Most of the U.S.-based respondents reacted with less enthusiasm. The debates attracted such interest that the journal continued to publish commentaries into the early 1970s (Duerr et al. 1970; Kobben et al. 1971).

Another key text of the era was *Reinventing Anthropology*, edited by Dell Hymes (1972). This collection of essays reflects something of the intellectual diversity associated with the critical reevaluation of anthropology in the U.S. Themes included, among others, critical evaluations of anthropology's relationship to racism and imperialism (Willis 1972; Caulfield 1972), strategies for studying power and domination (Nader 1972), epistemological reflections on the discipline (Diamond 1972), and the identification of new topics such as ecological crisis (Anderson 1972). Participants in the volume came from multiple generations and most had affiliations with the University of California at Berkeley, Columbia, or the University of Pennsylvania as either faculty or former PhDs. Half had received their PhDs in the 1950s and some—for example,

Dell Hymes, Eric Wolf, Stanley Diamond—were quite prominent figures. The critique of anthropology, though energized by student movements and political radicalization, was by no means simply a youth rebellion.

The movement was also not confined to the U.S. and was particularly encouraged by scholars from the Global South. In Mexico, for example, a cadre of anthropologists analyzed the complicity of anthropology with the "internal colonialism" of a Mexican state subordinate to U.S. imperialism, drawing on the dependency theories they had helped develop over the previous decade (Rosemblatt 2014). A group of Latin American anthropologists that included some of those Mexican anthropologists issued the "Declaration of Barbados" promoting revolutionary social transformation in defense of indigenous peoples.[5] Black South African anthropologists Archie Mafeje (1971) and Bernard Magubane (1971) explored the ideological underpinning of anthropological approaches to social change and concepts such as tribe. In the UK, a New Left critique of anthropology (Goddard 1969; Banaji 1970) led to debates over the discipline's relationship to British colonialism, gathered in *Anthropology and the Colonial Encounter* (Asad 1973). Although the focus of this chapter is the U.S., the discussion there developed in an international and transnational context.

The overall movement toward a reevaluation of the discipline did not have a name. Diane Lewis identified it as "the critical view" (1972, 50), whereas Herbert Lewis has recently referred to it, disapprovingly, as the "radical transformation of anthropology" (2014, 27). However we label the various strands of intervention at play—critical, decolonial, anti-imperial, revisionist, radical—the moment entailed, as Clifford put it, a "relentless questioning of anthropological orthodoxies" (2003, 97–98). In U.S. anthropology, this included critical explorations of: the relationship between anthropology and colonialism; the politics of cultural representation; the ethical and political relationships between anthropologists and research subjects; the epistemological foundations of the discipline; the limitations of fieldwork; the possibility of "objective" knowledge. The critical turn included calls for "activist," "advocate," or "radical" anthropology that would contribute to political struggles of the oppressed, advocacy of "native" or "insider" anthropology, and the promotion of self-reflexivity in ethnography. Feminist anthropology, named as such, also began to emerge at this time (Leacock 1982, 261). At the most general level, the movement involved an effort to conceptualize anthropology as a form of knowledge production implicated in power relations. Reevaluations of the history of the discipline thus emerged as a central feature of the critical turn.

Black Power, Black Studies, and Anthropology

How did the critical turn impact anthropology's approaches to race and racism? Increasing attention to the discipline's past brought to the fore the role anthropologists played in the promotion of scientific racism, particularly in the nineteenth century (Harris 1968; Stocking 1968). Struggles for civil rights and Black liberation led to increased anthropological interest in African American culture in the United States. Anthropological studies devoted to Black cultural expression in the U.S. (e.g., Abrahams 1964; Keil 1966; Liebow 1967; Hannerz 1969) sought to counter stereotypes of African American culture even if, as Valentine argued, they did not escape dominant paradigms of evaluation (see below). Reconsiderations of the Black family explicitly sought to counter images of cultural pathology (Stack 1970; 1974). The politics of representing African American culture itself became a subject of attention (Szwed 1972; Valentine 1972), and efforts to retheorize New World Black cultures reflected those politics.[6] For the first time, anthropologists began to ponder in print why in the U.S. the discipline had focused primarily on Native American Indians to the neglect of African Americans (Fisher 1969; Mintz 1970b, 13–14; Willis 1970).

If such efforts expanded anti-racist initiatives within anthropology, most anthropologists of the era do not appear to have taken racism and/or white supremacy as subjects of major theoretical concern for the discipline. Sidney Mintz, for example, edited a book called *Slavery, Colonialism and Racism* (1974) but dedicated little attention to developing an analytic of racism in his formidable corpus of work on Afro-Caribbean peoples and cultures in the era, including his insightful account of Black ("Afro-American") Studies as fundamental to American Studies and an understanding of the modern West (1970a; 1971). The prominent scholars most readily identified with the critical turn in anthropology (e.g., Gough, Hymes, Berreman, Diamond, Wolf) used terms such as colonialism, imperialism, and capitalism as their primary frames for critical analysis of the discipline. While these frames often implicated racism and white supremacy, the latter concepts were rarely at the explicit center of analysis; they often appeared as ancillary concerns derivative of the core frames. An interesting example can be found in the work of Gough, who illustrated her charge that anthropologists were blind to the implications of imperialism by pointing out the limitations of Boasian anti-racism.

> I would argue that while Boas and his students did invaluable work on race differences and race prejudice, they did not systematically explore the relationship

of race prejudice to the world-wide historical and structural development of White nations' imperialism. Had they done so they might have concluded that a complete shift in the power relations between White and colored races would be necessary to undermine White racism, rather than concluding—as I think they tended to do—that the solution lay mainly in the education of White people. (1968, 428–429)

For Gough, the limitations of Boasian anti-racism—the lack of a structural account of racism in favor of a liberal one—illustrated anthropological blindness to the effects of imperialism. This argument, which in turn implicated imperialism as a project of "White nations," nonetheless appeared only to illustrate the importance of rethinking anthropology in light of imperialism. The question of racism as an enduring feature of white dominant nations and their imperialism, or of anthropology, was not central to her analytic framework. For other scholars, less well known, it would be.

If opposition to the Vietnam War, the rise of the "counter-culture," and decolonization were all crucial elements of the context for the emergence of a sense of crisis in U.S. anthropology, so too was mobilization by people of color. Anthropologists of color would increasingly demand greater inclusion within the discipline and strive to hold anthropology accountable as a white-dominated discipline. Black student mobilization and the Black Studies movement played a crucial role. Between 1968 and 1969 Black students held protests on almost two hundred campuses across the country (Biondi 2012, 1). They sought not merely to expand the number of African American students and faculty but to transform the university. Crucially, this entailed "exposing the whiteness disguised as universalism" pervasive in the academy (4). In seeking to incorporate Black perspectives into knowledge production, proponents of Black Studies envisioned radical revisions of prevailing understandings of U.S. history and society. They interrogated prevailing notions of objectivity, promoted interdisciplinary and transnational approaches, and insisted that all knowledge had political ramifications. St. Clair Drake noted: "The Black Studies movement forced us all to critically reexamine the desirability and possibility of 'integration' and 'assimilation' as goals for colored ethnics in racist America" (1978, 101).

These views reflected intellectual and political currents that had crystallized in the broader Black Power movement. Black Power, emerging immediately out of the political energies and frustrations of the civil rights movement but rooted in diverse strands of political radicalism in the African Diaspora, represented a profound challenge to liberal perspectives on race (Singh 2005). This challenge went far beyond a critique of the failures of integration and the contradictions that ongoing racism posed to the "American creed" of individual opportunity and democratic inclusion. Black Power intellectuals identified American democracy as deeply compromised by racism and conceptualized white supremacy as a constitutive feature of U.S. society and its institutions. Whereas the civil rights movement relied on rhetorics of American civic nationalism to promote integration, Black Power discourse challenged prevailing understandings of integration. The Black Panthers, for example, "argued that the civil rights leadership had missed the main lesson of anti-imperialism, that the United States was not a nation into which black people could successfully integrate, but an empire they needed to oppose—not a beloved community of shared traditions and aspirations, but a coercive state to be overthrown" (197). From a Black Power perspective, African Americans were colonial subjects of a white power structure. In their widely read *Black Power*, Stokely Carmichael and Charles Hamilton referred to integration as "subterfuge for the maintenance of white supremacy" (1967, 54) because it maintained the superiority of white institutions over Black institutions and required that Blacks abandon Black identity to be accepted as American (32). They explicitly critiqued key tenets of U.S. liberal discourse on race, including the notion of color blindness (54), comparisons of Blacks to white immigrants (25, 51), and the interpretation of racism as a moral contradiction or "American dilemma." From a Black Power perspective, racism was not a conflict between creed and practice but a systemic feature of U.S. culture and society, saturating its institutions. Carmichael and Hamilton suggested that institutional racism—the term they coined to refer to the systemic rather than merely individual aspects of racism—constituted an integral "tradition" within U.S. society (56).

The challenges Black Power and Black Studies posed to U.S. institutions and white liberalism made an impact on U.S. anthropology and the AAA. In the early to mid-1960s, the AAA had reiterated scientific objections to racial determinism in public statements but had done little to promote changes in what Willis would call the "lily white" profile of the profession (1970, 38). With the explosion of the Black student movement the discipline would face its first concerted internal challenge as a white profession. Institutionally, anthropologists of color demanded not only greater inclusion in the discipline but transformations in pedagogy, organizational structures, research, and cultural representations. At the 1968 AAA meetings, Councill Taylor organized an experimental session on developing a "Black curriculum in Anthropological Studies" (Lewis 2014, 38).[7] The following year, Taylor and Johnnetta Cole organized a panel on "Ethnographic Research in Black Communities in the U.S.," while Belvie Rooks led the "Experimental Session of the Minority Curriculum Committee on the Implications of the Current Ethnic Studies Controversy." In 1970, the AAA meetings included a "Symposium on Racism and Ethnocentrism in Anthropology."[8] These initiatives were accompanied by the creation of the Third World Congress of Anthropologists and the Caucus of Black Anthropologists; the latter became the Association of Black Anthropologists (Harrison 1987).

Critical dissent was not confined to African American anthropologists. Native American activist historian Vine Deloria, whose aunt Ella Deloria had worked and studied with Boas, produced a scathing satire of anthropologists in Indian country (Deloria 1969). UC Berkeley anthropology PhD Octavio Romano critiqued distorted representations of Mexican American history and culture in the anthropological and sociological literature.[9] Francis Hsu, a senior Chinese American anthropologist at Northwestern University, took white anthropologists to task for various forms of prejudice, from neglect of the work of non-white anthropologists to the reproduction of Western biases: "There is a world of difference between a truly cross-cultural science of man and a White centered science of man with cross-cultural decorations" (Hsu 1973, 1). The critical turn in anthropology could thus include a critique of its universalist pretensions not only on ideological but on racial grounds.

Without extensive archival research it is difficult to gauge the reaction of most white anthropologists to the challenges posed by anthropologists of color and the racial politics of the era. A statement by the Northeast Anthropological Association on the assassination of Martin Luther King is perhaps illustrative of some of the contradictory currents.

> The Northeastern Anthropological Association, meeting in Hanover, New Hampshire on April 6, 1968, is both concerned and shocked with the assassination of Dr. Martin Luther King and the symbol it is of the destructive tendencies of racism against which anthropologists have so long fought. We request that the American Anthropological Association explore the ways in which anthropologists can become more effective in understanding the essential nature of this tragic situation, for only through such understanding can a resolution of these difficulties occur. (Gruber 1968, 10)

The ironies of the statement are worth noting: in asserting that anthropologists had "long fought" against racism, it ignored how anthropologists had also long contributed to scientific racism; in calling for the AAA to find more effective ways to understand racism, it tacitly admitted the discipline's weakness in conceptualizing and combating racism. Clifford Geertz, called upon by the *New York Times* to address violence in U.S. society after the assassination of King, could muster only the tepid response that violence was not inherent to American culture:

> The fact is that the present state of domestic disorder in the United States is not the product of some destructive quality mysteriously ingrained in the substance of American life. It is a product of a long sequence of particular events whose interconnections our received categories of self-understanding are not only inadequate to reveal but are designed to conceal. We do not know what kind of history we have had, what kind of people we are. (Geertz 1968, 24–25)

If Geertz implied the necessity for some sort of deep (self) examination of "America" and "Americans," he managed here to avoid the role of racism and the color line in the republic, its institutions, and its violence (De Genova 2007, 254). Many anthropologists, proud of the discipline's anti-racist traditions, appeared to have little ability to address the racial violence, domination, and rebellion in their midst.

Some anthropologists did begin to actively promote a more diverse discipline. In 1969 Dell Hymes and George Foster sponsored a resolution at the AAA urging the "vigorous recruitment of students of Black, Chicano, American Indian, Asian and other backgrounds into anthropology in universities and colleges, and vigorous efforts to hire and facilitate the careers of such persons in the profession" (quoted in Lewis 2014, 40). When Elliott Skinner wrote from Stanford asking Marvin Harris to identify potential applicants from Columbia, Harris replied:

> Our Department long ago recognized this need in a professional sense. It is unreasonable to suppose that the nature of ethnographic research is not influenced by the ethnic and racial identity of the field anthropologist. However, we are as short in supply of such students as you are. Of course, in our case it is a little more inexplicable given the richness of the metropolitan area in this human resource. It is not merely idle bluster to assert that Columbia and other elite universities have been pursuing de facto racist policies over the years.[10]

Stanford published a statement in the AAA newsletter announcing the introduction of four-year fellowships for all graduate students and "special consideration to applicants from such minority members as Black Americans,
Mexican-Americans, Puerto Ricans and American Indians" (Gibbs 1969, 5).[11]
An archaeologist at Florida State reacted with indignation that this entailed the
"reverse side of a racism which we, in anthropology particularly, have fought
since the time of Boas" (Smith 1969, 2). Modest efforts to overcome "de facto
racist policies" and entrenched passivity on diversifying the profession could
thus produce accusations of reverse racism that have become common in the
post–civil rights era, here justified by an appeal to Boasian anti-racism.[12]

Critical Race Currents Within the Critical Turn: Willis, Lewis, and Valentine

In the following pages I explore how several scholars radicalized by the politics
of the 1960s articulated the crisis facing anthropology and how their efforts
to reimagine anthropology involved efforts to rethink race and racism within
and beyond the discipline. I focus on William Willis, Diane Lewis, and Charles
Valentine because of the breadth of their interventions and the influence of
Black Studies perspectives on their relationship to anthropology. Their programmatic essays were products of considerable experience in the discipline
(all had received PhDs by 1962) and their radicalization with the emergence of
Black Power and Black Studies. Read together, these essays explored the relationship between anthropology and racism, both in the sense of the complicity
of anthropology with racism and of contributing to anthropological accounts
of racism. All three authors approached anthropology as a white-dominated
discipline from non-white perspectives. Willis and Lewis did so as anthropologists of color. Valentine wrote as a white anthropologist engaging Black Studies critiques of the social sciences and U.S. society. I will discuss each in turn,
starting with the shared concerns of Willis and Lewis that anthropology faced
a crisis precipitated by the demands of people of color, at home and abroad.

William Willis (1921–1983) was raised in a wealthy African American family based in Waco and Dallas, Texas. He completed his undergraduate degree
at Howard University, where he studied Black history and culture under the
prominent African American intellectuals Rayford Logan, E. Franklin Frazier,
Alain Locke, Sterling Brown, and Ralph Bunche. He entered Columbia University in 1945, shifting from political science to anthropology. His teachers
included Ruth Benedict, Charles Wagley, Gene Weltfish, Harry Shapiro, and

Julian Steward. Some of his fellow students—for example, Morton Fried, Marvin Harris, Sidney Mintz, Robert Murphy, and Eric Wolf—became prominent anthropologists. Willis chose anthropology, he later said,

> because I assumed that this discipline was the vanguard in the attack against racist thought. I tried to reconcile the concentration on North American Indians that then prevailed in anthropology with my strong interests in history and the study of Black people by selecting Black-Indian relations in Southeastern North America as the problem of my dissertation.... I soon discovered that this problem could not be handled adequately until a more satisfactory knowledge existed about sociocultural change among 18th century Indians in this region. (quoted in Lévy Zumwalt and Willis 2008, 2)

He completed his dissertation, *Colonial Conflict and the Cherokee Indians, 1710–1760*, in 1955 (Willis 1955) and subsequently published on southeastern Indian ethnohistory and Indian-Black relations, with a focus on the divide-and-conquer strategies of white colonialists (e.g., Willis 1963).

Willis could not secure full-time employment in a white-dominant university in the 1950s (Sanday 1999, 250). He self-financed research and taught as an adjunct at Columbia and the City University of New York until 1965, when he was the first Black faculty member hired at Southern Methodist University in Dallas. From a review of his correspondence, it is clear that Willis viewed his move as an experiment in integration. He initially reported receiving a warm reception at SMU but soon began to describe the strains of being what he called "the first Negro" and conflicts with other anthropologists, particularly the department chair. By late 1967 he identified his own "radicalization," writing to Elliott Skinner: "It is strange and revealing that I—after three years of smiling cooperation—now have a greater appreciation of black power." His assessment of his personal situation echoed a larger political stance on the need to confront white power: "It seems to me that 'real' integration can only come as a function of black power. Then the integration is not a gift, but the surrender to an irrestible [*sic*] demand."[13] Willis followed closely student activism at Columbia, where he taught during the summers, and played a mediating role between the Black Student movement and the administration at SMU, participating in the establishment of its Institute for African American Studies.

Willis' political radicalization informed his growing interest in the history of anthropology, and he initiated an intensive study of Boas and African Americans. In 1968, he gave a lecture at the University of Texas at Austin that began by exploring the question of why U.S. anthropology had neglected the study of Blacks (1970). Willis resigned from SMU in 1972 after a series of conflicts with the department chair, who circulated a racist flyer targeting him and sought to turn a one-year leave into a permanent termination of Willis' appointment. Ironically, Willis had helped the department secure a National Science Foundation graduate training grant on urban ethnography and minority issues. As a senior scholar with few publications, Willis felt another permanent appointment was unlikely and spent the latter years of his career continuing research on Boas (Sanday 1999; Lévy Zumwalt and Willis 2008, 1–40).

In the midst of the strife at SMU, Willis wrote "Skeletons in the Anthropological Closet" for the volume *Reinventing Anthropology* at the invitation of Dell Hymes and John Szwed. He initially considered titling the piece "The Anthropologist as Vulture."[14] Willis examined anthropology from what Richard Wright called "the frog perspective," the position of the oppressed (Willis 1972, 121). This perspective brought attention to "the importance of color" and exposed the "skeletons" of a discipline that took pride in its racial progressivism (121). Willis provided a provocative "minimal definition" of anthropology as historically practiced: "*To a considerable extent, anthropology has been the social science that studies dominated colored peoples—and their ancestors—living outside the boundaries of modern white societies*" (123). Anthropology was (and still is) typically defined as the study of humans or the study of culture. In actual practice, Willis asserted, anthropology was the social science of white-dominated societies devoted to the study of non-white peoples, especially those who could be seen as representatives of non-modern ways of life.

Willis' use of race-color terms was fundamental to his perspective. He spoke of the relationship between anthropology and colonialism, imperialism, and capitalism but also of "white rule with its color inequality" (122). Much as Black Power analytics called out white power within the U.S. social, cultural, and political order, Willis defined anthropology in terms of racial objectifications. The implications of this move are profound. It upset the imagination of anthropology as a racially neutral discipline, demanding an accounting of racial location, privilege, and subordination within the social order and discipline itself. Identified as a white discipline devoted to producing knowledge about non-whites, anthropology could no longer be imagined in any simple fashion as a progressive, anti-racist field of knowledge production.

Writing in the mode of an exposé, Willis sketched in broad strokes how anthropology had contributed to white domination. Some British anthropologists, for example, argued for the utility of anthropology in imperial administration and were employed directly by colonial governments. In the United States, the expansion of anthropological attention to the South Pacific, Latin America, Asia, and Africa followed, as Willis put it in an earlier essay, "the national flag and the national currency" (1970, 34). Anthropologists provided information on the colored world, occasionally acted as spies, and, while not necessarily directly serving imperial interests, always operated within the "framework of imperialism" and never advocated its overthrow (1972, 129). In general, Willis argued, anthropological paradigms followed the imperatives of colonial rule. Nineteenth-century scientific racism corresponded to the phase of securing territorial expansion. Cultural relativism emerged in the first half of the twentieth century as colonial reform efforts reflected the needs of securing the labor and consumption of colored colonial subjects. In the post–World War II era, as anthropologists argued that colonial subjects should share more of the wealth produced in the colored world, "imperialists were adopting a similar policy in order to salvage white economic interests" in response to revolutionary movements (130). Efforts by anthropologists to advocate on behalf of the people they studied or promote reform within colonial rule stopped short of supporting struggles for liberation. Willis thus called into question an anthropological self-image of defending non-Western peoples and cultures. His mention of scandalous revelations such as Malinowski's racist language in his recently published diary and Boas' robbing of Native American graves for skulls and bones—the literal skeletons of anthropology's past—bolstered the critique.

Willis' exposure of anthropology's skeletons was, to be sure, a polemic, but it involved more than creating a scandal; it entailed an intellectual-political analysis of the discipline as a formation of the white West. He paid particular attention to core concepts of the discipline—primitive, culture, cultural relativism—and the various kinds of political work they could perform. The idea of the primitive could be used to justify capitalist domination and racial hierarchy and, in more recent uses, to "condemn some conditions in white societies and some aspects of white domination of the colored world" (124). In either case it remained a projection that prevented most anthropologists from "seeing contemporary colored peoples as real human beings enmeshed in their intricate depths" (126). Similarly, anthropological uses of the concepts of culture and cultural relativism challenged some aspects of white superiority yet reproduced projections of radical alterity between whites and non-white peoples and maintained the hierarchy between them.

> [A]nthropologists have constructed imaginary counter cultures to serve white needs and thereby obtain reaffirmations. In the nineteenth century, anthropologists used an explicit racist ideology to make colored peoples into different human beings than white people. Later, when scientific racism became less popular, anthropologists achieved almost the same result with the concepts of culture and of cultural relativism. The enculturation inherent in the culture concept was seen as having the power to mold most human beings into accepting and internalizing almost any kind of sociocultural arrangement. These arrangements, whatever their nature and political and economic basis, were then justified by the "dignity" that was accorded them by cultural relativism. Thus, colored peoples, having been construed as simply culturally different, could be manipulated as things in the "laboratory" of the colored world. Hence Du Bois described the black man as the "football of anthropology." (126)

The reference to "laboratory" recalled a famous passage in *Patterns of Culture*, in which Benedict (with whom Willis had taken classes in the 1940s) referred to primitive cultures as "a laboratory in which we may study the diversity of human institutions" and thus come to understand "our" own cultural frameworks in order to change them (1934, 17). For Willis, the anthropological effort to conceive colored peoples as "other cultures" "we" study involved objectifications that reified differences between white and non-white peoples, perpetuated distorted representations of the colored world, and glossed over the power relations between the white world and the colored world. Despite the "liberal intent" of anthropology, its conceptual tool kit involved a "sleight of hand" that managed to avoid "the misery and distress of colored peoples." This, in turn, helped explain "the lack of outrage that has prevailed in anthropology until recent years" (1972, 126). It was perhaps this lack of outrage that most troubled Willis.

For Willis, even ostensibly anti-racist anthropology was, in practice, a project of the white world for the white world. Writing at a moment of intense interest in the history of the discipline—wherein the narrative was one of disciplinary progress on race thinking (largely as a result of Boas) in works as antagonistic as those of Stocking (1968) and Harris (1968)—Willis offered a critical (re)interpretation of Boasian anthropology. For Willis, the central concern of Boasian anthropology was not the condition of colored peoples but the improvement of white societies. He identified the basic prescription of Boas' politics as liberal—"the extension of individual freedom, unrestricted by the 'shackles' of tradition and the merging of individuals into social catego-ries" (Willis 1972, 134–135). Cultural diversity in the colored world provided, as Boas put it, "a freer view of our own lives and of our own life problems" (quoted in Willis 1972, 136). The Boasians did not, however, promote primitive cultures as offering alternative ways of life that might be adapted by anthro-pologists or the society at large. Rather they used cultural diversity to suggest the possibility of change in white societies by emphasizing the importance of cultural conditioning. Willis essentially identified Boasian anthropology as a white liberal project of domestic reform.

What then of Boasian scientific anti-racism, which had drawn Willis to an-thropology in the first place? Here too Willis took a critical view. He pointed out that Boas and those that followed him "increasingly minimized—but never completely excluded—the possible influence of racial factors on the sociocult-ural behavior of colored peoples, especially the black people" (138). He also charged that "*scientific anti-racism was concerned only secondarily with col-ored peoples*," giving primacy to racial discrimination among white groups—Nordicism and anti-Semitism (139, emphasis in the original).

> The minimal role assigned to race in regard to sociocultural patterns among colored peoples was used to establish *a fortiori*, as it were, the irrelevancy of racial explanations in regard to white groups. Hence, Boas concluded "there is no need of entering into a discussion of alleged hereditary differences in the mental characteristics of various branches of the white race." (138–139)

According to Willis, scientific anti-racism was an intellectual weapon used by predominately Jewish anthropologists against racist and anti-Semitic Protestant anthropologists struggling against the Boasians for control of the profession.

What should we make of the claims that Boasians showed only a "second-ary" concern for peoples of color and that opposition to racism against peoples of color was motivated by a concern for racial discrimination among whites? In Chapter 2, I critiqued the view that Boas' attacks on anti-Black racism served as a cover for his "real" target—anti-Semitism. Such a position reduces Boas' complex and contradictory thought on race and racism to readily discernible personal motivations as identity-driven interests. It can slide into a form of anti-Semitism that views Boasian anthropology as a *Jewish project*, a view long held within avowedly racist, white supremacist, and anti-Semitic circles (Baker 2010, 156–219). In my own view, the claim that Boasians were primarily con-cerned with anti-Semitism and discrimination against non-Nordic European immigrants is a red herring. It paints the critic into a corner of evaluating the Boasians on the basis of "true" versus "false" motivations, and it prompts the reader to question whether the critique (and the critic) are themselves anti-Semitic. It distracts from the possibility that Boasians were (sincerely) anti-racist *and* that their anti-racist interventions implied different things for those whom they understood to be white and non-white.

It is worth noting that after writing "Skeletons" Willis expressed a more complex view of Boas than could be gleaned from that article. The more he examined Boas' archive, the more he realized that Boas had taken a far greater interest in the study of African Americans and in training African American students than he or other scholars realized (Willis 1975).[15] In personal correspondence Willis articulated a deep respect for Boas and identified with him, asserting that "the strength and vision" of Boas had "played a crucial role in sustaining us [he and his wife] through the trauma of the last two years."[16] He also noted that the struggles of Jews within the profession were ignored in histories of anthropology, asserting that "anti-Semitism has yet to disappear entirely from anthropology even at some leading institutions" (1972, 150). Willis saw a contemporary analogue in Black struggles to find a home in anthropology. His complex attitude toward Boas was echoed by ambivalence toward his own perspective on the discipline. Upon submitting his third draft of "Skeletons" to Dell Hymes, he wrote, "I know that I would never have looked at things in quite this way without these 6 years in Dallas. This has given insights I might never have come to in New York. On the other hand, the bitterness must have caused a certain distortion."[17] But Willis never disavowed the insights of "Skeletons" gleaned, he felt, from his alienation from the discipline made evident by his experiences at SMU. His later work on Boas would both highlight Boas' efforts to articulate anthropology with anti-Black racism (describing him as "decades ahead of his times" [1975, 324]) and continue to identify failures and limitations in Boasian anthropology, including its inability to address white oppression and the "black struggle for survival, for freedom, and for equality" (327).

We need not accept Willis' contention in "Skeletons" that scientific anti-racism was only "secondarily" concerned with colored peoples to consider the importance of his critique of Boasian thought. It opened a space to consider how Boasian anti-racism thought worked differently in relation to whites and non-whites and how Boasian anthropology in general was produced primarily for a white audience. Perhaps most crucially, it raised probing questions about his own generation, the successors to the Boasians. If anthropology had an anti-racist heritage, where was the anger at the exploitation of people of color? Why was anthropological anti-racism reduced to the "catechism" of no inherent relationship between race language and color, "devoid of personal commitment"? Why did color prejudice persist among anthropologists and why did the discipline remain lily white, with resistance to any special commitment to recruit anthropologists of color? (1972, 140).

Willis provided one of the first elaborated critiques of Boasian scientific anti-racism, challenging a view of racial progressivism in twentieth-century U.S. anthropology. George Stocking had also identified limitations in Boas' anti-racism.

> Given the atmospheric pervasiveness of the idea of European racial superiority, it is hardly surprising that Boas wrote as a skeptic of received belief rather than as a staunch advocate of racial equipotentiality. Despite his basic liberal humanitarian outlook, he was a white-skinned European writing for other white-skinned Europeans at the turn of the century, and he was a physical anthropologist to boot. (1968, 189)

Stocking insisted on a historicist approach that attributed those limitations to the contemporary intellectual climate of racial thought, locating Boas on its progressive edge. There is, of course, much merit to such a perspective, but Stocking left the impression of decided scientific progress in which Boasians and their successors appeared to have largely left racism behind as the atavistic remnant of nineteenth-century science and politics. Willis questioned such a progressive narrative, refiguring Boasian liberalism as a departure from the biological determinism of scientific racism that nonetheless *maintained* and *rearticulated* anthropology as a white-dominant project implicated in subordinating peoples of color and white supremacy, at home and abroad, in new forms appropriate to changing conditions. Only with a thoroughgoing and painful confrontation with its racial past and present could anthropology aspire to a different future. This was the fundamental challenge he posed to the discipline.

U.S. anthropologists, then as today, often faced political changes to the discipline with the comfort of the conviction that the Boasians had left a progressive legacy of anti-racism. Morton Fried, a close friend and ally of Willis, self-consciously struggled to come to terms with the implications of the 1960s critiques in his overview of the discipline *The Study of Anthropology* (1972).[18] It is a text of its times, full of angst concerning the enduring relevance of anthropology in light of the crisis it, and U.S. society, faced. Yet Fried could reassure his readers: "Resisting the tendency to succumb to despair, it can be noted that whatever its liberal, bourgeois origins . . . anthropology has made contributions to enlightenment that may help produce a better world. No matter how obscured at present, it has been this discipline above all others that has made intellectual nonsense of racism" (1972, 54). Anti-racism was an anchor of anthropology's self-identity. Perhaps Willis' effort to expose in polemical terms the "skeletons in the anthropological closet"—its historic and enduring complicity with white domination—derived in part from his encounters with such disciplinary self-satisfaction with regards to racism, even among his closest allies.

Like Willis, Diane Lewis reexamined the relationship between anthropology and racism from a perspective informed by Black Studies and anti-colonial movements. Lewis (1931–2015) was born and raised in Los Angeles, completing a BA and an MA in anthropology from UCLA. She received a PhD from Cornell University in 1962, conducting fieldwork in Malaya (Malaysia). She was the third African American woman to earn a doctorate in anthropology (Bolles 2001, 31). Lewis joined the faculty at San Francisco State University (SFSU) in 1962. In an interview with a student a few years before her death, Lewis noted that it was not her fieldwork experiences in Southeast Asia that led her to write "Anthropology and Colonialism" but, rather, the challenges posed by the Black and Ethnic Studies movements. In 1968–1969, the Black Student Union and Third World Liberation Front led a strike at SFSU that endured nearly five months, the longest campus strike in U.S. history (Biondi 2012, 43–78). According to Lewis,

> Black students and other people of color were demanding that courses be relevant and help them cope with their own lives and bring about change in society. And this was the Ethnic Studies Movement where they were demanding courses more—first of all that were fair and secondly that represented their interests and their lives. And so I was teaching my course on the Peoples and Cultures of Malaysia . . . and the students came in, overturned chairs and demanded to know how this was relevant to their lives and experience. And that was what led to my rethinking of my professional goals as a teacher and in terms of research, because I couldn't see that it was that relevant. Then I began to question the whole process of what happens when you go in the field as a representa-

tive of the dominating culture, colonizing culture and how that whole process unfolds.[19]

In this period, Lewis participated in the political emergence of anthropologists of color within the AAA. She was a presenter at an experimental session on the Black curriculum in anthropology at the 1968 meeting and at a symposium on racism and ethnocentrism in the discipline in 1969 (Harrison 1987). She was also a member of the AAA Committee on Minorities in Anthropology. When she published "Anthropology and Colonialism" (1973), Lewis was a visiting professor at the University of California, Santa Cruz, where she soon took a full-time position to participate in an experimental college for non-traditional students led by Herman Blake, a sociologist who had co-written a book with Black Panther leader Huey Newton.[20]

In her prior dissertation fieldwork in the newly independent Malaya Federation, Lewis focused on the persistence of matrilineal customs of a Malay village in the face of sociocultural change and acculturative pressures from Islamic law and the state (Lewis 1962). This was articulated within a theoretical model inspired by Julian Steward, Morton Fried, and Alfred Kroeber emphasizing ecological adaptation and environmental organization at the core of cultural dynamics. Although we can see the seeds of her later feminist and anti-colonial positions in her concern with gender dynamics, political economy, and native cultural persistence/resistance, Lewis' dissertation fit a conventional anthropological paradigm of village-based study of sociocultural organization and acculturation. The larger politics of British colonialism, the transition to independence, and the insurgent war led by the communist party in Malaya remained in the backdrop. The contrast between her dissertation and "Anthropology and Colonialism" (1973), her first full-length publication since her graduate work, is striking. Lewis subsequently focused largely on race and gender in the U.S. from a Black feminist perspective, publishing on the Black family and gender roles (1975; 1977),[21] women, race, and prisons (1982; Bresler and Lewis 1983), and gender, race, and HIV (e.g., Lewis and Watters 1989).

If Willis sought to expose the racial skeletons in the anthropological closet and the complicity between anthropology and imperialism/colonialism, Lewis examined the "unacknowledged effect of colonialism on anthropology" (1973, 601). The question of whether anthropologists were direct agents of colonial rule was less important than coming to terms with anthropology as a field of knowledge production made possible by colonialism. The crucial issues involved: (1) the effects of colonialism on anthropological practice and theory and (2) the ways anthropology ignored the effects of colonialism on the people anthropologists studied, and thus on anthropology itself. This approach facilitated a greater degree of nuance than allowed by Willis' functionalist vocabulary of anthropology as an "instrument of white rule" (Willis 1972, 123) that served the "needs" (137) of imperialism. Lewis remarked:

> Undoubtedly most anthropologists were appalled by the colonial relationship and consciously rejected it. Therein lies the paradox; for no matter how great the anthropologist's aversion to the colonial system, he was, as a fieldworker, unable to function outside of it. It was as impossible from him as for other Europeans to remain in a colony without participating in the power and privileges of the dominant group. (1973, 583)

By virtue of being identified with the colonial power, the anthropologist occupied a position of superiority over colonized peoples, which provided access to subject peoples, who often affirmed that superiority. Even anthropologists who sought reform rarely questioned their position or the structure that made it possible. Structural affiliation with dominant political interests influenced anthropologists, "apparently unconsciously, to justifying the prevailing colonial system." Bringing this issue home, Lewis drew an analogy to "the somewhat ambiguous position of many liberals in our own society, who work to reform a situation from which they derive definite benefits" (583).

Lewis identified a tendency "for anthropologists who overtly fought racism at the same time to perpetuate formulations, attitudes, and behaviors which fostered it" (583). Here, she did not discuss racism in terms of a set of beliefs about biological differences but rather in terms of the culture concept. Drawing on the anti-colonial writer Albert Memmi (1967), she found anthropological corollaries to Memmi's three pillars of colonial racism: (1) the gulf posited between the cultures of the colonizer and colonized; (2) the exploitation of that gulf by the colonizer; (3) the reification of that gulf as determinative of the conditions of the colonized. Anthropologists documented cultural differences in ways that contributed to a sense of radical alterity between Western and non-Western cultures. They exploited these differences in pursuing careers as anthropologists. This was, Lewis implied, a structural issue as the discipline persistently privileged theory construction and professional advancement over the remuneration of knowledge to peoples studied or assistance to those peoples; thus the low esteem of applied anthropology. Moreover, the fieldwork experience often entailed the romanticization and exoticization of the primitive as a psychological means for anthropologists to cope with alienation from their own society (1973, 584). Anthropologists might be peculiar, unwitting, and even unwilling colonists, but colonists they were.

Like Willis, Lewis saw that the culture concept did not simply provide an alternative to racism understood as an ideology of biological determinism but could be deployed in ways that mirrored its objectifications. "It may be instructive to consider the anthropologist's reification of culture as similar in function to the racist's utilization of biological determinism to explain historical and social differences" (584). The attribution of behavior to culture, typically viewed as highly resistant to change, could not only reinforce a sense of absolute difference between dominant and subordinate peoples but, as with the culture of poverty thesis, could attribute the structural position of subalterns to their culture. Further, Lewis identified a certain hypocrisy in the anthropologist's idealization of primitive life as traditional, communal, and culturally determined, an idealization that was the inverse of the typical (liberal) stance of "personal freedom and self-determination he insists upon for himself" (584). The culture concept, deployed in these ways, ignored the structural relationships shaping the lives of subordinate peoples—whether colonized Africans or ghettoized African Americans.

> Anthropologists, then, have developed a conceptualization, *culture*, which in its analytical and theoretical usages seems dangerously reflective of the viewpoint of colonial racism. Both the anthropologist and the colonizer find in the cultural uniqueness of a people justification for perpetuating things as they are. The importance of the culture concept may help explain why anthropologists accepted so uncritically the colonial system in which they operated. (585)

These insights anticipated more elaborate critical accounts of culture as a successor to race developed by a later generation of anthropologists (e.g., Abu-Lughod 1991; Trouillot 2003; Visweswaran 1998).[22]

Central to Lewis' account of racism, anthropology, and colonialism was a critical concern with anthropology as a project of the "'objective' outsider" (1973, 585). Having identified the anthropologist's outsider status as a position of dominant privilege, she exposed the presumptions of objectivity associated with it. Drawing on arguments from the sociology of knowledge, she questioned the possibility of an impersonal, objective view of social reality and identified the consequences of embracing objectivity as the necessary stance of anthropology. Such a stance assumed the existence of a single, universal reality accessible to the outside observer and thus denied a multidimensional view of reality. It also objectified the people being studied, requiring alienation from the "other" and depersonalizing those studied. Anthropological objectification mirrored the dehumanization of colonialism and was a key source of disaffection on the part of nonwhites studied by anthropologists (585–586).

Such disaffection, as noted earlier, was a cause for considerable concern within the discipline. Margaret Mead, for one, interpreted it as a misdirected attack on anthropology, suggesting that colonized and oppressed peoples were being manipulated to turn against anthropologists who befriended them (Mead 1972, 23). Lewis called these remarks "insensitive" (1972, 48) and contested the implication that the critique of anthropology was the product of ideological manipulation. "Rather it represents a spontaneous grass-roots movement in which people are beginning to define their own reality. They are no longer content to have an anthropologist or sociologist do it for them" (48–49). Mead's position reflected the sort of liberal paternalism that the traditional subjects of anthropology, as well as students of color, rejected. As a counterpoint to the fictions of objective research conducted as if the anthropologist could produce a firewall between science and politics, Lewis advocated an "insider" anthropology oriented toward social transformation. From her anti-colonial perspective informed by a Black Studies critique, the crisis in anthropology represented an opportunity for a revitalized anthropology. I will return to these positions later but turn now to the most comprehensive effort to explicitly bring together Black Studies and anthropology, the work of Charles Valentine.

Charles Valentine (1929–1990) was a white anthropologist who came to research in African American communities via participation in the civil rights movement with his intellectual-political partner and wife, African American anthropologist Bettylou Valentine. Charles received his PhD from the University of Pennsylvania in 1958, conducting fieldwork in New Guinea. There is little hint of the self-described "radical" bent of Valentine's later writings in his early work; in fact, he sent the Australian colonial government of New Guinea reports on the cargo cult he studied (Jebens 2010, 38). By Valentine's own account, his political transformation from "left-liberalism" to "revolutionary radicalism" occurred through engagements with the civil rights and Black Power movements (1972, 1). He married Bettylou while teaching at the University of Washington in the early 1960s. He and Bettylou were active members of the Seattle chapter of the Congress for Racial Equality (CORE), and Charles published a report for CORE on the city's movement for employment equality (1964). Charles took a position at Washington University in St. Louis in 1965, but within a few years he and Bettylou had embarked on a long-term ethnographic project on life and oppression in an urban community they called Blackston (in Brooklyn) that ultimately involved five years of residence.

As their fieldwork began, Charles Valentine published the work for which he is best known, *Culture and Poverty: Critique and Counter-Proposals* (1968), an extended critique of the culture of poverty thesis first articulated by Oscar Lewis and adapted by others to imply that a minority group's cultural inheritance was a significant contributor to their inability to escape poverty. The Valentines further developed critical accounts of social science representations of African Americans (one article was sarcastically titled "It's Either Brain Damage or No Father" [Valentine 1971]), promoted activist scholarship, and contributed to theories of African American culture (Valentine and Valentine 1970; 1975). These agendas came together in *Black Studies and Anthropology* (Valentine 1972), a little-known work that, to my knowledge, was the only extensive attempt of the era by an anthropologist to wrestle with the potential impact of Black Studies on anthropology. Charles is listed as the sole author (and thus in my discussion of the text I refer only to him) but it is important to keep in mind that he acknowledged intensive intellectual collaboration with Bettylou as central to this and other works published under his name alone. Bettylou Valentine would go on to publish an ethnography of Blackston (1978) as sole author.

Whereas Willis and Lewis provided wide-ranging critical accounts of anthropology, particularly with regard to white domination of peoples of color, Valentine focused his critical analysis on the relationship between anthropology and U.S. African Americans. Valentine treated Black Studies as an intellectual project that provided a crucial counterpoint to the ideologically loaded presumption of separating knowledge and politics typical of the academy. Although institutionalized Black Studies in white universities was an emergent academic field, he recognized that forerunners such as Du Bois had long exposed the distortions and biases of mainstream scholarly currents dominated by white intellectuals. Recognition of the necessary relationship between knowledge and power had produced efforts to create alternative perspectives promoting a positive Black identity. Black Studies also produced an expansive understanding of racism as "a systemic condition of the society as a whole and its dominant culture" (1972, 4).

Much of *Black Studies and Anthropology* was devoted to a critical account of representations of African American culture in the social sciences. According to Valentine, mainstream scholarship over several decades had "denied the existence of an Afro-American cultural heritage" except as an incomplete imitation of white culture shaped by lower-class existence (9). An influential and representative text promoting this view was Swedish economist Gunnar Myrdal's *An American Dilemma* (1944). His account owed a major debt to the work of sociologist E. Franklin Frazier on the supposed deficiencies of African American kinship. In the 1960s such portrayals of Black culture remained popular and were retooled for the Johnson administration's war on poverty in what became known as the Moynihan Report. Therein sociologist Daniel Patrick Moynihan, serving as assistant secretary of labor, identified the so-called instability of the Black family as a prime determinant of Black inequality in U.S. society and argued that U.S. social policy must work not only to eliminate white racism but to transform African American culture. The report thereby reinforced scientifically certified stereotypes of Black culture—especially the "matriarchal" Black family—as the inverse of idealized assumptions of white middle-class norms.[23]

Valentine also briefly critiqued a social science tendency to analyze "the Black experience as analogous to the European immigrant story in America" (1972, 10). Like Herskovits (1941), Valentine argued that peoples of African descent, unlike European immigrants, were denied a valid cultural heritage and identity. He further elaborated that a political economy of racial distinction denied African Americans and Native Americans opportunities afforded European immigrants and even Asian immigrants.

> Only native American Indians have to live today under conquerors who will not return their stolen land, and only Afro-Americans must exist under domination by the grandchildren of slavers who remain reluctant to relinquish the privileges of the master's status. Euro-Americans and Asian-Americans are granted an honorable, if sometimes difficult, transition from separate cultural identification to acceptance in the United States mainstream. Native Americans and Afro-Americans are granted no effective, living cultural identity of their own, while at the same time they remain excluded from the mainstream. (1972, 10)

Although Valentine did not dwell on the point or recognize the importance of the immigrant analogy within Boasian thought on racism, he underscored key flaws in the effort to model Black inclusion on European assimilation. Any paradigm of ethnic comparison that did not confront the specific histories, forms of racialization, and political economies of inclusion/exclusion was likely to reproduce normative middle-class white standards of evaluating difference.[24] This problem was endemic to class-based models of interpreting African American culture.

Valentine argued that contemporary anthropology and related fields reproduced such standards of evaluation. At least partially in response to Black self-assertion and calls for positive appraisals of African American culture, studies of urban Black culture began to proliferate (Abrahams 1964; 1970; Hannerz 1969; Keil 1966). Valentine provided detailed accounts of how these studies, despite their authors' intentions, reproduced distorted representations of urban Black culture that emphasized its essential difference and ultimately deviance from white culture (1972, 15–20). He also asserted that this scholarship tended to (mis)represent the oppression of Blacks as a product of white "cultural misunderstanding" (17) rather than systemic racism structuring Black lives.

As a contrast, Valentine identified a "minorstream" (29) current in anthropology associated with the work of Zora Neale Hurston and Melville Herskovits that laid the potential basis for respectful, substantive accounts of African American culture. Valentine nonetheless provided an ambivalent evaluation of Herskovits and his successors. On the one hand, he lauded the work of Herskovits as a crucial point of reference for the theorization and documentation of New World Afro-American cultures that provided a crucial counterpoint to mainstream negations and denigrations of African American culture. On the other hand, he cast work in the Herskovitsian vein as a weak version of Black vindicationist scholarship (45), identifying the focus on cultural survivals as narrow compared to the work of Du Bois, whose theorization of Black culture and "double consciousness" in relation to the political economy of racism provided crucial orientations for Black Studies (30–31).

Drawing from that perspective, Valentine advocated a model of Black biculturalism linked to a critical analysis of the political economy of racism and Black subordination in a white-dominant social order. He used the work of Bryce-Laporte (1970) on the "contraculture" of West Indians in Panama and the work of Polgar (1960) on Native American "biculturation"—concepts resonant with Du Bois' discussion of double consciousness—to identify forms of "double cultural competence" developed by African Americans. African Americans were bicultural "in the sense that people regularly draw upon both an ethnically distinctive repertoire of beliefs and customs and, at the same time, make use of behavioral patterns from the Euro-American cultural mainstream"

(Valentine 1972, 33). The two patterns existed in dynamic tension in the context of white-dominant institutions that not only stigmatized Black cultural patterns but also worked "to inculcate mainstream goals and ideas without imparting the skills or providing the opportunities needed to make these goals realizable" (34). Structural constraints, rather than failure to assimilate, drove the (re)production of inequality. African Americans creatively developed a cultural repertoire to survive and resist marginalization yet were pressured to internalize norms of the Euro-American mainstream. For Valentine, scholarship that focused solely on Black "difference" misrepresented the active involvement of African Americans in mainstream white culture and misrecognized the marginalization produced by the dominant system.

Valentine's discussion of biculturalism reflects his theorization of cultural and racial discrimination as intimately bound up with, but not reducible to, class dynamics. Core to his objection to the dominant social science tradition was not only that it represented Black culture as deviant but that it treated racial and ethnic discrimination as a by-product of class distinctions. Valentine elaborated a complex account of the integral but non-reductive relationships between racism, ethnic prejudice, and class dynamics. He identified "a system of triple inequality, comprehending but also transcending class stratification" in U.S. society (13).

> The material condition and structural position of generally recognized groups are reflected in a threefold system of invidious comparisons that are part of mainstream Euro-American culture. The conventional wisdom of beliefs and values in the dominant folk culture rationalizes the collective fate of Afro-Americans and others on the grounds of physical group membership, plus the ethnic basis of cultural difference, as well as by reference to class criteria. The oppressive immobility of groups like Blacks is thereby maintained and perpetuated throughout the system as a whole, from its material base through its stratified institutional structure to its ruling ideological patterns. (13)

Valentine drew on Marxian distinctions between material base, institutional structure, and ideology in a total system, yet refused to designate race and ethnicity as effects of class. Practices of racial and ethnic stratification and discrimination "from education to the labor market" inhibited class mobility (13). The ideological justifications of racial, ethnic, and class inequality reflected and reinforced the practices of class, ethnic, and racial stratification. These forms of discrimination operated together (independently yet conjointly) in the structural subordination of African Americans and other peoples of color, and in the rationalizations for that subordination.

In refusing to reduce race either to class or ethnicity, Valentine highlighted the enduring importance of racial distinction in the post–civil rights era. He also embraced a structural view of the concept of racism promoted by intellectuals associated with Black Power. "Afro-American studies have had to confront the fact that Euro-American racism is . . . a systemic condition of the society as a whole and its dominant culture." Revolutionary thinkers from Frantz Fanon to Black Panther activist Eldridge Cleaver had "shown that racism is not an individual problem or a psychological aberration but systematic oppression in all spheres of social relations, inherent in all aspects of the social system" (4). From this perspective, racism served as a generalized label for modes of white domination that relied conjointly on stratification of non-whites along lines of class, physical difference, and culture. This theoretical perspective implied a potential agenda for an anthropology of structural racism beyond the confines of "caste" segregation.

Valentine, Lewis, and Willis all developed critical perspectives on anthropology, working with an understanding of racism as a social structural phenomenon rather than merely an ideology of biological difference. They challenged anthropology's self-image as a progressive, anti-racist discipline and, in so doing, cast into question the uses and abuses of its fundamental concept of culture. Willis and Lewis found that notions of cultural difference and relativism could be used to delineate essential differences that could in turn be used to "explain" the condition of subordinate, non-white peoples in lieu of providing analysis of white-controlled systems of domination. Valentine provided detailed expositions of how the social sciences, including anthropology, produced distorted representations of African American culture along these lines. These arguments revealed that the ideological projections of white domination took on forms beyond assertions of biological superiority and could be found even in cultural representations explicitly framed as non-pejorative and anti-racist.

In this work, the term racism itself took on expanded meanings beyond the belief in biological determinism and became linked not only to representations of cultural difference but also to wider structures of social inequality and domination. Valentine, in particular, promoted a non-reductive account of racial and ethnic discrimination as structural features of U.S. society and its class formations, and revealed how social science analytics of class could misrepresent the dynamics of ethnic and racial discrimination. In parallel with Willis' subversion of the discipline's story of progressive racial history, he followed the Black Studies identification of racism as a structural and cultural feature of the U.S. as a counterpoint to idealized figurations of "America" as an open, democratic, egalitarian, and assimilative society with a racial dilemma.

The Redemption of Anthropology?

Given the complicity of anthropology with white supremacy, colonialism, and imperialism, was there any hope for the discipline? Lewis posed the issue in this way:

> Is anthropology a truly universal discipline? Can it be utilized for explicit self-study and self-knowledge by all peoples? Is it able to meet the challenge of oppressed peoples who seek solutions to their problems? Or is it useful only in providing information about powerless peoples to those in power? Is it to remain an adjunct to Western exploitation and manipulation of Third World peoples? (1973, 590)

Lewis' hope for the discipline rested in the prospects of cultivating an "insider anthropology" with an activist commitment to radical social change. "I feel, along with a number of other Third World anthropologists, that the time has come for the study of culture from the inside, *by* the insider, as a dominant approach in the discipline" (1973, 588). Her self-identification as a Third World anthropologist reflected the distinction she made between Euro-American (white) and Third World anthropologists, and likely derived from the position embraced by radical Black and Chicano intellectuals that their communities were subjects of internal colonialism.[25]

Lewis identified multiple virtues of an insider perspective as a corrective to the fallacies and estrangement of an objectifying objective approach. Anthropologists studying their own oppressed group would generate different kinds of "perspectivistic" knowledge. They could produce work written for the people studied, in which those people could see something of their own experience reflected. Insider anthropologists would be more likely to share activist commitments with the group studied and more likely to be held accountable for their work. For Lewis, like others promoting activist anthropology, an activist orientation committed to radical social transformation necessarily involved "a radical change in the way in which problems are selected and formulated . . . so that the people themselves assume an important role in determining problems to be studied in terms of their own interests as they perceive them" (589). New theories of social change, in turn, could be generated out of efforts to confront social problems. In sum, an activist, insider, perspectivistic anthropology could help create a more egalitarian anthropology.

Lewis did not assume that insider anthropology would provide a cure-all for the discipline. She acknowledged that insider status did not guarantee that anthropologists would avoid perpetuating the oppression of those they studied. She also noted that "outsider" and "insider" perspectives were both valid and potentially complementary. Still, as the accompanying comments on her article reflected, her conceptualization of insider anthropology raised a number of thorny problems. For example, how was "insider" to be defined? (Was, say, the African American anthropologist working in Nigeria an insider? Was a Yoruba anthropologist studying Igbo people?) Should the governments of Third World nation-states be in control of the who and what of research, as Lewis suggested? Might they repress knowledge of their oppression of their own people? To the first question, Lewis replied that insider status depended on context, the identification of the anthropologist in question, and its acceptance by the people studied; it could depend upon ideological and class as well as ethnic considerations (599). This was a sensible response but left unexamined how U.S. anthropologists of color might, like their white counterparts, unwittingly participate in U.S. imperialism. On the second set of queries, she suggested that Western intellectuals were not in a position to understand the struggles of Third World countries (599). This response evaded the issue of which segments of a society a national government represented and the problems of conflating the struggles of people of color for self-determination in the U.S. with Third World state nationalism.

Lewis ultimately conceded that perspectival, activist, and insider approaches did not, in and of themselves, produce the theoretical and practical foundation for a revitalized and radical anthropology capable of comprehending and intervening in structures of power. She was, however, adamant that such approaches were necessary for the building of such a foundation. Her basic point was straightforward: if anthropology was the social science in which the West studied the non-West and whites studied non-whites, any significant transformation of the discipline would require that its traditional objects become active subjects of knowledge about themselves and the structures of power that oppressed them. She retained a faith that anthropology could become a site of such subject formation. Responding to the position that no liberatory anthropology was possible under the power relationships that conditioned its existence, she countered: "It is *because* of worldwide exploitation and oppression that a radical, activist social science is needed and is emerging. In these circumstances, should we sit silently and helplessly or attempt to contribute in some way to the revolution in consciousness which is making change possible?" (600).

Valentine also retained a faith in the radical possibilities of social science, ending *Black Studies and Anthropology* by identifying the contributions anthropology could make to Black Studies. What anthropology had to offer boiled down to the rather conventional suggestion that the hallmark anthropological method—intensive participant observation—could be usefully applied in African American communities. Key subjects of ethnographic inquiry included: documenting the strengths of African American culture; mapping the diversity of Black communities; analyzing dominant institutions from the standpoint of oppressed peoples; and studying Black liberation movements. Valentine's prescriptions followed from his critiques of mainstream scholarship and his attention to the political economy of racial-ethnic domination. Oppressed African American communities could not be studied in isolation from the structures of power that produced them; analysis of the operation of dominant institutions within those communities could ultimately contribute to discovering "the essentials of some basic social mechanisms which create and perpetuate ethnic inequality" (1972, 41).[26] Valentine hoped that this in turn could help in identifying and theorizing the entire range of ethnic hierarchization and stratification in the U.S.

He also reflected on the necessary subjective transformations of the researcher studying Black communities. He did not assume such researchers would be whites, but much of his discussion focused on white fieldworkers. He argued from his own experiences that white researchers could gain the trust of aggrieved communities. While Black communities were understandably leery of outside researchers, worries of "reverse racism" preventing whites access to African American communities appear "to owe much to fantasies of projections from overworked Euro-American imaginations" (38). The challenge for fieldworkers, rather, lay in the classical anthropological problem of overcoming biases. For middle-class researchers, white or Black, bourgeois preconceptions could prevent full participation in impoverished Black communities. For whites, recognition and overcoming of one's own ethnic and racial prejudices was of course essential. Beyond that, however, Valentine took the more provocative position that fieldwork in Black communities also required "a healthy degree of alienation from Euro-American culture" (39). Earlier he noted that "for Euro-Americans to free themselves" from ethnic biases they must "recognize, renounce, and repudiate their own present culture as racist through and through in its systemic exploitativeness and oppression" (22). Valentine's underlying perspective, drawn from radical Black scholarship, was that anti-Black racism was an integral feature of white or Euro-American culture. From this perspective, there could be no recourse, a la Benedict, to "American" values as a basis for racial equality and liberation.

But how was the repudiation of Euro-American culture to be achieved? Valentine admitted he did not have a clear answer. In initially raising the issue he noted: "It may well be that to do this effectively and thoroughly requires a revolutionary ideology, but such considerations are beyond the scope of this essay" (22). He later highlighted the potentially transformative affects of politically conscious participant observation:

> It is not that one must be a complete philosophical dropout or a committed political revolutionary to carry out insightful, valid participant research within underclass communities. The desirable social and cultural disjunction is neither a process which must be complete before meaningful fieldwork is possible nor an event which happens all at once. To begin participatory work in a serious way is an initial disconnection in itself. Scholars who carry through the process thus begun will be exposed to ample and rich concrete experience which can continue to free them from preconceptions and open the way to further insights in whatever directions that experience may lead. (39)

Valentine asserted that it was via his own fieldwork experience that he was able to attain an appreciation of both counter-hegemonic precepts of Black culture and the crushing structural oppression of Black communities.

Did Valentine reproduce the classical anthropological, liberal faith that the reasoned individual could shed the shackles of tradition through becoming familiar with the other? On the one hand, his affirmation of the subjective transformation produced by fieldwork echoed that sentiment. From this orientation, the problem with most anthropology of African America was the failure of white anthropologists to develop the kind of intensive, long-term, experiential participation in Black communities required for truly valid research. Valentine also had faith that individual scholars could responsibly navigate the competing demands of commitments to the people among whom they worked and the institutional politics of funders and the academy. On the other hand, Valentine also understood the problems associated with research on African Americans as theoretical, political, and ideological. Counter-hegemonic anthropological research required a philosophical and political perspective oriented toward understanding anti-Black racism as a structural phenomenon unconsciously instantiated in white precepts about the world. From this perspective, participant observation alone could not provide the estrangement from Euro-American culture necessary to apprehend anti-Black racism.

Ultimately, Valentine's reflections on anthropological method, estrangement, and racism left unanswered questions. Was it possible for the U.S. anthropologist, particularly the white anthropologist, to fully recognize, repudiate, and renounce Euro American culture? Was such repudiation a condition of productive research and struggle with African American communities, an outcome of such research and struggle, or both? Were white anthropologists really needed to study African-American communities? If Valentine did not have all the answers, his sensibility that anthropology needed to both identify and subvert white supremacy as endemic to (Euro) American culture and society— and by implication U.S. anthropology itself—offers an enduring provocation to the discipline.

Willis was less sanguine than either Lewis or Valentine in the prospects for anthropology. For him, the reformism of anthropological liberalism ran against the aspirations of the colored world. Its focus on individual freedom opposed the strong governments decolonial nationalists aspired to build (1972, 142). Its gradualism opposed revolutionary aspirations and the possibility of violence as a tool of liberation. "Since the vast majority of anthropologists are white people, they are especially opposed to colored peoples using violence to overthrow white rule" (143). Meanwhile, they largely ignored the violence of white rule. Although these judgments were harsh ones, recall how readily anthropologists could adhere to paradigms oriented more to alleviating racial "conflict" than understanding and subverting racial oppression. Willis' optimism lay in the prospects of the end of imperialism, which he called a "probable contingency" (146). Since anthropology was historically based on the subordination of colored people in white-dominant imperialism, the end of white-dominant imperialism would mean the end of anthropology.

However, Willis' sense of the end of imperialism relied both on a dubious faith in processes of national consolidation and economic modernization in the Global South and an underestimation of enduring white capitalist imperial power and coloniality. He did, however, qualify his position in ways that suggested a future for anthropology.

> There is still some hope for anthropology. The present disarray among colored peoples and the still immense power of the imperialists means that the end of imperialism is only a probability. Even if the end of imperialism is certain it will not end quickly nor at the same time around the world. Even if imperialism does not end everywhere, new conditions in the colored world mean that anthropologists cannot proceed in the old way. It is time for anthropologists to make drastic changes. If they make these changes, then perhaps a new kind of anthropology can survive in a new world in which colored peoples enjoy bona fide freedom and equality. (146)

In a final section Willis offered a few brief suggestions on how anthropologists might contribute to the making of that world. He urged them to continue to expose skeletons in the disciplinary past, develop theories of sociocultural change, and engage in new forms of research praxis, focusing on urban ethnography in the U.S. Like Valentine, he suggested the "ghetto" was a crucial crucible for creating a new relationship between anthropology and the oppressed and, like Lewis, he insisted that to adapt to the times anthropology must cultivate activist-oriented anthropologists of color. "The ghetto will not tolerate only white anthropologists" (147). Creating cohorts of anthropologists of color would reduce their isolation and potentially contribute to a "separate force in anthropology, distinctive in personality, race, and especially politics." Willis embraced white participation in a new urban ethnography, though with ambivalence about the prospects.

> Perhaps they (anthropologists of color) and white anthropologists working in the ghetto can achieve a new identity in political ideology that can overcome the divisiveness of the uniform of color. But white anthropologists must make the first moves, and one such move is to refrain from any kind of demand for ideological subservience. Perhaps even then, this new kind of identity is a pipe dream. (147)

Willis was not at all confident that a white-dominated discipline produced to study non-whites could move beyond its role in securing liberal white rule. Why should he have been?

Conclusion: Confronting the (White) Americanism of U.S. Anthropology

In December 1973, Eric Wolf wrote a new introduction to *Anthropology* (1974), an overview of U.S. anthropology from World War II up to 1964, when the book was first published. In 1964 Wolf had expressed the hopeful view that the discipline could both take the point of view of a "world culture, struggling to be born" (1974, 96) and contribute to its birth. Nearly a decade later, he identified that dream as a false illusion shattered by repudiations of American colonialist hegemony.

> Suddenly an unrequited past—a past of Indian wars, slavery, of colonial and neo-colonial expansion—rose up to plague the living. A host of forgotten victims and dissenters from the American Dream pressed demands which dispelled the easy-going assumptions of a universal societal consensus. It became clear that Americans were linked to one another not only by tacit agreements to "split the difference," but by feuds and hatreds of long standing for which no wergild had as yet been paid. At the same time, in the fiery light cast by burning villages and towns in Southeast Asia, the American past and present seemed no longer so privileged, so singular, so splendid in isolation. (1974, x–xi)

Suddenly, the post-war image of a science of man promoting freedom and progress now appeared as something else altogether: "a reflex of a falsely confident movement of American society towards global hegemony, of an onward march towards 'modernization' on the American model" (xi). Challenges to U.S. hegemony abroad and the American Dream at home forced a realization of the latent Americanism of U.S. anthropology and exposed its pretensions to universalism. Wolf himself played a key role in this reckoning through his opposition to U.S. imperial warfare and anthropological complicity with it (Jorgensen and Wolf 1970), through his theorization of peasant revolution (Wolf 1969b), and through his historical reflections on the political economic determinants of U.S. anthropology (1969a). Looking to the future in his preface, written while working on his monumental *Europe and the People Without History* (1982), Wolf articulated the approach for which he is now most famous: "Having long seen cultures and societies as isolated and distinctive, we must learn to see them in interchange and cultural synthesis. We have stressed order, equilibrium, negative feedback; now we must come to terms with opposition, contradiction, conflict, rebellion, and revolution" (1974, xii).

Wolf's rendering of the implications of a crisis in American hegemony for American anthropology was eloquent and powerful, yet, read by the illumination of the critics I have considered here, it also reproduced one of the problems he sought to confront—the problem of a particular perspective imposing itself as a universal. He effectively wrote an unmarked account of white America from the perspective of a white American. How else does it make sense that the "living" would be plagued by victims and dissenters of the American Dream and the republic's unrequited past of slavery, genocide, and colonialism? Had all Americans shared an easy sense of collective consensus? That past was, among other things, a past of racial distinction, division, and domination of whites over peoples of color. Wolf of course knew this, and he did not imply that only whites were Americans. Nonetheless, as author he narrated an account of white American reactions to social division without acknowledging that perspective. The temporality of the account reinforced this perspective. If for white Americans the uprisings appeared as the return of the dead to plague the living in a present that was supposed to transcend the past (exactly the type of history Wolf acknowledged as in question), people of color struggling to overturn their subordination in U.S. society continued to live their racial oppression. As Baldwin insisted in his dialogue with Mead, the past was present.

The anthropologists at the heart of this chapter demanded that anthropology reckon directly with the problem of the color line in the discipline and in the world. Their contributions to the broader critical movement in the discipline relied on a racial vocabulary to articulate a key modality of power: the power of racial distinctions and racism within colonialism, imperialism, and white-dominant nations, particularly the U.S. As I have shown at several points in this book, the play of marked and unmarked categories, particularly "American," haunts anthropological engagements with race. In part, this reflects the power of racial distinctions and the centrality of whiteness within the terms of U.S. identity formation; "America" readily equates to white (Perry 2001; Hill 2008). Even in efforts to render an account of division within the U.S. social body, as in the passage from Wolf, the tacit equation between white and America readily persisted. A significant achievement of the Black Power and Black Studies movement was to call attention to the power of terminology. No less important than the embrace of the term "Black" was the relentless identification of "white" with a system of domination. Take the use of terms like "white supremacy" by Lewis or "white rule" by Willis. White supremacy can index more than fanatical racism associated with hate groups. As De Genova asserts, the term

> has the advantage of establishing plainly that what we are considering is a so-cial and political order of domination and subordination that systematically generates and upholds inequalities of wealth, power, and prestige by privileg-ing racialized whiteness over and above all other categories of "racial" identity. (2007, 249)

Willis was particularly invested in the use of race-color terminology as a direct reflection of his conviction of the importance of white domination to an un-derstanding of anthropology—past, present and future—when viewed from perspectives of racial subordination. As his own radicalization embodied, the confrontational stance adopted by the Black Power and Black Studies move-ments enabled the public naming of white domination in a liberal discipline.

Willis, Lewis, and Valentine suggested that if U.S. anthropology was to be-come what it claimed to be and other than what it had been, it would have to reckon with the color line within U.S. society, the world at large, and within the discipline. A critical account of the discipline's relationship to colonialism and imperialism was incomplete until it analyzed the relationship between the whiteness of U.S. anthropology and white domination in U.S. society and the world at large. The anthropologist was not, any more than the American, a universal subject. White anthropologists—the overwhelming majority in the discipline—had to confront their privileged subject position and the Euro-American culture that sustained it. Anthropologists of color would have to play a major role in redefining the methods, theories, and politics in any process of decolonizing anthropology. The version of the critical turn articulated by Willis, Lewis, and Valentine implied that any account of the modern world had to analyze racial and ethnic stratifications as political economic and ideologi-cal phenomena integral to it. It charged that in practice anthropology—the Western discipline charged with understanding its others as non-white, non-modern peoples—was itself a modern, largely white-dominant project that, de-spite its critiques of racism, participated in white supremacy. It thus suggested that any project to decolonize anthropology must reckon with anthropological contributions to American liberal anti-racism as a paradoxical project of racial inclusion that left the normalization of whiteness intact.

Conclusion

Anti-Racism, Liberalism, and Anthropology
in the Age of Trump

I BEGAN WORK on what became this book before the first election of Barack Obama, and I drafted much of the manuscript during the presidential campaign of 2016. The election of Obama was interpreted by many as an indication of the racial progress of the nation and a symbolic affirmation of its core values. Obama encouraged this interpretation in soaring rhetoric affirming his campaign as embodying the ideals of the republic and the legacy of the civil rights struggle. Some imagined Obama's victory as a sign the U.S. had entered a post-racial era. But the liberal hope associated with Obama was contested on several fronts. On the one hand, critical race activists and intellectuals called attention to the persistence of racism and imperialism as endemic to the country. Black Lives Matter protested police violence against African Americans, and the impunity repeatedly afforded its perpetrators. Black student organizing surged on college campuses in response to enduring marginalization and a rise in anti-Black hate speech. As I delved into the history of the long sixties, the resonances between contemporary movements and Black Power became evident. Black Power had, after all, emerged precisely at the height of the civil rights movement, forcefully articulating the inadequacy of anti-racist liberalism in dismantling white supremacy.

On the other hand, the political right fueled a politics of white racial resentment that has been one of its calling cards throughout the post-civil rights era. It bears remembering that Obama—like every other Democratic presidential candidate since Lyndon Baines Johnson—lost the white vote, and by margins similar to those in prior elections (Figure 5).

Figure 5 White voting behavior in U.S. presidential elections since 1968

Election Year	Republican		Democrat		Other Significant Candidate	
2016	Trump	58%	H. Clinton	37%		
2012	Romney	59%	Obama	39%		
2008	McCain	55%	Obama	43%		
2004	G. W. Bush	58%	Kerry	41%		
2000	G. W. Bush	55%	Gore	42%		
1996	Dole	46%	W. Clinton	44%	Perot	9%
1992	G. H. W. Bush	41%	W. Clinton	39%	Perot	21%
1988	G. H. W. Bush	60%	Dukakis	40%		
1984	Reagan	66%	Mondale	34%		
1980	Reagan	56%	Carter	36%	Anderson	8%
1976	Ford	52%	Carter	48%		
1972	Nixon	68%	McGovern	32%		
1968	Nixon	47%	Humphrey	38%	Wallace	15%

The source of the figures for 1968 and 1972 is http://www.gallup.com/poll/9457/election-polls-vote-groups-19681972.aspx. The source of the figures from 1976 to 2016 is https://ropercenter.cornell.edu/polls/us-elections/how-groups-voted/.

These figures[1] ignore variation in class, gender, sexuality, region, religion, and age among white voters and tell us nothing about the complex motivations of white voters in any particular election. But they have the virtue of highlighting something often either ignored or taken for granted in the parsing done in election analysis: for over fifty years a majority of U.S. whites have voted for the candidate of the political party most associated with the retrenchment of civil rights, gay rights, and gender equality, with anti-Black, anti-Muslim, anti-immigrant, and homophobic discourses, with the dismantling of the welfare state, with opposition to affirmative action, and with the expansion of the military state. From this perspective, the election of Trump fits a persistent pattern of white voting behavior along party lines.

Why, then, did the election of Trump come as such a shock to many of us on the liberal-left? I will admit it surprised me, even though I was writing a book critical of how liberal anti-racism had proven unable to fully face the realities of American racism and white supremacy. In a brief but probing reflection on anthropological reactions to the election, Jonathan Rosa and Yarimar Bonilla 2017) urge us to "deprovincialize" Trump and refuse the narrative that his election represents a form of exceptionalism, an aberrant process that threatens to undermine U.S. democracy. "On what grounds is this election a breach of justice versus a logical outcome of the forms of racial democracy and racial capitalism that are fundamental to the US nation-state project?" (202). When, they ask, did institutions such as public education, the military and security apparatus, and the criminal justice system transcend racism and coloniality? (204). To be sure, candidate and President Trump breached forms of public decorum and etiquette in ways that made even many Republican politicians wince: calling Mexican immigrants rapists; questioning the impartiality of a judge because he was Mexican-American; referring constantly to "the Blacks"; deriding Fox News interviewer Megyn Kelly by referring to menstruation; encouraging supporters to violently expel protesters—the list goes on. The audacity of his exclusionary programs—the border wall, the Muslim ban—appeared beyond the pale of normalized Islamophobia and xenophobia. His campaign encouraged expressions of jingoistic nativism, racial vitriol, and white supremacy many presumed were forever banished from public discourse. All this and more contributed to the sense of shock following his victory. But, as Rosa and Bonilla imply, that shock should serve as both an awakening and a call to self-reflection. Granted that Trump lost the popular vote, Clinton ran a horrible campaign, the Russians meddled, and the neoliberal policies pursued by successive administrations have failed almost everyone but the elite, we should nonetheless resist an exceptionalist interpretation of the Trump victory to ask what it teaches us about U.S. democracy and society. What does it say about the country? For those of us shocked or surprised by the rise of Trump, what does that say about us and our distorted imagination of the republic?

Rosa and Bonilla implicate anthropology in reproducing an intellectual and social climate of misrecognition of our U.S. reality. Rather than make the typical anthropological gesture—"more and better ethnography of X" (e.g., whites, politics, neoliberalism)—they urge anthropologists to unsettle the discipline. In particular they ask anthropologists to search our past for decolonizing precedents and to engage those fields—e.g., ethnic studies, Black studies, indigenous studies—that often provide a more critical purchase on the U.S. than the traditional disciplines. These calls resonate with what I have attempted to do in this history of anthropological thought on race and racism, a story of how an influential stream of largely white anthropologists helped cultivate an Americanist liberal anti-racism and how, in the 1960s, some anthropologists—most of color—sought to critique and move beyond it as part of wider efforts to reinvent the discipline. Each part of the story has, I hope, lessons for the present, within and beyond anthropology.

In the age of Trump, there is an enormous temptation to defend liberal anti-racism as the unfulfilled promise of America, to link the promotion of the values of racial freedom, equality, and justice to national identity, heritage, and culture, to reclaim the nation from a resurgence of overt white supremacist nationalism. My account of anthropological anti-racism brings to the fore some of the problems associated with that orientation. If the Boasian intervention is best known for its reconceptualization of race and culture and its attacks on scientific racism and racial determinism, the efforts by Boas and his students to imagine the overcoming of racism in the U.S. also brought to the fore questions of the composition of American nationality, the social character of racial prejudice and discrimination, and the relationship between racial consciousness and American culture. The Boasians sought to extend the application of liberal norms to European immigrants and non-whites, and to promote a future in which race would become irrelevant to citizenship and national belonging. They knew that abstract arguments about race and culture and the debunking of scientific racism were not enough to transform white racial consciousness and overcome racial discrimination. They also struggled to imagine a more liberal American future and what it would take to get there. That they had to struggle is hardly surprising, but scrutiny of their struggles has revealed some of the problems the nation, as a racialized construct, poses for liberal anti-racism.

Boas' thought on the "Negro problem" became trapped by the conflict between his projection of an abstract liberal future where individuals treated each other as individuals and his recognition that American whites were socialized into a racial consciousness that denied individuality to those perceived as "other." As long as American nationality was white, those perceived as non-white would be subject to illiberal treatment. These premises led Boas to conclude that the long-term solution to the race problem was the whitening of Black racial difference via miscegenation between white men and Black women. This line of thought called attention to the imbrication between race and nation at the heart of the race problem yet displaced the problem back onto Black bodies, leaving intact the equation between American nationality and whiteness.

Benedict redirected the problem of race, nation, and liberalism in ways that affirmed American exceptionalism. She attempted to reconcile liberal values, American nationalism, and racial difference by identifying the nation as having a characteristic pattern of cultural assimilation built on liberal foundations and by figuring racism as the illiberal product of a reactionary defense of privilege and power on the part of "Old Americans" against Blacks, Asians, and the "new" immigrants of Europe. Liberalism became rendered more than a future ideal for America; it was part of the bedrock of American culture. White supremacy was thus made exceptional to American democracy; the solution to racism was "making democracy work." Perhaps we should not take Benedict too literally here. Her account of American culture and history can be read as a kind of mythical charter, an effort to *create* a liberal American identity that wed nationalism and anti-racism. Even so, in her formulation the subject of address and the progenitor of American identity was implicitly white, the descendants of European settlers and immigrants. The effort to promote liberal anti-racism through an appeal to the nation reproduced the whiteness of the nation. Moreover, it precluded the possibility that racism was a perpetual product of historically and actually existing U.S. democracy.

In the wake of the Boasian intervention and in the midst of the U.S. consolidation of a hegemonic position in the global order, Wagley and Harris developed comparative analytics of social race in the Americas that perpetuated the contradictions of liberal Americanist anti-racism. The ethnography Harris conducted in Brazil had the potential to illuminate how racial discrimination and white supremacy (via the supreme value placed on whiteness) can exist even without "caste-like" race relations or even racially defined social groups. Yet he, like Wagley, came to conclude that, unlike in the U.S., "systematic" discrimination did not, indeed could not, exist in Brazil because race was not the prime definer of social categories. Caste segregation in the U.S. provided the contrast for a relatively benign assessment of the social life of race in Brazil. This benign view, in turn, implicitly reflected the liberal hope that the ongoing dismantling of legal segregation would subvert systemic discrimination in the U.S. These anthropologists underestimated the pervasive power of racism in nation-states defined from their foundation by the oppositions between Black, Indian, and white. Indeed, Wagley and Harris deferred an examination of white supremacy throughout the Americas via liberalist evocations of "competition," prejudicial culturalist evaluations of minority adaptability, and immigrant analogies that glossed over the power of the color line.

If I have eschewed some of the nuance of earlier chapters to put a fine point on the critical assessment of these anthropological engagements with race, it is not to deny either their anti-racism or their public import for liberalizing racist thought; the point is to highlight the contradictions of liberal anti-racism itself, in which the problem of the nation—in particular the United States as racial nation—looms large. In a world in which citizenship and belonging are defined foremost by a political order of nation-states, thinking about the relationship between racism and liberalism requires attention to the nation-state, and thus to the construct of the nation in whose name it governs. In the U.S. that construct has, from its foundation, been deeply racialized by whiteness. I have argued that liberal anthropological anti-racist discourses not only failed to fully reckon with the whiteness of the national construct; they tended to reinscribe its normative whiteness. They helped lay the intellectual foundation for a post–civil rights democratic order that simultaneously contests, instantiates, and denies white domination. A mere defense of the racially egalitarian ideals of American liberalism—however necessary that is in the current moment—does not address the paradoxes it bequeathed. Critically interrogating the "contradictions of American dreams and social mobility" (Cox 2015, 16) is as urgent now as ever.

The conjunction between whiteness and America, combined with the public power of nationalist discourse, creates acute political conundrums. Should those committed to racial justice understand and attack white racism as a problem "in" the nation or a problem "of" the nation? Can a viable politics of racial justice be constructed in the name of America, or is an attachment to America an obstacle to racial justice? Renouncing America as irredeemable from its foundation forward presents rather obvious problems. To publicly take such a position is to court excommunication from the body politic; imagine a politician running with the slogan "America was never great." Moreover, it cedes the enormously potent affective construct of the nation to whites. The right understands this all too well. Conservative radio personality Rush Limbaugh, for example, characterizes left-liberal anti-racism as an "ongoing effort to erase America by discrediting the entire premise of our culture, our history, our founding. The objective is to create in as many American minds as possible that America as founded is not worth defending."[2] The right banks on the defense of America to shore up the power of whiteness. White resentment is an effect of white hegemony; only those who can assume their privileged place in America can react with such indignation to its perceived loss. The only viable response appears to be to reclaim America from whiteness, but we should not underestimate the difficulties of trying to do so.

It is possible to imagine robust versions of Americanist anti-racist liberalism. One can, for example, recognize the existence of racism within the republic from the foundational moment and affirm traditions of anti-racist struggles for inclusion, viewing both as part of an ongoing saga, equally "American."[3] One can affirm that whites hold no monopoly on being American and claiming America. One can hold out the symbolic liberal promise associated with America while understanding it has never been fulfilled and may never be fulfilled, refusing color-blind and post-racial discourses. These are ways to affirm America and recognize the white racism that speaks in its name. They refuse to grant whites exclusive claim to America. But are they sufficient? Whiteness, always-already produced in relation to non-whiteness, is a form of privilege and property imbricated with the construct of the nation. Attempting to make whites one group of many in a multiracial America asserts a false equivalence between them and others. Can a civic nationalism that views social solidarity as cohering despite racial distinctions speak in the name of America and fully confront the whiteness of its civil institutions? Can the link between whiteness and America be severed without the deconstruction of the nation as we know it?

As should be apparent, I do not have an answer to the conundrums presented here, but they must be confronted. Perhaps the election and presidency of Trump will at least have the virtue of dispelling the fantasy that the nation has moved toward a post-racial future. Perhaps it will prompt widespread critical engagement with the social life of race in new forms of social mobilization across the color line. Or perhaps the rise of overt white supremacy will become part of a new normal in the public discourse of U.S. society. Perhaps its resurgence will leave many left-liberal white detractors newly assured of their own progressiveness, unable to come to terms with the normalization of whiteness that fuels white resentment across the political spectrum. The outcomes depend, of course, on the struggles to come.

What lessons does this book hold for how anthropologists today might understand disciplinary history and its relationship to the present? Just as it is imperative to overcome satisfaction in the anti-racist achievements of liberalism, it is crucial that anthropologists resist self-satisfaction with disciplinary anti-racism, past and present. This was a key message of the critical turn of the 1960s, a moment of crisis in American liberalism when an array of anthropologists, drawing on Marxist, feminist, Black Power, and anti-colonial paradigms, tried to redirect the discipline toward liberatory politics with due concern for the relationship between knowledge and power. The lack of detailed histories of that moment, and what happened afterward, is a major lacuna in disciplinary history that can only be filled from a multiperspectival engagement. My contribution to that history is only a beginning but it will, I hope, help us think more deeply about the temporality of projects to reinvent and "decolonize" anthropology in ways that foreground questions of racism and white supremacy.

The authors I consider—Willis, Lewis, and Valentine—self-consciously struggled against the terms of engagement that defined disciplinary knowledge production (e.g., "objective" knowledge produced by distant outsiders). They identified the "lily white" composition of the profession, demanding that it not only expand its ranks to include more scholars of color but transform research, scholarship, and teaching to reflect non-white perspectives. They did for U.S. anthropology what Black Power did for the U.S. imperial nation-state, exposing the whiteness of the normalized liberal subject. The polemics of the era should not blind us to their insights. Indeed, their theoretical insights on race, culture, and racism were more extensive and provocative than anyone seems to have acknowledged. Drawing on Black radical traditions, they promoted structural analytics of racism that brought together race and class without reducing race to class. They refused a straightforward opposition between race and culture by identifying the reifying work that cultural relativism and representations of culture could do. In their hands, Euro-American culture ceased to be the implicit benchmark of civilizational achievement and American belonging—a notion that endured in many anthropological assumptions about integration—and was revealed as a source of oppression anthropologists had to confront lest they reproduce its terms of domination. All of these arguments represented efforts to wrestle with the endurance of racism in the early post–civil rights era, and they remain relevant two generations later.

This raises a question deferred from Chapter 6: What effects did the critical turn have in U.S. anthropology? Answering this question fully would require an extensive look at anthropology from the mid-1970s to the present, a task beyond my powers. I can, however, offer some general observations. Many of the suggestions for reinventing anthropology associated with the broad critical turn were eventually taken up in the discipline. Critiques of the discipline's past, the limitations of objectivity, and a focus on power are now central to the disciplinary mainstream. Activist anthropology and native/insider anthropology—though by no means dominant tendencies—are no longer anathema. Feminist anthropology and Marxist anthropology emerged as subfields in the 1970s. The critique of anthropological complicity with colonialism ultimately led to an anthropology of colonialism and helped generate a self-reflexive turn

attuned to the continuities between colonial and post-colonial politics of cultural representation. But what happened to the study and theorization of race
and racism in the cultural wing of the discipline?

Until the mid to late 1980s there appears to have been little anthropological
work on the social life of race, perhaps because of the predominance of an ethnicity paradigm that tended to displace race (Sanjek 1994, 8; Williams 1989).
By the mid-1990s, however, race and racism had become subjects of increased
anthropological attention. In a 1995 review article, Faye Harrison noted that
"within the past decade, anthropologists have revitalized their interest in the
complex and often covert structures and dynamics of racial inequality" (1995,
47). Steven Gregory and Roger Sanjek (1994) edited an expansive volume on
race, and the majority of its contributors were cultural anthropologists. The
revitalized interest in racism reflected, in part, the increased number of anthropologists of color in the post–civil rights era and responded to the appropria-
tion of color-blind discourse by the political right in the "culture wars" of the
Reagan years. Anthropologists tackled a series of topics such as the political
economy of racism, race and cultural representation, and the relationships between race, transnationalism, and diaspora. They examined the historical relationship between anthropology, race, and racism (e.g., Baker 1998; Smedley
1993; Visweswaran 1998). They insisted that anthropology cease to be what
Shanklin (1998) called "the profession of the color blind." They promoted,
once again, the decolonization of anthropology (Harrison 1991a) and contributed to the new field of whiteness studies (e.g., Brodkin 1998; Frankenberg
1993; Hartigan 1999). In Latin Americanist anthropology—my original field—
anthropologists articulated critiques of "racial democracy" and examined the
nuances of racial identification, politics, and discrimination (e.g., Gordon 1998;
Hale 1994; Wade 1993). All of these currents have informed this book—indeed
made it possible—and laid the foundation for contemporary anthropologies of
race that have become increasingly concerned with the intersectional analysis
of race, gender, sexuality, and class and that have introduced topics such as
race and the environment, and race and genomic science. Whether this has
amounted to what we might call a "critical race turn" within the discipline as a
whole is up for debate.

The precise relationship between the critical turn of the late 1960s/early
1970s and the anthropologies of race and racism since the 1980s is difficult to
ascertain, but some of the connections are readily discernible. Take *Decolonizing Anthropology* (Harrison 1991a), a text that Allen and Jobson (2016) use to

highlight how a generation of under-acknowledged Black and allied anthropologists—what they call the "decolonizing generation"—developed an extensive (race) critical engagement with anthropological theory, method, and pedagogy. The collection was edited by Faye Harrison, who has played a central role in the anthropology of race and racism and in documenting African American contributions to anthropology.[4] She opened the volume with a call to reassess the discipline at the approach of the new millennium, noting, "Since the late 1960s, critiques of anthropology's collusion with and complicity in colonial and imperialist domination and proposals for more socially and politically responsible disciplinary agendas have been numerous" (1991b, 1). She and others extensively cited the work of this previous generation, including Willis and Lewis. A representative of that earlier generation, Delmos Jones, wrote the afterword. The very subtitle of *Decolonizing Anthropology*, "Moving Further Toward an Anthropology for Liberation," acknowledged the debt.

Recognizing the first "decolonizing generation" of the 1960s and 1970s is important today not merely to pay homage to forebears but to reflect on the project of decolonizing anthropology. That is, it is important to recognize that *a collective anthropological project of decolonization imbued with critical race analytics has been around for approximately half a century.* That project, like Black Studies, had antecedents but, like Black Studies, it was new in the sense that it represented a concerted collective struggle to transform the institutions of knowledge production. It was a self-conscious effort to refashion the discipline, including its theories, methods, pedagogy, research subjects, research agents, and professional organization. I call particular attention to the work of Willis, Lewis, and Valentine as representatives of that project because they issued far-reaching critical and programmatic statements on the discipline, but this is only a beginning. Far more work needs to be done to document the energies, struggles, politics, and intellectual innovations of the era, and to identify their shortcomings.

If we view decolonizing anthropology as an ongoing project undergoing constant renewal and reinvention, certain questions emerge. Why do projects of decolonizing anthropology have to be repeatedly called forth anew? How are elements of those projects accepted, rejected, appropriated, contained, deferred, and/or marginalized in the disciplinary mainstream? How do those projects build from each other and proliferate? What institutional transformations could help them endure? Having written a history that ends with an account of the birth of decolonizing projects in institutional anthropology in the

U.S., I do not pretend to have the answers to these questions. I hope this history might inspire others to explore them. I will conclude, however, with a few reflections on an issue raised by Willis, namely, the whiteness of anthropology.

Anthropology remains, if not lily white, awfully white. How white, demographically speaking, is difficult to discern with precision. The American Anthropological Association does not keep data on the racial-ethnic makeup of its membership or faculty in anthropology departments. Earlier reports document growth in the number of non-white faculty in the last decades of the twentieth century. Recall that the 1973 report of the AAA Committee on Minorities and Anthropology estimated that only 3 percent of anthropologists were non-white (Hsu et al. 1973). By the late 1980s the percentage of faculty of color in anthropology was approximately 11 percent, where it remained over the subsequent decade (Brodkin, Morgen, and Hutchinson 2011, 548).[5] I have not been able to find figures beyond that time frame. The National Science Foundation maintains data on PhD graduates that shows an increase in minority anthropology PhDs over the past several decades from approximately 10 percent in 1990 to 21 percent in 2015. Figure 6 compares the composition of 2015 PhDs by race

Figure 6 Percentage of PhDs in the U.S. (citizens and permanent residents) by social science discipline, 2015

Race/Ethnicity	Anthropology	Economics	Political Science	Psychology	Sociology
African American	4.3	2.7	7.4	7.8	8.9
American Indian or Alaska Native	1	0.4	0.2	0.4	0.2
Asian	6.3	13.2	4.7	6.1	5.5
Hispanic or Latino	9.6	6.2	5.8	7.9	8.4
White	72.5	71.7	75.2	72.7	71.2
More than One Race	2	2.7	2.6	2.6	4.2

https://www.nsf.gov/statistics/2017/nsf17306/data/tab24.pdf

Figure 7 U.S. population by race/ethnicity in 2016 according to the U.S census

Race/Ethnicity	Percentage of U.S. Population
African American	13.3
American Indian or Alaska Native	1.3
Asian	5.7
Hispanic or Latino	17.8
White	61.3
More than One Race	2.9

https://www.census.gov/quickfacts/fact/table/US/PST045216

Figure 8 Comparison of percentage of anthropology PhDs by race/ethnicity to U.S. population, using figures from figures 6 and 7

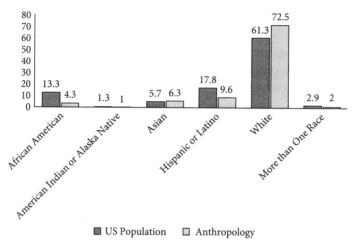

■ US Population   □ Anthropology

and ethnicity across the social sciences, followed by numbers for the overall racial-ethnic makeup of the United States in Figure 7. Figure 8 compares the composition of 2015 anthropology PhDs to the overall makeup of the United States.

Across the social sciences, white PhDs represent over 70 percent of the total and are over-represented in comparison to their population in the country, whereas Native Americans, Latinxs, and African Americans are underrepresented. In anthropology the paucity of African Americans is particularly notable in comparison with other disciplines (economics excepted) and their relative population in the country. Indeed, the percentage of African American anthropology PhDs has barely increased since the 1980s (Thorkelson 2009). Moreover, we should not assume that the overall increase in minority PhDs translates into a concomitant increase in minority representation in the faculty of anthropology departments. A survey conducted at the turn of the decade suggested that many anthropologists of color with academic positions held them in departments outside of anthropology and that they advanced in the ranks more slowly than their white colleagues (Brodkin, Morgen, and Hutchinson 2011, 548–549). On the whole there has been but modest diversification of the discipline's population over the past several decades.

Beyond the numbers, the experiences of anthropologists of color reveal that many anthropology departments continue to operate as "white public space"

(Brodkin, Morgen, and Hutchinson 2011). In 2007, the AAA created an ad hoc Commission on Race and Racism in Anthropology (CRRA). The commission conducted focus groups and surveys of graduate students and faculty of color (Hutchinson and Patterson 2010). Graduate students reported a series of adverse conditions in anthropology departments; among others: "lip service to diversity"; devaluation of their research interest; "subtle forms of racism that make them feel isolated, invisible, excluded, vulnerable, unworthy, unwanted or treated as research subjects"; lack of recognition of and response to racism; insensitivity to intersecting gender, class, and family realities (2010, 3–4). In an article based on survey responses, Brodkin, Morgen, and Hutchinson (2011) highlighted the challenges faced by faculty of color in the discipline. Many respondents reported encountering disciplining strictures on what counted as anthropology. Studies of racism and communities of color were deemed inappropriate while curriculum and canon formation marginalized non-white scholarship and theory production. Anthropologists of color also confronted a "racial division of department labor" that inhibited professional advance (545). Often being the only or one of two faculty of color in a department, they became over-burdened with various forms of "diversity duty"—e.g., recruiting, retaining, and mentoring students of color; doing extensive committee work so that faculty of color will be represented on committees—not expected of white faculty (550). Meanwhile, race-evasive and color-blind discourses obscured the racial inflections of what defines proper anthropology while denying non-white experiences of discrimination and rejection. In sum, the Commission on Race and Racism found that the experiences of faculty of color in the twenty-first century were similar to their experiences reported in 1973 by the Committee on Minorities and Anthropology.[6]

As with the election of President Trump, this should not come as a shock. William Willis articulated a similar sentiment in his excavation of anthropological skeletons. "These revelations should not be surprising: white anthropologists are members of racist societies" (1972, 140). Juxtaposing the election of Trump with the institutional life of anthropology may seem like a stretch, but the provocation here is to refuse denial. Anthropology, like America, is not as racially progressive as many of us (especially whites) think it is or hope that it is. All anthropologists should confront the prospect that the racial makeup of anthropology, like that of the other traditional social science disciplines, is the expected outcome of the institutional and structural dynamics of a racial order characterized by white supremacy. This does not mean that efforts to diversify and decolonize anthropology are perforce futile or that nothing has changed. Nor does it negate the need to continue to develop new theoretical tools to comprehend the subtleties and complexities of race and racism in the post–civil rights era (Hartigan 2010; Jackson 2008). It does mean that anthropologists cannot assume the inevitable racial progress of their discipline any more than they can assume racial progress in the U.S. and the world at large, in which the U.S. plays such a powerful role.

Notes

Prologue

1. The phrase comes from Ruth Benedict (1929, 648).

Introduction

1. This is, essentially the narrative told in a review of a recent book on Margaret Mead (Turner 2013); see also Jackson (2001, 17). It echoes a broader "canonical narrative" of the historical relationship between race and science, in which science supposedly came to disavow race (Reardon 2005, 17–44).

2. Many of these positions were developed in the midst of a perceived disciplinary malaise on these topics at a moment (the 1980s and 1990s) when it had become apparent that culture had become essentialized in a manner aligned with racialization and that the most critical, cutting-edge work on race, racism, and culture was appearing in multidisciplinary fields such as cultural studies, post-colonial studies, and ethnic studies rather than anthropology (Abu-Lughod 1991; Visweswaran 1998). As I argue in Chapter 6, they had largely unacknowledged precursors among anthropologists influenced by the Black Studies movement.

3. To be clear, that is an important project. For many years, Faye Harrison has played a prominent role in bringing Drake, Davis, W. E. B. Du Bois, and other African American scholars to the attention of anthropologists (e.g., 1992; 2008b; 2013). The volume *African American Pioneers in Anthropology* (Harrison and Harrison 1999) provides an overview of the work and careers of African American anthropologists who receive their PhDs before 1955. An expanded edition of that volume is in the works, as is a volume focused on a later generation of African American anthropologists.

4. For analysis of Boasians in relation to Du Bois and other Black intellectuals see Baker (1998), Lamothe (2008), and Liss (1998).

5. Scholars offer differing interpretations of the invention of race and origins of racial thinking (see, for example, Goldberg 1993; Malik 1996; Seth 2010; Smedley 1993; Wynter 2003). I view twentieth-century discourses on race as rooted in the formation of modernity, with the European colonization of the Americas and enslavement of Africans providing the backdrop for the development of the scientific racial taxonomies of the eighteenth century and the biological determinism of the nineteenth century.

6. Examples of this now vast literature include Brodkin (1998), Goldstein (2006), Guglielmo (2003), Ignatiev (1995), and Roediger (2005).

7. Important works exploring various dimensions of cultural, social, political, and intellectual interchange across the African Diaspora across different disciplines include, among others, Gilroy (1993), Edwards (2003), Matory (2005), and Matera (2015).

8. In addition to the literature on immigration noted above, see, for example, Frankenberg (1993), Lipsitz (1998), and Perry (2001).

Chapter 1

1. Unconquered indigenous peoples were declared enemies of the state. In California, federally sponsored killings reduced the Indian population from 310,000 in 1850 to 50,000 in 1855 (Menchaca 2001, 223).

2. Daniel Folkmar (1861–1932) received his PhD in anthropology from the University of Paris after studying at Harvard, Clark, and the University of Chicago. He was a lieutenant governor of a province in the Philippines from 1903 to 1907 during the U.S. occupation and published a photographic album of Philippine racial "types." He subsequently joined the United States Immigration Commission (Perlmann 2011, 11–12).

3. Harvard accounted for 35.4% of anthropology PhDs, Columbia 31.7%, the University of Chicago 11%, the University of California, Berkeley 9.75%, the University of Pennsylvania 4.88%, Clark University 3.66%, and 1.22% each for George Washington University, the University of Minnesota, and the University of Michigan. See Bernstein (2002) for a complete listing.

4. Columbia PhD Alfred Kroeber was the first professor in anthropology at UC Berkeley (hired in 1901), leading the program until his retirement in 1946. Boas' student Frank Speck chaired the University of Pennsylvania program from 1913 until 1949.

5. Hurston's relationship to anthropology is a subject of considerable treatment and debate in the voluminous scholarship on her life and work. As a starting point, see Carby (1994), Hernandez (1995), Lamothe (2004), Mikell (1983; 1999) and Walters (1999).

6. The term "social race" is often viewed as the coinage of Charles Wagley in the late 1950s (see Chapter 5) so it is noteworthy that Locke used the phrase decades ear-

lier. Locke's engagement with Boasian theories of race merits more treatment than I can give it here.

7. Herskovits' turn toward examining the enduring African cultural heritage of the "New World Negro" had multiple influences, including Harlem Renaissance intellectuals and scholars of Black culture in the Caribbean and Brazil (Gershenhorn 2004; Jackson 1986; Yelvington 2006).

8. Sidney Mintz and Richard Price (1992) would develop an anthropological approach to Afro-American cultures with a similar emphasis in the early 1970s.

9. The term "caste" was previously deployed by sociologists at the University of Chicago in the 1920s to describe Black-white relations in the U.S. Du Bois had earlier used the term to refer to "a definite place, preordained in custom, law and religion, where all men of black blood must be thrust," and identified the origins of the caste position of African Americans in the conflation between slavery and blackness in the U.S. South that persisted after abolition (Visweswaran 2010, 112).

10. Scholars have widely divergent evaluations of *Deep South* as a representative text of the "caste school of race relations." Compare, for example, Harrison (2008b, 70–72) and Visweswaran (2010, 119–125) with O'Connor (2001, 84–88).

Chapter 2

1. This essay was retitled "The Negro in America" in a posthumous collection of Boas' work. I retain the original title in my discussion of the essay.

2. Key texts include Baker (1998; 2010), Barkan (1992), Stocking (1968; 2001, 3–48), Teslow (2014), and Williams (1996).

3. For overviews of Boas' social and political activism, see Baker (2004), Darnell et al. (2015), Hyatt (1990), and Stocking (1979).

4. For a discussion of Boas' views on nationalism see Liss (2015).

5. He thus opposed the imposition of tariffs on foreign countries because of the harm they caused the people of those countries. He generally opposed immigration restrictions on similar grounds, though it is significant that he wavered on the question of what he called "East Asiatic immigration." In a lecture to Barnard students in 1917, Boas asserted:

> From a general human point of view, I should wish that all barriers against human migration could be abolished. It is clear, however, that in a sparsely settled country with unrestricted immigration of a cultural type entirely distinct in character, that type of life we call our civilization may be swamped completely by that of the foreign immigrant. Here I think is a point in which the members of a nation have the right to defend their national life against the inroad of foreign ideas and of foreign mode of life, provided this can be done without injustice. (1945, 181)

The lack of reconciliation in Boas' thought between a "human point of view" and the right of nations to defend their cultural integrity hints at a profound contradiction between humanism and nationalism, but he did not belabor the point. It was, however, no mere coincidence that *Asian* immigration raised the specter of an "entirely distinct" culture swamping American civilization.

6. See also Boas (1904; 1905). Lévy Zumwalt and Willis (2008) provide a detailed account of Boas' trip to Atlanta.

7. Stocking contends, correctly I think, that over time Boas grew increasingly skeptical of racial differences in endowment. Nonetheless, he did not abandon the possibility of "fewer men of genius" among Blacks (Williams 1996, 10). In the 1938 edition of *The Mind of Primitive Man*, Boas modified the statement "it seemed possible that perhaps the race would not produce quite so many men of highest genius as other races" (1911a, 268) to read "it seemed barely possible . . ." (1965, 238).

8. In *Anthropology and Modern Life*, Boas briefly noted the consequence of the power of masters over slaves in determining patterns of interracial mixture (1928, 70–71). In her work on African American genealogies in the late 1920s and early 1930s, Carolyn Bond Day noted the pain white ancestry raised for her informants, who sometimes "did not want to talk about their ancestry because it involved abusive White ancestors and memories of trauma" (Curwood 2012, 84).

9. Gershenhorn provides an account of this work (2004, 27–57). Herskovits published two books on the results, one popular (1928) and one technical (1930c).

10. He repeated a similar assertion in the substantially revised 1938 edition of *The Mind of Primitive Man* (Boas 1965, 241).

11. Gilberto Freyre, a student of Boas in the early 1920s, would go on to elaborate a highly influential thesis of Brazil as a racial democracy born of racial mixture (Sánchez-Eppler 1992).

12. Boas reworked his discussion of nationality in the 1932 edition of *Anthropology and Modern Life*, suggesting both the importance of the concept to his thought and the difficulties he had with it.

13. See, for example, Evans (2006), Frank (1997), Glick (1982), and Stocking (1979). Bunzl (2003) provides a particularly informative account of the Jewish influence on German anthropology in the second half of the nineteenth century.

14. See Williams (1996, 37–53) for a rebuttal to Hyatt's argument that focuses on Boas' relationship to African American intellectuals and struggles.

15. This brief biography is based on Ferguson (2005).

16. George Schuyler to Melville Herskovits, June 15, 1927, Melville J. Herskovits Papers, Box 21, Folder 12.

17. Melville Herskovits to George Schuyler, November 3, 1931, Melville J. Herskovits Papers, Box 21, Folder 12.

18. J. A. Rogers was a Jamaican-American intellectual and friend of Schuyler who contributed articles to *The Messenger*. His writings on interracial sex influenced

Schuyler (Ferguson 2005, 138–139). A. A. Goldenweiser was Boas' former student Alexander Goldenweiser.

Chapter 3

1. Ruth Benedict to Franz Boas, November 5, 1939, Franz Boas Papers, B.B61.

2. Benedict and her husband grew apart from each other, separating in 1930 (Caffrey 1989, 183–185). In the mid-1920s Benedict had a relationship with Margaret Mead, and her subsequent partners were women.

3. Ruth Benedict to David Zablodowsky, June 13, 1940, Ruth Fulton Benedict Papers, Folder 51.4. The UK version of the book bore Benedict's preferred title.

4. For an account of the origins of racism in Christian constructions of biological descent and social differentiation associated with "blood," see Anidjar (2014).

5. Cox was a sociologist and economist originally from Trinidad who received a PhD at the University of Chicago and taught at various Black colleges over a long career. He is best known for his Marxian critique of race relations theories developed in *Caste, Class and Race* (1948), which incorporated the article cited here.

6. Visweswaran locates the source of this position in the Boasian distinction between race and culture, defined in opposition to each other. Race, objectified as biology, had an ontological reality prior to racism, viewed as a false interpretation of biological reality. The constructed reality of race as a product of social-historical formations became impossible to theorize, on the very grounds that made the Boasian intervention possible. Without minimizing the importance of the race/culture distinction in Boasian thought, I would counter that the distinction in itself did not prohibit a social-cultural inquiry into the social life of race even if it did not, as Visweswaran contends, entail a view of biology and race as socially constructed. Since Benedict viewed racism, racial prejudice, and racial conflict as sociocultural problems and "social facts," her argument that they were products of other social dynamics involved a claim about the ontological status of different kinds of *sociocultural* phenomena.

7. In the U.S., Benedict argued, racism remained a question of distinctions internal to the nation and not a "doctrine of the superiority of nations" (Benedict 1940, 191).

8. For further reflections by Benedict on American culture, see "Can Cultural Patterns Be Directed?" (Benedict 1948) and also an unpublished work, "The Growth of the Republic," n.d., Ruth Fulton Benedict Papers, Folder 54.8.

9. "America's Racial Myth," Ruth Fulton Benedict Papers, Folder 58.3.

10. "American Melting Pot, 1941," Ruth Fulton Benedict Papers, Folder 54.1.

11. Gene Weltfish studied under Boas and Benedict in the 1920s and taught at Columbia as a lecturer from 1935 until 1953, when the administration canceled her

contract a few days ahead of her appearance before the Senate Committee on Government Operations Permanent Subcommittee on Investigations, led by Joseph McCarthy. Weltfish was a target of repression because of her leftist political history and anti-racist activism and had difficulty securing employment after her "public show trial" (Price 2004, 110–135).

12. Although Benedict was listed as a co-author of *In Henry's Backyard*, Teslow identifies it as the work of Weltfish and Violet Edwards, under Benedict's supervision. The Cranbrook Institute's exhibition was advised by, among others, Weltfish and other Columbia anthropologists including Ralph Linton, John Adams, and Harry Shapiro (Teslow 2014, 251).

13. This was a recurrent theme in other popular media derived from *The Races of Mankind*. The Cranbrook Institute of Science Exhibition had an opening panel with photographs of a Black, a white, and an Asian child—the white in the center—in front of a figure of Adam and Eve (the biblical trope of the original unity of humanity also present in *The Races of Mankind*) (Jacobson 1998, 106–108; Teslow 2014, 247–249). In the children's book *In Henry's Backyard* (Benedict and Weltfish 1948), a tripartite division between white, Black, and Asian races appears in thirteen of the fifty-seven illustrations.

Chapter 4

1. For analysis of the nexus between Cold War politics, anti-colonialism, and U.S. civil rights politics, see Anderson (2014), Plummer (1996), and Von Eschen (1997).

2. A number of anthropologists, including Boas' students Gene Weltfish and Ashley Montagu, lost their academic jobs as a result of government persecution. The American Anthropological Association did not advocate for them and some anthropologists informed on them (Price 2004).

3. For overviews of theoretical trends in U.S. anthropology in the 1950s and 1960s, see Patterson (2001, 103–134) and Wolf (1974).

4. These calculations are suggestive, not definitive. They are derived from data I compiled on PhDs awarded in 1954, 1955, and 1956 compared to 1966–1967 and 1967–1968, taken from the American Anthropological Association's *Guide to Graduate Departments of Anthropology* for 1964–1965 (for the data on PhDs in 1954–1956), 1967–1968, and 1968–1969 (American Anthropological Association 1965; 1968; 1969).

5. This was not a comprehensive survey of all anthropologists but an effort by the AAA Minority Committee, established in 1972, to conduct a survey of (self-identified) minority anthropologists, most of whom had either a PhD or an MA degree. Of the 122 minority anthropologists they identified, 60 were of Black background, 26 of Asian background, 19 of Spanish-speaking background, and 17 of Native American background.

6. Laurence Foster (PhD, University of Pennsylvania, 1931), Mark Hanna Watkins (PhD, University of Chicago, 1933), and Irene Diggs (PhD, University of Havana, 1944) taught at Black colleges. Louis Eugene King completed his dissertation at Columbia in 1932 but could not afford the requirement to publish his dissertation, finally receiving the PhD in 1965. He and Arthur Huff Fauset (PhD, University of Pennsylvania, 1942) did not work in the university system. Zora Neale Hurston and Katherine Dunham were graduate students in anthropology who did not complete the PhD or work full-time in academia (Harrison and Harrison 1999).

7. According to Drake, a least a dozen African American Africanists with intellectual roots in anthropology emerged between 1953 and 1970. The Ford Foundation established an African fellowship fund in 1953, opening the doors to African Americans who had previously found little support in conducting research in Africa (1980, 24–25). Examples of African American anthropologists who conducted fieldwork in an African country include Elliott Skinner (PhD, Columbia, 1955), James Gibbs (PhD, Harvard, 1961), William Shack (PhD, London School of Economics, 1961), Niara Sudarkasa (PhD, Columbia, 1964), Johnnetta B. Cole (PhD, Northwestern, 1967), and Audrey Smedley (PhD, University of Manchester, 1967).

8. Councill Taylor (PhD, Yale, 1955) and Vera Green (PhD, University of Arizona, 1969) worked in the Caribbean on interethnic, class, and color relations. John Langston Gwaltney (PhD, Columbia, 1967) worked in Mexico. Delmos Jones (PhD, Cornell, 1967) did research in Thailand, and Diane Lewis (PhD, Cornell, 1962) focused on Malaya.

9. Further research is needed to shed light on the experiences of Black—as well as Asian, Native American, and Latinx—anthropologists in the not-so-distant past of the discipline. As a starting point, see Harrison and Harrison (1999), Hsu and Xu (1999), Medicine (2001), and Norcini (2007).

10. These comments followed Diamond's critique of a statement on racism by the American Association of Physical Anthropologists. Diamond chided physical anthropologists for stating "there is nothing in science that justifies the denial of opportunities or rights to any group by virtue of race" rather than offering a more positive statement against racism that would assert "the doctrine of racial equality is fully supported by scientific and historical inquiry" (1963, 323).

11. David Mandelbaum (1952) and Edward T. Hall (1947) discussed the adverse effects of segregation in the U.S. military.

12. Landes also conducted research on race relations in post-war Britain (Nava 2013), as did Drake (1954).

Chapter 5

1. The statement generated considerable controversy among physical anthropologists and biologists for questioning the term race, rejecting meaningful biological

differences between races, and asserting that humanity was inclined to cooperation. In 1951, UNESCO produced a new statement that implied the probable existence of innate differences, including in intelligence, between races (Brattain 2007, 1401–1405; Hazard 2012, 35–62).

2. In an excellent analysis of the U.S., UNESCO, and the politics of race, Hazard (2012) argues that UNESCO's agenda in the 1940s and 1950s was deeply informed by the U.S. government, which provided the principal source of funding.

3. The Brazil project was initially limited to the state of Bahia but was later expanded to include the cities of São Paulo and Rio de Janeiro, where racism was in evident ascendance. For an account of the evolution of the project see Maio (2001).

4. Another team of researchers based in São Paulo was led by French sociologist Roger Bastide and Brazilian sociologist Florestan Fernandes. As discussed later, their analysis of racial discrimination in Brazil differed significantly from that of the U.S. anthropologists. For an overview, see Wade (2010, 52–59).

5. Marvin Harris to Neal Wood, October 30, 1962, Marvin Harris Papers, Box 1, Off-Campus Before 1965, Folder 1.

6. Harris noted, "it is one of the fundamental axioms of life in Minas Velhas that the girls are very particular whom they will dance with" (1952, 72), but he did not elaborate further on the dynamic relationships between gender, class, and race.

7. In his larger ethnography of Minas Velhas, published in 1956, Harris asserted that "race helps to produce the town's most important social cleavage" (1971, 128).

8. In a preface to the second edition, Wagley reiterated: "racial origin has not become a serious point of conflict in Brazilian society. Brazilians can still call their society a racial democracy" (1963, 2).

9. Bastide was best known for his studies of Afro-Brazilian religion. A professor at the Universidade de São Paulo since 1938, he had contacts with Afro-Brazilian organizations, including the Teatro Experimental do Negro, whose leader was the important activist Abdias do Nascimento.

10. Marvin Harris to R. A. Schermerhorn, July 23, 1963, Marvin Harris Papers, Box 1, Off-Campus Before 1965, Folder 2.

11. This work originated as a televised lecture for the Columbia Lectures in International Studies. Robert Bass to Marvin Harris, February 7, 1963, Marvin Harris Papers, Box 32, Walker & Co., Correspondence regarding Patterns of Race in the Americas.

12. In his essay "On the Concept of Social Race in the Americas" Wagley hinted that in the nineteenth century the new nation-states of the Americas produced simplified systems of racial classification in ways that ensured the power of the white elite (1965, 536). He also suggested that elite whites in contemporary Latin America and the Caribbean retained an investment in demonstrating their own racial purity

(540). He did not, however, pursue the implications of these suggestions for a potential anthropological analytics of white domination/dominant whiteness across the Americas.

13. "The Anthropology of Racial Prejudice—unfinished," Marvin Harris Papers, Box 32.

Chapter 6

1. For overviews of the critique of anthropology generated in this era see Desai (2001), Lewis (2014), Marfleet (1973), Silverman (2005, 310–317), and Trencher (2000).

2. Diane Lewis (1973, 590) explicitly referred to the "'decolonization' of the social sciences," drawing on Mexican anthropologist Rodolfo Stavenhagen (1971).

3. Levi-Strauss would also assert that "it is precisely because the so-called primitive peoples are becoming extinct that their study should now be given absolute priority" (1966, 125), echoing the salvage orientation of U.S. anthropology in the late nineteenth and early twentieth centuries. See Mafeje (1976, 328–329) and Visweswaran (2010, 74–102) for critical discussions.

4. Rather than submit the files of investigation to the Executive Committee, Mead reportedly burned them. For a full account of the whole affair see Watkin (1992). Micaela di Leonardo offers a scathing portrait of Mead as an embodiment of "the American anthropological tradition of pronouncing on American culture in deep ignorance of United States history and political economy" (1998, 95) and refers to her "long record as a Cold Warrior—her condemnation of antinuclear protest, her red-baiting of unions, and her postwar promilitary propagandizing, not to mention her efforts to quash protest against anthropological complicity in the war in Southeast Asia" (258).

5. The 1971 Declaration of Barbados is available at www.lacult.unesco.org/lacult _en/docc/Barbados_1971.doc.

6. An early version of the influential creolization model of Afro-American culture (Mintz and Price 1992) was articulated by Mintz (1970a) in an article promoting a pan-hemispheric vision of Afro-American Studies. Mintz participated in a symposium on Black Studies at Yale occasioned by Black student protests (Mintz 1969) and helped create the African American Studies program there. See also the edited volume *Afro-American Anthropology* (Whitten and Szwed 1970).

7. The panelists included Taylor, Delmos Jones, Johnnetta Cole, and Oliver Osborne. Taylor was a professor at UCLA who had received his PhD from Yale in 1955, writing a dissertation on color and class in Jamaica. Jones had done fieldwork in Thailand and was in the thick of many streams of the critical movement in the discipline, including debates over anthropological complicity with counter-insurgency (1971), the promotion of "native anthropology" (1970), and the development of an urban

anthropology that focused on dominant institutions (1972). Johnnetta Cole received her PhD from Northwestern in 1967 (based on research conducted in Liberia) and would soon run the newly formed Black Studies program at Washington State University. Her long list of accomplishments includes co-editing special issues on Black anthropology for the *Black Scholar* (Cole and Walker 1980a, 1980b) and eventually becoming president of Spelman College. Oliver Osborne was a self-described nurse-anthropologist who made a career in the social science of health care.

8. Participants included Vine Deloria (author of a scathing portrayal of anthropology from a Native American perspective [Deloria 1969]), Audrey Smedley (who presented her paper "History and Racism in Anthropology," a forerunner to her book *Race in North America* [1993]), Diane Lewis, and Jack Stauder (who both would soon publish on the relationship between anthropology and colonialism [Lewis 1973; Stauder 1972]).

9. Octavio Romano (1923–2005) received his PhD in anthropology at UC Berkeley in 1965, where he subsequently taught in the School of Public Health. Romano played a key role in the development of Chicano Studies. He was the founder and editor of the journal *El Grito* and the publishing house Quinto Sol. Beginning in the late 1960s, he authored a series of essays critical of social science representations of Mexican Americans and their "traditional culture" (Romano 1973).

10. Marvin Harris to Elliott Skinner, December 10, 1968, Marvin Harris Paper, Box 2, Folder 3.

11. The author was James Gibbs, an African American anthropologist who organized the African and Afro-American Studies program at Stanford in 1968.

12. In the late 1960s, Columbia faculty were divided on whether to make a special effort to recruit Black anthropologists. Some, including Charles Wagley, felt that the proper position was to ignore race, whereas others, including Marvin Harris and Morton Fried, urged a more proactive stance. Elliott Skinner to William Willis, December 27, 1967, William S. Willis Papers, Series I, Correspondence and Academic Papers.

13. William Willis to Elliott Skinner, December 18, 1967, William S. Willis Papers, Series I, Correspondence and Academic Papers.

14. William Willis to Dell Hymes, October 23, 1970, William S. Willis Papers, Series I, Correspondence and Academic Papers.

15. See also the unpublished essays "Franz Boas and the Origins of Afro-American Studies" and "Franz Boas, Black Students and the Study of Black Problems," William S. Willis Papers, Series III, Works.

16. William Willis to Morton Fried, March 17, 1973, William S. Willis Papers, Series I, Correspondence and Academic Papers. Interestingly, Willis was responding to Fried's criticisms of an early draft of his paper on Boas and Black folklore that Willis was "presentist" in his evaluation of Boas. Willis responded that his goal was a

balance between a historicist appreciation of Boas and a presentist evaluation of his limitations. He refuted an exclusively historicist position as letting "individuals off the hook" and, more importantly, excusing an "evil social system."

17. William Willis to Dell Hymes, June 17, 1971, William S. Willis Papers, Series I, Correspondence and Academic Papers.

18. Fried was one of two professors thanked by Willis in "Skeletons" and he in turn thanked Willis in *The Study of Anthropology*. As chair of the Columbia anthropology department, Fried hired Willis to teach summer courses; at one point they shared an office. Upon Willis' death in 1983, Fried wrote an obituary for *American Anthropologist* that began: "Though most anthropologists prefer to believe that their discipline is and has been relatively free of that ideological scourge known as racism, the life and career of Dr. William S. Willis, Jr. offers evidence to the contrary" ("William Shedrick Willis, Jr.," William S. Willis Papers, Series I, Correspondence and Academic Papers, Morton Fried, 1973–1983). The obituary was not published.

19. Kirin Rajagopalan, "Interview with Dr. Diane K. Lewis (2/21/2013)," Oakes Oral History Project, University of California Santa Cruz, 3.

20. Kirin Rajagopalan, "Interview with Dr. Diane K. Lewis (2/21/2013)," Oakes Oral History Project, University of California Santa Cruz, 5.

21. Lewis published the first article by a Black woman in the premier feminist journal *Signs* (1977).

22. Fanon (1967) had, in the 1950s, provided an account of how discourses of culture succeeded biological racism; see also Caulfield (1972).

23. For discussion of the Moynihan report, including its origins and legacies, see Greenbaum (2015) and O'Connor (2001).

24. It is notable that Valentine placed Asian Americans and Euro-Americans on one side of the racial-ethnic-social divide and African Americans and Native Americans on the other. Later in the text he suggested that Asian Americans occupied an intermediate position between whites, on one end of the spectrum, and Blacks and Indians, on the other (1972, 41–42).

25. The concept of internal colonialism figured prominently in Carmichael and Hamilton's *Black Power* (1967) and in Black Power analysis more generally. For reflections on the use of the concept in the 1960s and 1970s and its origins in Latin American dependency theory, see Gutiérrez (2004).

26. Delmos Jones developed a similar orientation in his fieldwork in urban Black communities (1972).

Conclusion

1. I consider those in the column "Other Significant Candidate" to be those receiving more than 5% of white votes.

2. "Rush Limbaugh: 'We Are on the Cusp of a Second Civil War.'" http://www
.breitbart.com/video/2017/08/18/rush-limbaugh-cusp-second-civil-war/

3. St. Clair Drake (1963) provided such an account in lectures delivered on the occasion of the 100th anniversary of the Emancipation Proclamation.

4. Harrison studied under St. Clair Drake at Stanford University, as did two of the other African American contributors, Glenn Jordan and Edmund T. Gordon. Drake had relocated to Stanford in 1969 to direct the newly created African and African American studies program. It is not clear if he participated directly in the early phases of Black mobilization in the American Anthropological Association, but in the late 1970s he wrote articles on anthropology and the Black experience (1978; 1980) that were clearly influenced by Black Studies paradigms he helped forge.

5. The breakdown was Native American 1%, African American 3%, Latinx 4%, Asian 3%.

6. See also Smedley and Hutchinson (2012).

References

Abrahams, Roger. 1964. *Deep Down in the Jungle: Negro Narrative Folklore from the Streets of Philadelphia.* Hatboro, PA: Folklore Associates.

Abrahams, Roger. 1970. *Positively Black.* Englewood Cliffs, NJ: Prentice-Hall.

Abu-Lughod, Lila. 1991. "Writing Against Culture." In *Recapturing Anthropology: Working in the Present*, edited by Richard Fox, 137–162. Santa Fe, NM: School of American Research Press.

Allen, Jafari Sinclaire, and Ryan Cecil Jobson. 2016. "The Decolonizing Generation: (Race and) Theory in Anthropology Since the Eighties." *Current Anthropology* 57(2):129–148.

American Anthropological Association. 1965. *Guide to Graduate Departments for the Year 1964–1965.* Washington, DC: American Anthropological Association.

American Anthropological Association. 1968. *Guide to Graduate Departments for the Year 1967–1968.* Washington, DC: American Anthropological Association.

American Anthropological Association. 1969. *Guide to Graduate Departments for the Year 1968–1969.* Washington, DC: American Anthropological Association.

Anderson, Carol. 2014. *Bourgeois Radicals: The NAACP and the Struggle for Colonial Liberation, 1941–1960.* New York: Cambridge University Press.

Anderson, E. N., Jr. 1972. "The Life and Culture of Ecotopia." In *Reinventing Anthropology*, edited by Dell Hymes, 264–283. New York: Random House.

Anderson, Mark. 2008. "The Complicated Career of Hugh Smythe, Anthropologist and Ambassador . . . The Early Years, 1940–1950." *Transforming Anthropology* 16(2):128–146.

Anderson, Mark. 2009. *Black and Indigenous: Garifuna Activism and Consumer Culture in Honduras.* Minneapolis: University of Minnesota Press.

Anderson, Mark. Forthcoming. "Hugh Smythe: Anthropologist, Sociologist, Ambassador, Public Intellectual." In *African American Pioneers in Anthropology, Expanded Edition*, edited by Ira E. Harrison, Faye V. Harrison, and Deborah Johnson-Simon. Urbana: University of Illinois Press.

Anidjar, Gil. 2014. *Blood: A Critique of Christianity.* New York: Columbia University Press.

Arendt, Hannah. 1944. "Race-Thinking before Racism." *Review of Politics* 6(1):36–73.

Asad, Talal, ed. 1973. *Anthropology and the Colonial Encounter.* Atlantic Highlands, N.J.: Humanities Press.

Baker, Lee. 1998. *From Savage to Negro: Anthropology and the Construction of Race, 1896–1964.* Berkeley: University of California Press.

Baker, Lee. 2000. "Daniel G. Briton's Success on the Road to Obscurity, 1890–99." *Cultural Anthropology* 15(3):394–423.

Baker, Lee. 2004. "Franz Boas Out of the Ivory Tower." *Anthropological Theory* 4(1):29–51.

Baker, Lee. 2010. *Anthropology and the Racial Politics of Culture.* Durham, NC: Duke University Press.

Baker, Lee. 2016. "Adversary as Ancestor: Fear, Panic, and Anthropology for Civil Rights." *Hau: Journal of Ethnographic Theory* 6(3):376–381.

Balandier, Georges. 1966. "The Colonial Situation: A Theoretical Approach." In *Social Change: The Colonial Situation*, edited by Immanuel Wallerstein, 34–61. New York: John Wiley & Sons. First published (in French) 1951.

Banaji, Jairus. 1970. "The Crisis of British Anthropology." *New Left Review* 64:71–86.

Barkan, Elazar. 1992. *The Retreat of Scientific Racism: Changing Concepts of Race in Britain and the United States Between the World Wars.* New York: Cambridge University Press.

Bastide, Roger. 1957. "Race Relations in Brazil." *International Social Science Bulletin* 9(4):495–512.

Bauman, Richard, and Charles Briggs. 2003. *Voices of Modernity: Language Ideologies and the Politics of Inequality.* New York: Cambridge University Press.

Beals, Ralph. 1955. "Indian-Mestizo-White Relations in Spanish America." In *Race Relations in World Perspective*, edited by Andrew W. Lind, 412–432. Honolulu: University of Hawaii Press.

Beardsley, Edward. 1973. "The American Scientist as Social Activist: Franz Boas, Burt G. Wilder, and the Cause of Racial Justice, 1900–1915." *Isis* 64(1):50–66.

Benedict, Ruth. 1922. "The Vision in Plains Culture." *American Anthropologist* 24(1):1–23.

Benedict, Ruth. 1929. "The Science of Custom: The Bearing of Culture on Contemporary Thought." *Century Magazine* 1:641–649.

Benedict, Ruth. 1934. *Patterns of Culture.* Boston: Houghton Mifflin.

Benedict, Ruth. 1940. *Race: Science and Politics.* New York: Modern Age Books.

Benedict, Ruth. 1941. "Race Problems in America." *Annals of the American Academy of Political and Social Science* 216:73–78.

Benedict, Ruth. 1942a. "We Can't Afford Race Prejudice." *Frontiers of Democracy,* October 15, 2.

Benedict, Ruth. 1942b. "American Melting Pot, 1942 Model." In *Americans All: Studies in Intercultural Education,* 14–24. Washington, DC: Department of Supervisors and Directors of Instruction of the National Education Association.

Benedict, Ruth. 1946. *The Chrysanthemum and the Sword: Patterns of Japanese Culture.* Boston: Houghton Mifflin.

Benedict, Ruth. 1948. "Can Cultural Patterns Be Directed?" *Intercultural Education News* 9(2):1–3.

Benedict, Ruth. 1959. "Postwar Race Prejudice." In *An Anthropologist at Work: Writings of Ruth Benedict,* edited by Margaret Mead, 361–368. Boston: Houghton Mifflin.

Benedict, Ruth, and Mildred Ellis. 1942. *Race and Cultural Relations: America's Answer to the Myth of a Master Race.* Washington, DC: National Education Association.

Benedict, Ruth, and Gene Weltfish. 1943. *The Races of Mankind.* Public Affairs Pamphlet, No. 85. New York: Public Affairs Committee.

Benedict, Ruth, and Gene Weltfish. 1948. *In Henry's Backyard: The Races of Mankind.* New York: Henry Schuman.

Bernstein, Jay. 2002. "First Recipients of Anthropological Doctorates in the United States, 1891–1930." *American Anthropologist* 104(2):551–564.

Berreman, Gerald. 1960. "Caste in India and the United States." *American Journal of Sociology* 66(2):120–127.

Berreman, Gerald. 1967. "Stratification, Pluralism and Interaction: A Comparative Analysis of Caste." In *Caste and Race: Comparative Approaches,* edited by Anthony de Reuck and Julie Knight, 45–73. London: J. & A. Churchill.

Berreman, Gerald. 1968. "Is Anthropology Alive? Social Responsibility in Social Anthropology." *Current Anthropology* 9(5):391–396.

Biondi, Martha. 2012. *The Black Revolution on Campus.* Berkeley: University of California Press.

Boas, Franz. 1904. "What the Negro Has Done in Africa." *Ethical Record* 5(2):106–109.

Boas, Franz. 1905. "The Negro and the Demands of Modern Life." *Charities* 15(1):85–88.

Boas, Franz. 1910. "The Real Race Problem." *The Crisis* 1(2):22–25.

Boas, Franz. 1911a. *The Mind of Primitive Man.* New York: Macmillan.

Boas, Franz. 1911b. Foreword to *Half a Man: The Status of the Negro in New York,* by Mary White Ovington, vii–ix. New York: Longmans, Green.

Boas, Franz. 1912. "Changes in the Bodily Form of Descendants of Immigrants." *American Anthropologist* 14(3):530–562.

Boas, Franz. 1925. "What Is Race?" *The Nation* 120(3108):89–91.

Boas, Franz. 1928. *Anthropology and Modern Life*. New York: W. W. Norton.

Boas, Franz. 1934. "Race." In *Encyclopedia of Social Sciences*, Volume 13, 25–36. New York: Macmillan.

Boas, Franz. 1938. "An Anthropologist's Credo." *The Nation* 147(9):201–204.

Boas, Franz. 1945. *Race and Democratic Society*. New York: Biblo & Tannen.

Boas, Franz. 1962. *Anthropology and Modern Life*. New York: W. W. Norton. First published 1932.

Boas, Franz. 1965. *The Mind of Primitive Man, Revised Edition*. New York: The Free Press. First published 1938.

Boas, Franz. 1966. *Race, Language and Culture*. New York: The Free Press. First published 1940.

Boas, Franz. 1974. "The Outlook for the American Negro." In *A Franz Boas Reader: The Shaping of American Anthropology, 1883–1911*, edited by George Stocking Jr., 310–316. Chicago: University of Chicago Press. First published 1906.

Bolles, A. Lynn. 2001. "Seeking the Ancestors: Forging a Black Feminist Tradition in Anthropology." In *Black Feminist Anthropology: Theory, Politics, Praxis and Poetics*, edited by Irma McClaurin, 24–48. Piscataway, NJ: Rutgers University Press.

Bonfil Batalla, Guillermo. 1966. "Conservative Thought in Applied Anthropology: A Critique." *Human Organization* 25(2):89–92.

Bonilla Silva, Eduardo. 2017. *Racism Without Racists: Color-Blind Racism and the Persistence of Racial Inequality in America*, 5th ed. Lanham, MD: Rowman & Littlefield.

Brattain, Michelle. 2007. "Race, Racism, and Antiracism: UNESCO and the Politics of Presenting Science to the Postwar Public." *American Historical Review* 112(5):1386–1413.

Bresler, Laura, and Diane Lewis. 1983. "Black and White Women Prisoners: Differences in Family Ties and Their Programmatic Implications." *Prison Journal* 63(2):116–123.

Brodkin, Karen. 1998. *How Jews Became White Folks and What That Says About Race in America*. New Brunswick, NJ: Rutgers University Press.

Brodkin, Karen, Sandra Morgen, and Janis Faye Hutchinson. 2011. "Anthropology as White Public Space?" *American Anthropologist* 113(4):545–556.

Bryce-Laporte, Roy. 1970. "Crisis, Contraculture, and Religion Among West Indians in the Panama Canal Zone." In *Afro-American Anthropology: Contemporary Perspectives*, edited by Norman Whitten and John Szwed, 103–118. New York: Macmillan.

Bunzl, Mati. 2003. "Völkerpsychologie and German-Jewish Emancipation." In *Worldly Provincialism: German Anthropology in the Age of Empire*, edited by Glenn Penny and Mati Bunzl, 47–85. Ann Arbor: University of Michigan Press.

Burkholder, Zoë. 2010. "From 'Wops and Dagoes and Hunkies' to 'Caucasian': Changing Racial Discourse in American Classrooms During World War II." *History of Education Quarterly* 50(3):324–358.

Burkholder, Zoë. 2011. *Color in the Classroom: How American Schools Taught Race, 1900–1954*. New York: Oxford University Press.

Caffrey, Margaret. 1989. *Ruth Benedict: Stranger in this Land*. Austin: University of Texas Press.

Carby, Hazel. 1994. "The Politics of Fiction, Anthropology, and the Folk: Zora Neale Hurston." In *History and Memory in African-American Culture*, edited by Robert O'Meally and Geneviève Fabre, 28–44. New York: Oxford University Press.

Carmichael, Stokely, and Charles Hamilton. 1967. *Black Power: The Politics of Liberation in America*. New York: Vintage Books.

Caulfield, Mina Davis. 1972. "Culture and Imperialism: Proposing a New Dialectic." In *Reinventing Anthropology*, edited by Dell Hymes, 182–212. New York: Random House.

Clifford, James. 2003. *On the Edges of Anthropology (Interviews)*. Chicago: Prickly Paradigm Press.

Cole, Douglas. 1999. *Franz Boas: The Early Years, 1858–1906*. Seattle: University of Washington Press.

Cole, Johnnetta, and Sheila Walker, eds. 1980a. *The Black Scholar, Special Issue, Black Anthropology, Part 1*, 11(7).

Cole, Johnnetta, and Sheila Walker, eds. 1980b. *The Black Scholar, Special Issue, Black Anthropology, Part 2*, 11(8).

Cox, Aimee. 2015. *Shapeshifters: Black Girls and the Choreography of Citizenship*. Durham, NC: Duke University Press.

Cox, Oliver. 1944. "The Racial Theories of Robert E. Park and Ruth Benedict." *Journal of Negro Education* 13(4):452–463.

Cox, Oliver. 1948. *Caste, Class, & Race: A Study in Social Dynamics*. Garden City, NY: Doubleday.

Curwood, Anastasia. 2012. "Carolyn Bond Day (1889–1948): A Black Woman Outsider Within Physical Anthropology." *Transforming Anthropology* 20(1):79–89.

Darnell, Regna. 1998. *And Along Came Boas: Continuity and Revolution in Americanist Anthropology*. Philadelphia: John Benjamins.

Darnell, Regna, Michelle Hamilton, Robert L. A. Hancock, and Joshua Smith, eds. 2015. *The Franz Boas Papers, Volume 1: Franz Boas as Public Intellectual—Theory, Ethnography, Activism*. Lincoln: University of Nebraska Press.

Davis, Allison, and John Dollard. 1940. *Children of Bondage: The Personality Development of Negro Youth in the Urban South*. Washington, DC: American Council on Education.

Davis, Allison, Burleigh Gardner, and Mary Gardner. 1941. *Deep South: A Social Anthropological Study of Caste and Class*. Chicago: University of Chicago Press.

De Genova, Nicholas. 2005. *Working the Boundaries: Race, Space, and "Illegality" in Mexican Chicago*. Durham, NC: Duke University Press.

De Genova, Nicholas. 2007. "The Stakes of an Anthropology of the United States." *CR: The New Centennial Review* 7(2):231–277.

De Reuck, Anthony, and Julie Knight, eds. 1967. *Caste and Race: Comparative Approaches.* London: J. & A. Churchill.

De Vos, George, and Hiroshi Wagatsuma. 1966. *Japan's Invisible Race: Caste in Culture and Personality.* Berkeley: University of California Press.

Degler, Carl. 1989. "Culture Versus Biology in the Thought of Franz Boas and Alfred L. Kroeber." *German Historical Institute Annual Lecture Series No. 2,* 1–19. New York: Berg.

Deloria, Vine, Jr. 1969. *Custer Died for Your Sins: An Indian Manifesto.* New York: Macmillan.

Desai, Gaurav. 2001. *Subject to Colonialism: African Self-Fashioning and the Colonial Library.* Durham, NC: Duke University Press.

Di Leonardo, Micaela. 1998. *Exotics at Home: Anthropologies, Others, American Modernity.* Chicago: University of Chicago Press.

Diamond, Stanley. 1962. "Culture and Race." *Science* 135(3507):961–964.

Diamond, Stanley. 1963. "Statement on Racism." *Current Anthropology* 4(3):323.

Diamond, Stanley. 1964. "Reply." *Current Anthropology* 5(2):108.

Diamond, Stanley. 1972. "Anthropology in Question." In *Reinventing Anthropology,* edited by Dell Hymes, 121–152. New York: Random House.

Drake, St. Clair. 1951. "The International Implications of Race and Race Relations." *Journal of Negro Education* 20(3):261–278.

Drake, St. Clair. 1954. *Value Systems, Social Structure and Race Relations in the British Isles.* PhD Dissertation, University of Chicago.

Drake, St. Clair. 1963. *The American Dream and the Negro: 100 Years of Freedom? The Emancipation Proclamation Centennial Lectures.* Chicago: Roosevelt University.

Drake, St. Clair. 1978. "Reflections on Anthropology and the Black Experience." *Anthropology & Education Quarterly* 9(2):85–109.

Drake, St. Clair. 1980. "Anthropology and the Black Experience." *Black Scholar* 11(7): 2–31.

Drake, St. Clair, and Horace Cayton. 1962. *Black Metropolis: A Study of Negro Life in a Northern City.* New York: Harper Torchbooks. First published 1945.

Du Bois, W. E. B. 1992. "Letter by W.E.B. Du Bois to Edward Weeks, Atlanta, Georgia, October 2, 1941." In *African-American Reflections on Brazil's Racial Paradise,* edited by David Hellwig, 117–120. Philadelphia: Temple University Press.

Du Bois, W. E. B. 1995. *The Souls of Black Folk.* New York: Penguin Books. First published 1903.

Dudziak, Mary. 2004. "*Brown* as a Cold War Case." *Journal of American History* 91(1): 32–42.

Duerr, Hans Peter, Ruth Gruhn, F. C. Madigan, K. Paddayya, Harold K. Schneider, and Gutorm Gjessing. 1970. "On the Social Responsibilities Symposium." *Current Anthropology* 11(1):72–79.

Edwards, Brent Hayes. 2003. *The Practice of Diaspora: Literature, Translation, and the Rise of Black Internationalism.* Cambridge, MA: Harvard University Press.

Evans, Brad. 2006. "Where Was Boas During the Renaissance in Harlem? Race, Diffusion, and the Culture Paradigm in the History of Anthropology." In *Central Sites, Peripheral Visions: Cultural and Institutional Crossings in the History of Anthropology*, edited by Richard Handler, 69–98. Madison: University of Wisconsin Press.

Fanon, Franz. 1967. "Racism and Culture." In *Toward the African Revolution*, translated by Haakon Chevalier, 39–54. New York: Penguin Books. First published (in French) 1956.

Favor, J. Martin. 1999. *Authentic Blackness: The Folk in the New Negro Renaissance.* Durham, NC: Duke University Press.

Ferguson, Jeffrey. 2005. *The Sage of Sugar Hill: George S. Schuyler and the Harlem Renaissance.* New Haven, CT: Yale University Press.

Fisher, Ann. 1969. "The Personality and Subculture of Anthropologists and Their Study of U.S. Negroes." In *Concepts and Assumptions in Contemporary Anthropology*, edited by Stephen A. Tyler, 12–17. Southern Anthropological Society Proceedings, No. 3.

Frank, Gelya. 1997. "Jews, Multiculturalism, and Boasian Anthropology." *American Anthropologist* 99(4):731–745.

Frankenberg, Ruth. 1993. *White Women, Race Matters: The Social Construction of Whiteness.* Minneapolis: University of Minnesota Press.

Frazier, E. Franklin. 1942. "The Negro's Cultural Past." *The Nation* 154:195–196.

Freyre, Gilberto. 1946. *The Masters and the Slaves: A Study in the Development of Brazilian Civilization*, translated by Samuel Putnam. New York: Alfred A. Knopf. First published (in Portuguese) 1933.

Fried, Morton. 1972. *The Study of Anthropology.* New York: Thomas Y. Crowell.

Geertz, Clifford. 1968. "We Can Claim No Special Gift for Violence." *New York Times Magazine*, April 28, 24–25.

Geertz, Clifford. 1988. *Works and Lives: The Anthropologist as Author.* Palo Alto, CA: Stanford University Press.

Gershenhorn, Jerry. 2004. *Melville J. Herskovits and the Racial Politics of Knowledge.* Lincoln: University of Nebraska Press.

Gerstle, Gary. 2001. *American Crucible: Race and Nation in the Twentieth Century.* Princeton, NJ: Princeton University Press.

Gibbs, James. 1969. "University Opportunities." *Anthropology News* 10(3):4-5.

Gilkeson, John. 2010. *Anthropologists and the Rediscovery of America, 1886–1965.* New York: Cambridge University Press.

Gilliam, Angela. 1992. "From Roxbury to Rio—and Back in a Hurry." In *African-American Reflections on Brazil's Racial Paradise*, edited by David Hellwig, 173–181. Philadelphia: Temple University Press. First published 1970.

Gilroy, Paul. 1993. *The Black Atlantic: Modernity and Double-Consciousness.* Cambridge, MA: Harvard University Press.

Gjessing, Gutorm. 1968. "The Social Responsibility of the Social Scientist." *Current Anthropology* 9(5):397–402.

Glick, Leonard. 1982. "Types Distinct from Our Own: Franz Boas on Jewish Identity and Assimilation." *American Anthropologist* 84(3):545–565.

Goebel, Michael. 2016. "Immigration and National Identity in Latin America, 1870–1930." *Oxford Research Encyclopedia, Latin American History.* Accessed August 10, 2017. http://latinamericanhistory.oxfordre.com/view/10.1093/acrefore/9780199366439.001.0001/acrefore-9780199366439-e-288.

Goldberg, David Theo. 1993. *Racist Culture: Philosophy and the Politics of Meaning.* Cambridge, MA: Blackwell.

Goldenweiser, Alexander. 1923. "Racial Theory and the Negro." *Opportunity* 1 (August):229–231.

Goldenweiser, Alexander. 1924. "Race and Culture in the Modern World." *Journal of Social Forces* 3(1):127–136.

Goldenweiser, Alexander. 1925. "Can There Be a 'Human Race'?" *The Nation* 120[3120]:462–463.

Goldstein, Eric. 2006. *The Price of Whiteness: Jews, Race, and American Identity.* Princeton, NJ: Princeton University Press.

Goodard, David. 1969. "Limits of British Anthropology." *New Left Review* 58:79–89.

Goodman, Mary Ellen. 1946. "Evidence Concerning the Genesis of Interracial Attitudes." *American Anthropologist* 48(4):624–630.

Goodman, Mary Ellen. 1952. *Race Awareness in Young Children.* Cambridge, MA: Addison-Wesley.

Gordon, Edmund T. 1998. *Disparate Diasporas: Identity and Politics in an African-Nicaraguan Community.* Austin: University of Texas Press.

Gordon, Edmund T., and Mark Anderson. 1999. "The African Diaspora: Toward an Ethnography of Diasporic Identification." *Journal of American Folklore* 112(445):282–296.

Gossett, Thomas. 1963. *Race: The History of an Idea in America.* New York: Schocken Books.

Gough, Kathleen. 1968. "New Proposal for Anthropologists." *Current Anthropology* 9(5):403–435.

Grant, Madison. 1916. *The Passing of the Great Race.* New York: Charles Scribner's Sons.

Greenbaum, Susan. 2015. *Blaming the Poor: The Long Shadow of the Moynihan Report on Cruel Images About Poverty.* New Brunswick, NJ: Rutgers University Press.

Gregory, Steven, and Roger Sanjek, eds. 1994. *Race*. New Brunswick, NJ: Rutgers University Press.

Gruber, Jacob. 1968. "Correspondence." *Anthropology Newsletter*, September 10.

Guglielmo, Thomas. 2003. *White on Arrival: Italians, Race, Color, and Power in Chicago, 1890–1945*. New York: Oxford University Press.

Guterl, Matthew. 2001. *The Color of Race in America, 1900–1940*. Cambridge, MA: Harvard University Press.

Gutiérrez, Ramon. 2004. "Internal Colonialism: An American Theory of Race." *Du Bois Review* 1(2):281–295.

Hale, Charles R. 1994. *Resistance and Contradiction: Miskitu Indians and the Nicaraguan State, 1894–1987*. Palo Alto, CA: Stanford University Press.

Hall, Edward T. 1947. "Race Prejudice and Negro-White Relations in the Army." *American Journal of Sociology* 52(5):401–409.

Handler, Richard. 1990. "Boasian Anthropology and the Critique of American Culture." *American Quarterly* 42(2):252–273.

Handler, Richard. 2005. *Critics Against Culture: Anthropological Observers of Mass Society*. Madison: University of Wisconsin Press.

Handler, Richard. 2006. "Jules Henry and Ruth Landes on American Education." In *Visionary Observers: Anthropological Inquiry and Education*, edited by Jill Cherneff and Eve Hochwald, 149–166. Lincoln: University of Nebraska Press.

Handler, Richard. 2014. "Introduction." In *Boasian Critiques of Race in* The Nation *by Franz Boas, Melville Herskovits, Edward Sapir, Konrad Bercovici, Hendrik Willem Van Loon, Alexander Goldenweiser, and Harry Elmer Barnes*, edited by Alex Golub and Angela Chen. Savage Minds Occasional Paper Series 12. Accessed August 12, 2017. https://evols.library.manoa.hawaii.edu/bitstream/handle/10524/46197/SM%2012%20Boasian%20Critiques%20Of%20Race%20In%20The%20Nation.pdf?sequence=4.

Hannerz, Ulf. 1969. *Soulside: Inquiries into Ghetto Culture and Community*. New York: Columbia University Press.

Harris, Cheryl I. 1993. "Whiteness as Property." *Harvard Law Review* 106(8):1707–1791.

Harris, Marvin. 1952. "Race Relations in Minas Velhas, a Community in the Mountain Region of Central Brazil." In *Race and Class in Rural Brazil*, edited by Charles Wagley, 47–81. Paris: United Nations Educational, Scientific and Cultural Organization.

Harris, Marvin. 1958. *Portugal's African 'Wards.'* New York: American Committee on Africa.

Harris, Marvin. 1962. "Race Relations Research: Auspices and Results in the United States." *Social Science Information* 1:28–51.

Harris, Marvin. 1964a. *Patterns of Race in the Americas*. New York: W. W. Norton.

Harris, Marvin. 1964b. "Racial Identity in Brazil." *Luso-Brazilian Review* 1(2):21–28.

Harris, Marvin. 1968. *The Rise of Anthropological Theory*. New York: Thomas Y. Cromwell.

Harris, Marvin. 1970. "Referential Ambiguity in the Calculus of Brazilian Racial Identity." *Southwestern Journal of Anthropology* 26(1):1–14.

Harris, Marvin. 1971. *Town & Country in Brazil: A Socio-Anthropological Study of a Small Brazilian Town*. New York: W. W. Norton. First published 1956.

Harrison, Faye, ed. 1991a. *Decolonizing Anthropology: Moving Further Toward an Anthropology for Liberation*. Arlington, VA: American Anthropological Association.

Harrison, Faye. 1991b. "Anthropology as an Agent of Transformation: Introductory Comments and Queries." In *Decolonizing Anthropology: Moving Further Toward an Anthropology for Liberation*, edited by Faye Harrison, 1–15. Arlington, VA: American Anthropological Association.

Harrison, Faye. 1992. "The Du Boisian Legacy in Anthropology." *Critique of Anthropology* 12(3):239–260.

Harrison, Faye. 1995. "The Persistent Power of Race in the Cultural and Political Economy of Racism." *Annual Review of Anthropology* 24:47–74.

Harrison, Faye. 2008a. "Race and Anthropology." *International Encyclopedia of the Social Sciences*. Accessed August 10, 2017. http://www.encyclopedia.com/social-sciences/applied-and-social-sciences-magazines/race-and-anthropology.

Harrison, Faye. 2008b. *Outsider Within: Reworking Anthropology in the Global Age*. Urbana: University of Illinois Press.

Harrison, Faye. 2013. "Learning from St. Clair Drake: (Re)mapping Diasporic Connections." *Journal of African American History* 98(3):446–454.

Harrison, Ira. 1987. "The Association of Black Anthropologists: A Brief History." *Anthropology Today* 3(1):17–21.

Harrison, Ira, and Faye Harrison, eds. 1999. *African-American Pioneers in Anthropology*. Urbana: University of Illinois Press.

Hartigan, John, Jr. 1999. *Racial Situations: Class Predicaments of Whiteness in Detroit*. Princeton, NJ: Princeton University Press.

Hartigan, John, Jr. 2010. *Race in the 21st Century: Ethnographic Approaches*. New York: Oxford University Press.

Hartman, Saidiya. 1997. *Scenes of Subjection: Terror, Slavery, and Self-Making in Nineteenth-Century America*. New York: Oxford University Press.

Hazard, Anthony. 2012. *Postwar Anti-Racism: The United States, UNESCO and "Race," 1945–1968*. New York: Palgrave Macmillan.

Hazard, Anthony. 2014. "Wartime Anthropology, Nationalism, and 'Race' in Margaret Mead's *And Keep Your Powder Dry*." *Journal of Anthropological Research* 70:365–383.

Hegeman, Susan. 1999. *Patterns for America: Modernism and the Concept of Culture*. Princeton, NJ: Princeton University Press.

Helbling, Mark. 1999. *The Harlem Renaissance: The One and the Many*. Westport, CT: Greenwood Press.

Hernandez, Graciela. 1995. "Multiple Subjectivities and Strategic Positionality: Zora Neale Hurston's Experimental Ethnographies." In *Women Writing Culture*, edited by Ruth Behar and Deborah A. Gordon, 148–165. Berkeley: University of California Press.

Herskovits, Melville. 1925. "Brains and the Immigrant." *The Nation* 120[3110]:139–141.

Herskovits, Melville. 1927. "When Is a Jew a Jew?" *Modern Quarterly* 4(2):109–117.

Herskovits, Melville. 1928. *The American Negro*. New York: Alfred A. Knopf.

Herskovits, Melville. 1929. "Race Relations." *American Journal of Sociology* 34(6):1129–1139.

Herskovits, Melville. 1930a. "Race Relations." *American Journal of Sociology* 36(6):1052–1062.

Herskovits, Melville. 1930b. "The Negro in the New World: The Statement of a Problem." *American Anthropologist* 32(1):145–155.

Herskovits, Melville. 1930c. *The Anthropometry of the American Negro*. New York: Columbia University Press.

Herskovits, Melville. 1932. "Race Relations." *American Journal of Sociology* 37(6):976–982.

Herskovits, Melville. 1933. "Race Relations." *American Journal of Sociology* 38(6): 913–921.

Herskovits, Melville. 1941. *The Myth of the Negro Past*. New York: Harper & Brothers.

Herskovits, Melville. 1968. "The Negro's Americanism." In *The New Negro*, edited by Alain Locke, 353–360. New York: Atheneum. First published 1925.

Hill, Jane. 2008. *The Everyday Language of White Racism*. Malden, MA: Wiley-Blackwell.

Hsu, Francis. 1973. "Prejudice and Its Intellectual Effect in American Anthropology: An Ethnographic Report." *American Anthropologist* 75(1):1–19.

Hsu, Francis, Delmos Jones, Diane Lewis, Beatrice Medicine, James Gibbs, and Thomas Weaver. 1973. "Report of the Committee on Minorities and Anthropology." American Anthropological Association. Accessed September 1, 2017. http://www.americananthro.org/ParticipateAndAdvocate/Content.aspx?ItemNumber=1514.

Hsu, Francis, and Longde Xu. 1999. *My Life as a Marginal Man: Autobiographical Discussions with Francis L.K. Hsu*. Taipei: SMC.

Hutchinson, George. 1995. *The Harlem Renaissance in Black and White*. Cambridge, MA: Harvard University Press.

Hutchinson, Janis Faye. 2012. "Parallel Paradigms: Racial Diversity and Racism at Universities." In *Racism in the Academy: The New Millennium*, edited by Audrey Smedley and Janis Faye Hutchinson, 35–47. American Anthropological Association. Accessed September 1, 2017. http://www.americananthro.org/LearnAndTeach/Content.aspx?ItemNumber=2639.

Hutchinson, Janis Faye, and Thomas Patterson. 2010. "Final Report 2010, Commission on Race and Racism in Anthropology (CRRA)." American Anthropological Association. Accessed September 1, 2017. http://s3.amazonaws.com/rdcms-aaa/files/production/public/FileDownloads/pdfs/cmtes/commissions/upload/CRRA-final-report-19-Oct-2010-2.pdf.

Hyatt, Marshall. 1990. *Franz Boas, Social Activist: The Dynamics of Ethnicity.* New York: Greenwood Press.

Hymes, Dell, ed. 1972. *Reinventing Anthropology.* New York: Random House.

Ignatiev, Noel. 1995. *How the Irish Became White.* London: Routledge.

Jackson, John L., Jr. 2008. *Racial Paranoia: The Unintended Consequences of Political Correctness.* New York: Basic Books.

Jackson, John P., Jr. 2001. *Social Scientists for Social Justice: Making the Case Against Segregation.* New York: New York University Press.

Jackson, Walter. 1986. "Melville Herskovits and the Search for Afro-American Culture." In *Malinowski, Rivers, Benedict and Others: Essays on Culture and Personality*, edited by George Stocking Jr., 95–126. Madison: University of Wisconsin Press.

Jacobson, Matthew Frye. 1998. *Whiteness of a Different Color: European Immigrants and the Alchemy of Race.* Cambridge, MA: Harvard University Press.

Jebens, Holger. 2010. *After the Cult: Perceptions of Other and Self in West New Britain (Papua New Guinea).* New York: Berghahn Books.

Jhally, Sut, and Stuart Hall. 2002. *Race: The Floating Signifier.* Reference and class eds. Northampton, MA: Media Education Foundation.

Jones, Delmos. 1970. "Towards a Native Anthropology." *Human Organization* 29(4): 251–259.

Jones, Delmos. 1971. "Social Responsibility and the Belief in Basic Research: An Example from Thailand." *Current Anthropology* 12(3):347–350.

Jones, Delmos. 1972. "Incipient Organizations and Organizational Failures in an Urban Ghetto." *Urban Anthropology* 1(1):51–67.

Jorgensen, Joseph, and Eric Wolf. 1970. "A Special Supplement: Anthropology on the Warpath in Thailand." *New York Review of Books*, November 19, 27–35.

Keil, Charles. 1966. *Urban Blues.* Chicago: University of Chicago Press.

Kelly, John, and Martha Kaplan. 2001. *Represented Communities: Fiji and World Decolonization.* Chicago: University of Chicago Press.

Klineberg, Otto. 1935. *Race Differences.* New York: Harper & Brothers.

Klineberg, Otto, ed. 1944. *Characteristics of the American Negro.* New York: Harper & Brothers.

Kobben, Andre, Gerald Berreman, Gutorm Gjessing, and Kathleen Gough. 1971. "On the Social Responsibilities Symposium." *Current Anthropology* 12(1):83–87.

Kottack, Conrad. 2000. "Charles Walter Wagley." *Proceedings of the American Philosophical Society* 144(1):120–122.

Kuznick, Peter. 1987. *Beyond the Laboratory: Scientists as Political Activists in 1930s America.* Chicago: University of Chicago Press.

Lamothe, Daphne. 2008. *Inventing the New Negro: Narrative, Culture, and Ethnography.* Philadelphia: University of Pennsylvania Press.

Leacock, Eleanor. 1969. *Teaching and Learning in City Schools: A Comparative Study.* New York: Basic Books.

Leacock, Eleanor. 1982. "Marxism and Anthropology." In *The Left Academy: Marxist Scholarship on American Campuses,* edited by Bertell Ollman and Edward Vernoff, 242–276. New York: McGraw-Hill.

Levi-Strauss, Claude. 1966. "Anthropology: Its Achievements and Future." *Current Anthropology* 7(2):124–127.

Lévy Zumwalt, Rosemary, and William Willis. 2008. "Franz Boas and W. E. B. Du Bois at Atlanta University, 1906." *Transactions of the American Philosophical Society, New Series* 98(2):i–iii, vii–viii, 1–83.

Lewis, Diane. 1962. *The Minangkabau Malay of Negri Sembilan: A Study of Socio-Cultural Change.* PhD dissertation, Cornell University.

Lewis, Diane. 1972. "Comment." *Western Canadian Journal of Anthropology* 3(3):47–52.

Lewis, Diane. 1973. "Anthropology and Colonialism." *Current Anthropology* 14(5):581–602.

Lewis, Diane. 1975. "The Black Family: Socialization and Sex Roles." *Phylon* 36(3):221–237.

Lewis, Diane. 1977. "A Response to Inequality: Black Women, Racism, and Sexism." *Signs* 3(2):339–361.

Lewis, Diane. 1982. "Female Ex-offenders and Community Programs: Barriers to Service." *Crime and Delinquency* 28:40–51.

Lewis, Diane, and John Watters. 1989. "Human Immunodeficiency Virus Seroprevalence in Female Intravenous Drug Users: The Puzzle of Black Women's Risk." *Social Science and Medicine* 29(9):1071–1076.

Lewis, Herbert. 2014. *In Defense of Anthropology: An Investigation of the Critique of Anthropology.* New Brunswick, NJ: Transaction.

Lewis, Herbert. 2015. "The Individual and Individuality in Franz Boas's Anthropology and Philosophy." In *The Franz Boas Papers, Volume 1: Franz Boas as Public Intellectual—Theory, Ethnography, Activism,* edited by Regna Darnell, Michelle Hamilton, Robert L. A. Hancock, and Joshua Smith, 19–41. Lincoln: University of Nebraska Press.

Liebow, Elliot. 1967. *Tally's Corner: A Study of Negro Streetcorner Men.* Boston: Little, Brown.

Lipsitz, George. 1998. *The Possessive Investment in Whiteness: How White People Profit from Identity Politics.* Philadelphia: Temple University Press.

Liss, Julia. 1998. "Diasporic Identities: The Science and Politics of Race in the Work of Franz Boas and W. E. B. Du Bois, 1894–1919." *Cultural Anthropology* 13(2):127–166.

Liss, Julia. 2015. "Franz Boas on War and Empire: The Making of a Public Intellectual." In *The Franz Boas Papers, Volume 1: Franz Boas as Public Intellectual—Theory, Ethnography, Activism*, edited by Regna Darnell, Michelle Hamilton, Robert L. A. Hancock, and Joshua Smith, 293–328. Lincoln: University of Nebraska Press.

Locke, Alain. 1968a. "The New Negro." In *The New Negro*, edited by Alain Locke, 3–16. New York: Atheneum. First published 1925.

Locke, Alain. 1968b. "The Negro Spirituals." In *The New Negro*, edited by Alain Locke, 199–210. New York: Atheneum. First published 1925.

Locke, Alain, 1989a. "The Concept of Race as Applied to Social Culture." In *The Philosophy of Alain Locke: Harlem Renaissance and Beyond*, edited by Leonard Harris, 187–199. Philadelphia: Temple University Press. First published 1924.

Locke, Alain, 1989b. "Who and What Is 'Negro.'" In *The Philosophy of Alain Locke: Harlem Renaissance and Beyond*, edited by Leonard Harris, 209–228. Philadelphia: Temple University Press. First published 1942.

Losurdo, Domenico. 2011. *Liberalism: A Counter-History*, translated by Gregory Elliott. New York: Verso.

Lowie, Robert. 1923. "Psychology, Anthropology, and Race." *American Anthropologist* 25(3):291–303.

Mafeje, Archie. 1971. "The Ideology of Tribalism." *Journal of Modern African Studies* 9:253–261.

Mafeje, Archie. 1976. "The Problem of Anthropology in Historical Perspective: An Inquiry into the Growth of the Social Sciences." *Canadian Journal of African Studies* 10(2):307–333.

Magubane, Bernard. 1971. "A Critical Look at Indices Used in the Study of Social Change in Colonial Africa." *Current Anthropology* 12(4/5):419–445.

Maio, Marcos Chor. 2001. "UNESCO and the Study of Race Relations in Brazil: Regional or National Issue?" *Latin American Research Review* 36(2):118–136.

Malik, Kenan. 1996. *The Meaning of Race: Race, History and Culture in Western Society*. New York: New York University Press.

Mandelbaum, David. 1952. *Soldier Groups and Negro Soldiers*. Berkeley: University of California Press.

Maquet, Jacques. 1964. "Objectivity in Anthropology." *Current Anthropology* 5(1):47–55.

Marfleet, Philip. 1973. "Bibliographical Notes on the Debate." In *Anthropology & the Colonial Encounter*, edited by Talal Asad, 273–281. Atlantic Highlands, NJ: Humanities Press.

Matera, Marc. 2015. *Black London: The Imperial Metropolis and Decolonization in the Twentieth Century*. Berkeley: University of California Press.

Matory, J. Lorand. 2005. *Black Atlantic Religion: Tradition, Transnationalism, and Matriarchy in the Afro-Brazilian Condomblé*. Princeton, NJ: Princeton University Press.

Matory, J. Lorand. 2015. *Stigma and Culture: Last-Place Anxiety in Black America*. Chicago: University of Chicago Press.

McKee, James. 1993. *Sociology and the Race Problem: The Failure of a Perspective*. Urbana: University of Illinois Press.

Mead, Margaret. 1928. *Coming of Age in Samoa: A Psychological Study of Primitive Youth for Western Civilization*. New York: Blue Ribbon Books.

Mead, Margaret. 1942. *And Keep Your Powder Dry: An Anthropologist Looks at America*. New York: William Morrow.

Mead, Margaret, ed. 1959. *An Anthropologist at Work: Writings of Ruth Benedict*. Boston: Houghton Mifflin.

Mead, Margaret. 1972. "Changing the Requirements in Anthropological Education." *Western Canadian Journal of Anthropology* 3(3):19–23.

Mead, Margaret, and James Baldwin. 1971. *A Rap on Race*. New York: J.B. Lippincott.

Medicine, Beatrice. 2001. *Learning to Be an Anthropologist & Remaining "Native": Selected Writings*, edited with Sue-Ellen Jacobs. Urbana: University of Illinois Press.

Memmi, Albert. 1967. *The Colonizer and the Colonized*, translated by Howard Greenfeld. Boston: Beacon Press.

Menchaca, Marta. 2001. *Recovering History, Constructing Race: The Indian, Black, and White Roots of Mexican Americans*. Austin: University of Texas Press.

Métraux, Alfred. 1950. "UNESCO and the Racial Problem." *International Social Science Bulletin* 2(3):384–394.

Mikell, Gwendolyn. 1983. "The Anthropological Imagination of Zora Neale Hurston." *Western Journal of Black Studies* 7(1):27–35.

Mikell, Gwendolyn. 1999. "Feminism and Black Culture in the Ethnography of Zora Neale Hurston." In *African-American Pioneers in Anthropology*, edited by Ira E. Harrison and Faye V. Harrison, 51–69. Urbana: University of Illinois Press.

Mintz, Sidney. 1969. "Summary and Commentary." In *Black Studies in the University: A Symposium*, edited by Armstead Robinson, Craig Foster, and Donald Ogilvie, 202–206. New Haven, CT: Yale University Press.

Mintz, Sidney. 1970a. "Creating Culture in the Americas." *Columbia University Forum* 13:4–11.

Mintz, Sidney. 1970b. "Forward." In *Afro-American Anthropology: Contemporary Perspectives*, edited by Norman Whitten and John Szwed, 1–16. New York: Free Press.

Mintz, Sidney. 1971. "Toward an Afro-American History." *Journal of World History* 13(2):317–332.

Mintz, Sidney, ed. 1974. *Slavery, Colonialism, and Racism*. New York: W. W. Norton.

Mintz, Sidney. 1981. "Ruth Benedict." In *Totems and Teachers: Perspectives on the History of Anthropology*, edited by Sydel Silverman, 141–170. New York: Columbia University Press.

Mintz, Sidney, and Richard Price. 1992. *The Birth of Afro-American Culture: Anthropological Perspectives.* Boston: Beacon Press.

Modell, Judith Schacter. 1983. *Ruth Benedict: Patterns of a Life.* Philadelphia: University of Pennsylvania Press.

Montagu, Ashley. 1945. *Man's Most Dangerous Myth: The Fallacy of Race,* 2nd ed. New York: Columbia University Press.

Moore, John. 1971. "Perspective for a Partisan Anthropology." *Liberation,* December, 34–43.

Mullings, Leith. 2005. "Interrogating Racism: Toward an Antiracist Anthropology." *Annual Review of Anthropology* 34:667–693.

Myrdal, Gunnar. 1944. *An American Dilemma: The Negro Problem and Modern Democracy.* New York: Harper & Brothers.

Nader, Laura. 1972. "Up the Anthropologist—Perspectives Gained from Studying Up." In *Reinventing Anthropology,* edited by Dell Hymes, 284–311. New York: Random House.

Nash, Manning. 1962. "Race and the Ideology of Race." *Current Anthropology* 3(3): 285–288.

Nava, Mica. 2013. "American Anthropologist Ruth Landes and Race Relations Research in Postwar Britain: A Research File." University of East London. Accessed September 1, 2017. http://roar.uel.ac.uk/3200/.

Ngai, Mae. 2004. *Impossible Subjects: Illegal Aliens and the Making of Modern America.* Princeton, NJ: Princeton University Press.

Norcini, Marilyn. 2007. *Edward P. Dozier: The Paradox of the American Indian Anthropologist.* Tucson: University of Arizona Press.

O'Connor, Alice. 2001: *Poverty Knowledge: Social Science, Social Policy, and the Poor in Twentieth-Century U.S. History.* Princeton, NJ: Princeton University Press.

Painter, Nell Irvin. 2010. *The History of White People.* New York: W. W. Norton.

Patterson, Thomas. 2001. *A Social History of Anthropology in the United States.* New York: Berg.

Peretz, Henri. 2004. "The Making of *Black Metropolis.*" *Annals of the American Academy of Political and Social Science* 595:168–175.

Perlmann, Joel. 2011. "Views of European Races Among the Research Staff of the US Immigration Commission and the Census Bureau, ca. 1910." Levy Economics Institute of Bard College Working Paper No. 648. Accessed August 12, 2017. http://www.levyinstitute.org/pubs/wp_648.pdf.

Perry, Pamela. 2001. "White Means Never Having to Say You're Ethnic: White Youth and the Construction of 'Cultureless' Identities." *Journal of Contemporary Ethnography* 30(1):56–91.

Pierson, Donald. 1942. *Negroes in Brazil: A Study of Race Contact at Bahia.* Chicago: University of Chicago Press.

Plummer, Brenda Gayle. 1996. *Rising Wind: Black Americans and U.S. Foreign Affairs, 1935–1960.* Chapel Hill: University of North Carolina Press.

Polgar, Steven. 1960. "Biculturation of Mesquakie Teenage Boys." *American Anthropologist* 62(2):217–235.

Price, David. 2004. *Threatening Anthropology: McCarthyism and the FBI's Surveillance of Activist Anthropologists.* Durham, NC: Duke University Press.

Price, David. 2016. *Cold War Anthropology: The CIA, the Pentagon, and the Growth of Dual Use Anthropology.* Durham, NC: Duke University Press.

Putnam, Lara. 2010. "Eventually Alien: The Multigenerational Saga of British West Indians in Central America and Beyond, 1880–1940." In *Blacks and Blackness in Central America: Between Race and Place*, edited by Lowell Gudmundson and Justin Wolfe, 278–306. Durham, NC: Duke University Press.

Putnam, Lara. 2011. "Unspoken Exclusions: Race, Nation and Empire in the Immigration Restrictions in North America and the Greater Caribbean." In *Workers Across the Americas: The Transnational Turn in Labor History*, edited by Lean Fink, 267–294. New York: Oxford University Press.

Randolph, A. Philip, and Chandler Owen. 1920. "The New Negro—What Is He?" *The Messenger* 2(August):73–74.

Rauch, Jerome. 1955. "Area Institute Programs and African Studies." *Journal of Negro Education* 24(4):409–425.

Reardon, Jennifer. 2005. *Race to the Finish: Identity and Governance in an Age of Genomics.* Princeton, NJ: Princeton University Press.

Roediger, David. 2005. *Working Toward Whiteness: How America's Immigrants Became White: The Strange Journey from Ellis Island to the Suburbs.* New York: Basic Books.

Romano, Octavio, ed. 1973. *Voices: Readings from El Grito, a Journal of Contemporary Mexican American Thought, 1967–1973.* Berkeley: Quinto Sol.

Rosa, Andrew. 2012. "The Roots and Routes of 'Imperium in Imperio': St. Clair Drake, the Formative Years." *American Studies* 52(1):49–75.

Rosa, Jonathan, and Yarimar Bonilla. 2017. "Deprovincializing Trump, Decolonizing Diversity, and Unsettling Anthropology." *American Ethnologist* 44(2):201–208.

Rosemblatt, Karin. 2014. "Modernization, Dependency and the Global in Mexican Critiques of Anthropology." *Journal of Global History* 9(1):94–121.

Ross, Dorothy. 1991. *The Origins of American Social Science.* New York: Cambridge University Press.

Sahlins, Marshall. 1967. "The Established Order: Do Not Fold, Spindle, or Mutilate." In *The Rise and Fall of Project Camelot: Studies in the Relationship Between Social Science and Practical Politics*, edited by Irving Horowitz, 71–79. Cambridge, MA: Massachusetts Institute of Technology Press.

Sánchez-Eppler, Benigno. 1992. "Telling Anthropology: Zora Neale Hurston and Gilberto Freyre Disciplined in Their Field-Home-Work." *American Literary History* 4(3):464–488.

Sanday, Peggy Reeves. 1999. "Skeletons in the Anthropological Closet: The Life and Work of William S. Willis Jr." In *African-American Pioneers in Anthropology*, edited by Ira E. Harrison and Faye V. Harrison, 243–264. Urbana: University of Illinois Press.

Sanjek, Roger. 1994. "The Enduring Inequalities of Race." In *Race*, edited by Steven Gregory and Roger Sanjek, 1–17. New Brunswick, NJ: Rutgers University Press.

Sapir, Edward. 1921. *Language: An Introduction to the Study of Speech*. New York: Harcourt, Brace.

Sapir, Edward. 1924. "Culture, Genuine and Spurious." *American Journal of Sociology* 29(4):401–429.

Sapir, Edward. 1925. "Let Race Alone." *The Nation* 120(3112):211–213.

Schneider, Mark Robert. 2002. *"We Return Fighting": The Civil Rights Movement in the Jazz Age*. Boston: Northeastern University Press.

Schuyler, George. 1926. "The Negro-Art Hokum." *The Nation* 122 (3180):662–663.

Schuyler, George. 1927. "Our White Folks." *American Mercury* 12(48):385–392.

Schuyler, George. 1929a. *Racial Intermarriage in the United States: One of the Most Interesting Phenomena in Our National Life*. Girard, KS: Haldeman-Julius.

Schuyler, George. 1929b. "Emancipated Women and the Negro." *Modern Quarterly* 5(3):361–363.

Schuyler, George. 1930. "A Negro Looks Ahead." *American Mercury* 17(74):212–220.

Schuyler, George. 1934. "When Black Weds White." *Modern Monthly* 8(1):11–17.

Schuyler, George. 1971. *Black No More: Being an Account of the Strange and Wonderful Workings of Science in the Land of the Free, A.D. 1933–1940*. New York: Collier Books. First published 1931.

Seigel, Micol. 2009. *Uneven Encounters: Making Race and Nation in Brazil and the United States*. Durham, NC: Duke University Press.

Seigel, Morris. 1953. "Race Attitudes in Puerto Rico." *Phylon* 14(2):163–178.

Seth, Vanita. 2010. *Europe's Indians: Producing Racial Difference, 1500–1900*. Durham, NC: Duke University Press.

Shanklin, Eugenia. 1998. "The Profession of the Color Blind: Sociocultural Anthropology and Racism in the 21st Century." *American Anthropologist* 100(3):669–679.

Sieber, R. Timothy. 1994. "The Life of Anthony Leeds: Unity in Diversity." In *Cities, Classes and the Social Order*, edited by Roger Sanjek, 3–26. Ithaca, NY: Cornell University Press.

Silverman, Sydel. 2005. "The United States." In *One Discipline, Four Ways: British, German, French, and American Anthropology*, 257–347. Chicago: University of Chicago Press.

Simpson, George Eaton, and J. Milton Yinger. 1958. *Racial and Cultural Minorities: An Analysis of Prejudice and Discrimination*, rev. ed. New York: Harper & Row.

Singh, Nikhil Pal. 2005. *Black Is a Country: Race and the Unfinished Struggle for Democracy*. Cambridge, MA: Harvard University Press.

Skidmore, Thomas. 1990. "Racial Ideas and Social Policy in Brazil, 1870–1940." In *The Idea of Race in Latin America, 1870–1940*, edited by Richard Graham, 7–36. Austin: University of Texas Press.

Smedley, Audrey. 1993. *Race in North America: Origin and Evolution of a Worldview*. Boulder, CO: Westview Press.

Smedley, Audrey, and Janis Faye Hutchinson, eds. 2012. *Racism in the Academy: The New Millennium*. American Anthropological Association. Accessed September 1, 2017. http://www.americananthro.org/LearnAndTeach/Content.aspx?ItemNumber =2639.

Smith, M. E. 1969. "Reaction to Recent Events." *Anthropology Newsletter* 10(6):2.

Spiro, Jonathan Peter. 2009. *Defending the Master Race: Conservation, Eugenics, and the Legacy of Madison Grant*. Burlington: University of Vermont Press.

Stack, Carol. 1970. "The Kindred of Viola Jackson: Residence and Family Organization of an Urban Black American Family." In *Afro-American Anthropology: Contemporary Perspectives*, edited by Norman Whitten and John Szwed, 303–312. New York: Free Press.

Stack, Carol. 1974. *All Our Kin: Strategies for Survival in a Black Community*. New York: Harper & Row.

Stauder, Jack. 1972. "The 'Relevance' of Anthropology Under Imperialism." *Critical Anthropology* 2(2):65–87.

Stavenhagen, Rodolfo. 1971. "Decolonizing Applied Social Sciences." *Human Organization* 30(4):333–357.

Stepan, Nancy Leys. 1991. *"The Hour of Eugenics": Race, Gender, and Nation in Latin America*. Ithaca, NY: Cornell University Press.

Steward, Julian, Robert Manners, Eric Wolf, Elena Padilla Seda, Sidney Mintz, and Raymond Scheele. 1956. *The People of Puerto Rico: A Study in Social Anthropology*. Urbana: University of Illinois Press.

Stocking, George, Jr. 1968. *Race, Culture, and Evolution*. New York: Free Press.

Stocking, George, Jr. 1979. "Anthropology as Kulturkampf: Science and Politics in the Career of Franz Boas." In *The Uses of Anthropology*, edited by Walter Goldschmidt, 33–50. Washington, DC: American Anthropological Association.

Stocking, George, Jr. 2001. *Delimiting Anthropology: Occasional Inquiries and Reflections*. Madison: University of Wisconsin Press.

Szwed, John. 1972. "An American Anthropological Dilemma: The Politics of Afro-American Culture." In *Reinventing Anthropology*, edited by Dell Hymes, 153–181. New York: Random House.

Tannenbaum, Frank. 1946. *Slave & Citizen: The Negro in the Americas.* New York: Alfred A. Knopf.

Teslow, Tracy. 2014. *Constructing Race: The Science of Bodies and Cultures in American Anthropology.* New York: Cambridge University Press.

Thorkelson, Eli. 2009. "Race and White Dominance in American Anthropology." Decasia. Accessed September 1, 2017. https://decasia.org/academic_culture/2009/11/22/race-and-white-dominance-in-american-anthropology/.

Trencher, Susan. 2000. *Mirrored Images: American Anthropology and American Culture, 1960–1980.* Westport, CT: Praeger.

Trouillot, Michel-Rolph. 2003. *Global Transformations.* New York: Palgrave Macmillan.

Turner, Fred. 2013. "Margaret Mead's Countercultures." *Public Books,* November 1. Accessed September 1, 2017. http://www.publicbooks.org/margaret-meads-counter cultures/.

UNESCO. 1969. "Statement on Race, Paris, July 1950." In *Four Statements on the Race Question,* 30–35. Paris: United Nations Educational, Scientific and Cultural Organization. First published 1950.

United States Immigration Commission. 1911. *Dictionary of Races or Peoples.* Washington, DC: Government Printing Office.

Valentine, Bettylou. 1978. *Hustling and Other Hard Work: Life Styles in the Ghetto.* New York: Free Press.

Valentine, Charles. 1964. *Deeds: Background and Basis, a Report on Research Leading to the Drive for Equal Employment in Downtown Seattle.* Seattle: Congress of Racial Equality.

Valentine, Charles. 1968. *Culture and Poverty: Critique and Counter-Proposals.* Chicago: University of Chicago Press.

Valentine, Charles. 1971. "It's Either Brain Damage or No Father: The False Issue of Deficit vs. Difference Models of Afro-American Behavior." In *Toward Social Change: A Handbook for Those Who Will,* edited by Robert Buckhout and 81 concerned Berkeley students, 126–133. New York: Harper & Row.

Valentine, Charles. 1972. *Black Studies and Anthropology: Scholarly and Political Interests in Afro-American Culture.* Reading, MA: Addison-Wesley.

Valentine, Charles, and Bettylou Valentine. 1970. "Making the Scene, Digging the Action, and Telling It Like It Is: Anthropologists at Work in a Dark Ghetto." In *Afro-American Anthropology: Contemporary Perspectives,* edited by Norman Whitten and John Szwed, 403–418. New York: Free Press.

Valentine, Charles, and Bettylou Valentine. 1975. "Brain Damage and the Intellectual Defense of Inequality." *Current Anthropology* 16(1):117–150.

Visweswaran, Kamala. 1998. "Race and the Culture of Anthropology." *American Anthropologist* 100(1):70–83.

Visweswaran, Kamala. 2010. *Un/common Cultures: Racism and the Rearticulation of Cultural Difference*. Durham, NC: Duke University Press.

Von Eschen, Penny. 1997. *Race Against Empire: Black Americans and Anticolonialism, 1937–1957*. Ithaca, NY: Cornell University Press.

Wade, Peter. 1993. *Blackness and Race Mixture: The Dynamics of Racial Identity in Colombia*. Baltimore: Johns Hopkins University Press.

Wade, Peter. 2010. *Race and Ethnicity in Latin America*, 2nd ed. New York: Pluto Press.

Wagley, Charles, ed. 1952. *Race and Class in Rural Brazil*. Paris: United Nations Educational, Scientific and Cultural Organization.

Wagley, Charles. 1963. "Preface to the Second Edition." *Race and Class in Rural Brazil*, 2nd ed., edited by Charles Wagley, 1–2. Paris: United Nations Educational, Scientific and Cultural Organization.

Wagley, Charles. 1965. "On the Concept of Social Race in the Americas." In *Contemporary Cultures and Societies of Latin America*, edited by Dwight Heath and Richard Adams, 531–545. New York: Random House.

Wagley, Charles, and Marvin Harris. 1958. *Minorities in the New World: Six Case Studies*. New York: Columbia University Press.

Walters, Keith. 1999. "'He Can Read My Writing but He sho' Can't Read My Mind': Zora Neale Hurston's Revenge in *Mules and Men*." *Journal of American Folklore* 112(445):343–371.

Warner, Lloyd, J. O. Low, Paul Lunt, and Leo Strole. 1962. *Yankee City: One Volume, Abridged Edition*. New Haven, CT: Yale University Press.

Warren, Jonathan. 2000. "Masters in the Field: White Talk, White Privilege, White Biases." In *Racing Research, Researching Race: Methodological Dilemmas in Critical Race Studies*, edited by France Winddance Twine and Jonathan Warren, 135–164. New York: New York University Press.

Watkin, Eric. 1992. *Anthropology Goes to War: Professional Ethics and Counterinsurgency in Thailand*. Madison: University of Wisconsin Center for Southeast Asia Studies.

Whitten, Norman. 1969. "The Ecology of Race Relations in Northwest Ecuador." *Journal de la Société des Américanistes* 58:223–233.

Whitten, Norman, and John Szwed, eds. 1970. *Afro-American Anthropology: Contemporary Perspectives*. New York: Macmillan.

Wilder, Gary. 2005. *The French Imperial Nation-State: Negritude and Colonial Humanism Between the Two World Wars*. Chicago: University of Chicago Press.

Williams, Brackette. 1989. "A Class Act: Anthropology and the Race to Nation Across Ethnic Terrain." *Annual Review of Anthropology* 18:401–444.

Williams, Vernon. 1996. *Rethinking Race: Franz Boas and his Contemporaries*. Lexington: University Press of Kentucky.

Williams, Vernon. 2006. *The Social Sciences and Theories of Race*. Urbana: University of Illinois Press.

Williamson, Joel. 1980. *New People: Miscegenation and Mulattoes in the United States*. Baton Rouge: Louisiana State University Press.

Willis, William. 1955. *Colonial Conflict and the Cherokee Indians, 1710–1760*. PhD dissertation, University of Columbia.

Willis, William. 1963. "Divide and Rule: Red, White, and Black in the Southeast." *Journal of Negro History* 48(3):157–176.

Willis, William. 1970. "Anthropology and Negroes on the Southern Colonial Frontier." In *The Black Experience in America: Selected Essays*, edited by James Curtis and Lewis Gould, 33–50. Austin: University of Texas Press.

Willis, William. 1972. "Skeletons in the Anthropological Closet." In *Reinventing Anthropology*, edited by Dell Hymes, 121–152. New York: Random House.

Willis, William. 1975. "Franz Boas and the Study of Black Folklore." In *The New Ethnicity: Perspectives from Ethnology, 1973 Proceedings of The American Ethnological Society*, edited by John Bennett, 307–334. St. Paul, MN: West.

Wolf, Eric. 1969a. "American Anthropologists and American Society." In *Concepts and Assumptions in Contemporary Anthropology*, edited by Stephen A. Tyler, 3–11. Southern Anthropological Society Proceedings, No. 3.

Wolf, Eric. 1969b. *Peasant Wars of the Twentieth Century*. New York: Harper & Row.

Wolf, Eric. 1974. *Anthropology*. New York: W. W. Norton.

Wolf, Eric. 1982. *Europe and the People Without History*. Berkeley: University of California Press.

Wolfe, Brendan. 2015. "Racial Integrity Laws (1924–1930)." In *Encyclopedia Virginia*. Accessed August 13, 2017. https://www.encyclopediavirginia.org/Racial_Integrity _Laws_of_the_1920s.

Worsley, Peter. 1964. *The Third World*. London: Weidenfeld & Nicolson.

Wynter, Sylvia. 2003. "Unsettling the Coloniality of Being/Power/Truth/Freedom: Towards the Human, After Man, Its Overrepresentation—An Argument." *CR: The New Centennial Review* 3(3)257–337.

Yelvington, Kevin. 2006. "The Invention of Africa in Latin America and the Caribbean: Political Discourse and Anthropological Praxis, 1920–1940." In *Afro-Atlantic Dialogues: Anthropology in the Diaspora*, edited by Kevin Yelvington, 35–82. Santa Fe, NM: School of American Research Press.

Yelvington, Kevin. 2011. "Constituting Paradigms in the Study of the African Diaspora, 1900–1950." *Black Scholar* 41(1):64–76.

Young, Virginia Heyer. 2005. *Ruth Benedict: Beyond Relativity, Beyond Pattern*. Lincoln: University of Nebraska Press.

Manuscript Collections

Ruth Fulton Benedict Papers, 1905–1948, Archives and Special Collections Library, Vassar College.

Franz Boas Papers, American Philosophical Society, Philadelphia.

Melville J. Herskovits Papers, Northwestern University Archives, Northwestern University Library, Evanston, IL.

Papers of Marvin Harris, National Anthropological Archives, Smithsonian Institution, Washington, DC.

William Shedrick Willis Papers, American Philosophical Society, Philadelphia.

Index

Page numbers followed by f indicate material in figures.

Mongolian race, 33–34, 112, 118. *See also* race
Montagu, Ashley, 16, 111, 133
Moore, Sally Falk, 122
Moynihan, Daniel Patrick, 188
Mozambique, 136, 152
Murphy, Robert, 122, 175
Museums, role of, 37–38, 44
Myrdal, Gunnar, 105, 188
Myth of the Negro Past, The (Herskovits), 50–52
Mythology of progressive anthropology, 8–9

NAACP, 67, 68, 126, 151
Nash, Manning, 128
Nash, Philleo, 126
Nation, The, 29–30, 39, 44, 53, 82
National belonging, 17, 88; Boas/Boasians on, 61–62, 65–66, 77–81, 204; "civic nationalism," 6, 121, 171, 207; national character studies, 122; "nation," "nationality," and race, 78–79; and original racial distinctions, 30, 33; postwar studies of, 122; as source of cultural progress, 65
Nation-states, 25–26, 64–65, 120, 131, 193, 205–206
Native Americans: Baldwin's scalping comment, 4; Benedict on, 97–109; Boasians on, 44–45; case studies of, 147–150; Deloria's satire of anthropologists, 172; displacement of, 31; as "domestic dependent nations," 31; early twentieth century studies of, 38–39; as enemies of the state, 216n1; Indian Wars, 31; pre-conquest, 153; and "reverse racism," 174; slavery under Spain, 153
Naturalization Act (1790), 28
Nazism, 99, 108, 112
"Negro," use of term, 86–87
"Negro-Art Hokum, The" (Schuyler), 85
"Negro problem," Boas on, 60–61, 67
"Negro Spirituals," 49
Neo-evolutionary approach, 149
Neoliberalism, 203
New Negro, The (Locke), 46, 48, 52
"New Negro" scholars, 46–53, 85, 87
New Republic, 39, 44
Newton, Huey, 183
New York–centered artists, writers, 39
Nordics/Nordicism, 47; "anti-Nordics," 83; as Caucasian subdivision, 113; and Gobineau, 99; and Grant, 103; "Nordic

Myth" series *(The Nation)*, 29–30, 44; Nordic race, 24, 28–30, 33, 86; and scientific anti-racism, 179

Obama, Barack, 201
Objective knowledge, 47, 166, 168, 185–186, 192, 208
"Old Americans," 24, 104, 106–107, 205
"One drop" rule, 73, 86, 151. *See also* hypodescent
Opportunity journal, 44
Osborn, Henry Fairfield, 28
Osborne, Oliver, 223–224n7
Other, rejection of, 64–65
"Our White Folks" (Schuyler), 86
Owen, Clyde, 82

Pan-African movement, 119
Pan-Asian movement, 119
Parsons, Elsie Clews, 46, 93–94
Passing of the Great Race, The (Grant), 29, 103
Past as present, 199
Patterns of Culture (Benedict), 40, 90, 94–95, 112, 178
Patterns of Race in the Americas (Harris), 136–137, 153, 155, 158–160
Peretz, Henri, 55
"Perspectivistic" knowledge, 192–193
Phenotypical difference, 68–69, 71, 73, 89, 138, 140, 144
Philippines, 38, 216n2
Pierson, Donald, 133–134, 144
Pittsburgh Courier (Schuyler), 82
Pluralism versus assimilation, 81, 150–151, 161
Polgar, Steven, 189
Polygenic theory, 36
Portuguese colonization, 152, 156
Post-civil rights era, 201–202
"Postwar Race Prejudice" (Benedict), 107
"Poverty knowledge," 57
Powell, John Wesley, 37
Price, David, 121
Price, Richard, 217n8
"Primary" races, 29, 113. *See also* Caucasoid, Negroid, Mongoloid classification
"Primitive" societies. *See* early/"primitive" human society
"Problem of the American Negro, The" (Boas), 60, 70–71, 75, 87
Professionalization of anthropology, 36–39